A PROFILE
OF THE
NEGRO
AMERICAN

THE AUTHOR

Born in Richmond, Virginia, THOMAS PETTIGREW is currently Associate Professor of Social Psychology, Department of Social Relations, Harvard University. He graduated from the University of Virginia with an A.B. in Psychology in 1952; and, from Harvard University, he received an M.A. and a Ph.D. in Social Psychology, 1955 and 1956 respectively.

The author has served as Research Associate, Institute for Social Research, University of Natal (South Africa); Assistant Professor of Psychology, University of North Carolina; and Assistant Professor of Social Psychology, Harvard University. He is an Associate Editor of the *American Sociological Review;* an editorial board member of the *Journal of Social Issues;* and a Fellow of both The American Psychological Association and The American Sociological Association.

Co-author of "Christians in Racial Crisis: A Study of the Little Rock Ministry," Professor Pettigrew has also contributed numerous articles and reviews to leading scholarly publications—*Journal of Abnormal and Social Psychology, Journal of Experimental Psychology, American Sociological Review, Social Forces, American Journal of Sociology, Contemporary Psychology, Journal of Negro Education, Phylon, Public Opinion Quarterly, American Psychologist, Christian Century* and *Commentary.*

A Profile of

the Negro American

by THOMAS F. PETTIGREW

GREENWOOD PRESS, PUBLISHERS
WESTPORT, CONNECTICUT

Library of Congress Cataloging in Publication Data

Pettigrew, Thomas F.
  A profile of the Negro American.

  Reprint. Originally published: Princeton, N.J. :
Van Nostrand, 1964.
  Bibliography: p.
  Includes indexes.
  1. Afro-Americans--Psychology. 2. Afro-Americans--
Health and hygiene. 3. Afro-American criminals.
4. Intelligence levels--Afro-Americans. 5. Racism--
United States. 6. United States--Race relations.
I. Title.
E185.625.P4 1984   305.8'96073   84-10731
ISBN 0-313-24380-8 (lib. bdg.)

To

MY PARENTS

and

Miss Mildred Adams

PREFACE

"Of all vulgar modes of escaping from the consideration of the effect of the social and moral influences on
the human mind," wrote John Stuart Mill years ago,
"the most vulgar is that of attributing the diversities of
conduct and character to inherent natural differences."

Mill's words have special meaning for us today. Living through a time of revolution and change, we are
witnessing the last desperate gasp of the most "vulgar"
form of assertions of "inherent natural differences"—
racism and its assumptions of racial superiority. One
theme of this volume is that racism, in addition to its
vulgarity, is simply not supported by the empirical findings of the biological and social sciences.

Other approaches, other conceptions are required to
gain an adequate profile of today's Negro American.
The following pages briefly present some of these approaches and conceptions in a variety of critical realms
—personality, genetics, health, intelligence, crime, and
the current protest for change. An extensive bibliography
is provided for this discussion, both to suggest the type
of scientific evidence which supports these newer conceptions and to provide the interested reader with additional sources to explore the topic further.

I would like to acknowledge the cooperation of numerous authors and publishers in kindly permitting
important, copyrighted material to be reproduced
throughout the book: James Baldwin, Abraham Kardiner,
Herman Lehmann, Curt Stern, and George Stoddard;
and the American Academy of Political and Social Science, the American Psychological Association, Appleton-
Century-Crofts, Beacon Press, Dial Press, Inc., Free Press
of Glencoe, Harper & Row, Inc., Harcourt, Brace &
World, Inc., Houghton Mifflin Co., the Journal Press,

Alfred A. Knopf, Inc., Lea & Febiger, J. P. Lippincott Co., Macmillan Co., New American Library of World Literature, Inc., the *New York Times*, Public Affairs Press, Random House, Inc., W. B. Saunders Co., *Scientific American, Social Problems,* and John Wiley & Sons, Inc.

Many people helped me to produce this volume. I especially want to express my appreciation to: Gordon Allport, for suggesting such a book in the first place; Irving Gottesman, for providing vital suggestions for chapters 3 and 5; Dorothy Heid, for developing the name index; David McClelland, for supplying considerable practical advice; and Ronald Nuttall, for rendering invaluable bibliographical aid. I would also like to thank the Marshall Field Foundation and its executive, Maxwell Hahn, for granting Harvard University's Laboratory of Social Relations the funds for the research upon which much of this volume is based. The generosity of the Field Foundation is particularly appreciated because it came at a time when many other foundations were refusing to support race relations research. Finally, I wish to thank my wife, Ann Hallman Pettigrew, for her multiple roles as co-author of Chapter 4 plus editor and typist of the entire manuscript.

                                                                   T.F.P.

Cambridge, Massachusetts
April, 1964

TABLE OF CONTENTS

LIST OF FIGURES

INTRODUCTION

They are "a lazy, apathetic people, eating coarse food and indifferent to the arts and comforts of life." Backward and inferior, they have failed to produce "a good poet, a capable mathematician, or a man of genius in a single art or a single science." (141, pp. 14, 136)[1]

These charges sound suspiciously similar to the racist stereotype of the Negro American; but actually they were made by influential European writers of the late eighteenth and early nineteenth centuries against *all* Americans. Advanced by such men as Cornelius de Pauw, a Dutch scholar, Peter Kalm, a Swedish naturalist, and Abbé Raynal, a French scientist, these assertions were a part of a widely accepted theory of "American degeneration." (141) The central contention of this theory was simple in the extreme: the severe climate of North America led inevitably to physical and mental retardation and retrogression among every living thing—plants, animals, and humans. No people could prosper in such an environment; indolence, apathy, ill-health, and stupidity would forever mark Americans.

Naturally, Americans of revolutionary times did not take kindly to such ideas. Benjamin Franklin and Thomas Jefferson led the effort at disproving the stereotype, with Jefferson devoting a goodly portion of his famous *Notes on Virginia* to a refutation of the charges of American degeneration. Often these rebuttals betrayed a strong defensiveness. Much was made of unusually large animal skeletons. Far from degenerating, argued Americans, animals actually grew bigger and better in North America.

[1] Numbers in parentheses refer to the relevant bibliographical sources listed at the close of the volume.

The theme of "bigger and better" suggests an attempt by many American defenders to convince themselves as well as their critics. These indications of lurking self-doubt were due in some measure to the reality of the situation. After all, when compared to old Europe, young America *was* relatively "indifferent to the arts and comforts of life." Though it had produced men like Franklin and Jefferson, it could not yet boast of the Old World's array of poets, mathematicians, and men of genius. Could the European critics be right? Were Americans doomed to be always the inferiors of their well-established cousins?

The long-term consequences of such fears for American culture and national character are difficult to over-estimate. The "bigger and better" claims are still heard —and not only in Texas. Or, just as significant, some Americans still emulate slavishly the manners, customs, and fashions of the Old World.

If Americans consider their history, they should have no difficulty in understanding how other people feel and react to outside charges of inferiority. The Soviet Union's expansive claims to the world's chief inventions and to a society "bigger and better" than those of the West have a familiar ring. Similar claims are now emanating from the new nations of Africa. Each national group— whether American, Soviet, or African—has reacted strongly and, to some extent, defensively to charges of inferiority. Each has demanded a sense of dignity and feeling of worth.

If this generalization holds true for national peoples considered unworthy by outsiders, it must apply with special force to peoples so considered by insiders, by their fellow citizens. Such is the case with the Negro American. For years he has had to face the charges of racists in his own society, charges that ironically echo many of the old sneers against the New World in general. He is supposed to be innately lazy, unhealthy, un-intelligent, and criminal. (186, 421, 468, 556) The con-sequences of these allegations for Negro Americans are even more serious than similar charges against early Americans. The disparagement by Europeans did not prevent white Americans from achieving at least part of the "American dream"; but racist assertions and the restrictions which flow from them have deferred for centuries the Negro American's attainment of this same dream.

This volume attempts to understand the individual Negro American and to ascertain "what happens to a dream deferred."

What happens to a dream deferred?
        Does it dry up
        like a raisin in the sun?
        Or fester like a sore—
        And then run?
        Does it stink like rotten meat?
        Or crust and sugar over—
        like a syrupy sweet?

        Maybe it just sags
        like a heavy load.

        Or does it explode?

LANGSTON HUGHES

From *Selected Poems of Langston Hughes.* New York:

Alfred A. Knopf, Inc., 1959   USED WITH PERMISSION

Part I

NEGRO AMERICAN PERSONALITY

1

THE ROLE AND ITS BURDENS

A small Negro boy came regularly to his play therapy
sessions. Each week he entered the playroom, sat at the
table, propped back his chair, placed his feet upon the
table, and then folded his arms majestically over his
chest. Week after week, the child came to the playroom,
repeated the performance, and sat with an impassive
expression on his face until the session ended. Finally,
he asked the therapist if she knew what he had been
playing. Eagerly, she confessed that she had no idea.
"I've been playing white man!" he announced. (22)

This incident aptly illustrates the translation of societal racism into personal terms, the effect of racial
discrimination upon the individual Negro. But discrimination does not affect all Negroes in the same way. There
are, of course, as many Negro American personalities
as there are Negro Americans. As Gordon W. Allport
and others emphasize, each individual has his own
unique personality, shaped by his special endowments
and experiences. (4) But the ubiquity of racial prejudice
in the United States guarantees that virtually every
Negro American faces at some level the impersonal effects of discrimination, the frightening feeling of being
a black man in what often appears to him to be a white
man's world.

PLAYING THE ROLE OF "NEGRO"

Like all human interactions, discriminatory encounters
between whites and Negroes require that both parties
"play the game." As the small Negro boy astutely recognized, the white must act out the role of the "superior";

by direct action or subtle cue, he must convey the expectation that he will be treated with deference. For his part, the Negro must, if racist norms are to be obeyed, act out the role of the "inferior"; he must play the social role of "Negro." And if he should refuse to play the game, he would be judged by the white supremacist as "not knowing his place," and harsh sanctions could follow.

The terror such a subordinate role can have for a white person, inexperienced in its subtleties, is revealed by John Griffin in his *Black Like Me*. (207) Artificially darkening his skin and traveling in the South as a "Negro," Griffin discovered viscerally what it is like to play the lowly role. He describes the "hate stare" intensely bigoted whites cast upon Negroes:

> It came from a middle-aged, heavy-set, well-dressed white man. He sat a few yards away, fixing his eyes on me. Nothing can describe the withering horror of this. You feel lost, sick at heart before such unmasked hatred . . . (207, p. 53)

Griffin concludes:

> The Negro is treated not even as a second-class citizen, but as a tenth-class one. His day-to-day living is a reminder of his inferior status. He does not become calloused to those things—the polite rebuffs when he seeks better employment; hearing himself referred to as nigger, coon, jigaboo; having to bypass available rest-room facilities or eating facilities to find one specified for him. Each new reminder strikes at the raw spot, deepens the wound. (207, p. 47)

The socially-stigmatized role of "Negro" is the critical feature of having dark skin in the United States. "It is part of the price the Negro pays for his position in this society," comments James Baldwin, "that, as Richard Wright points out, he is almost always acting." (25, p. 68) At the personality level, such enforced role adoption further divides the individual Negro both from other human beings and from himself. Of course, all social roles, necessary as they are, hinder to some extent forthright, uninhibited social interaction. An employer and employee, for example, may never begin to understand each other as complete human beings unless they break through the formality and constraints of their role relationship, unless they "let their hair down." Likewise, whites and Negroes can never communicate as equals unless they break through the role barriers. As long as racial roles are maintained, both parties find it difficult to perceive the humanity behind the façade. Many whites who are by no means racists confuse the role of "Negro" with the people who must play this role. "Negroes are just like that," goes the phrase, "they are born that way." Conversely, many Negroes confuse the role of "white man" with whites. "Whites are just like that, they are born thinking they should be boss."

Intimately associated with this impairment of human relatedness is an impairment of the individual's acceptance and understanding of himself. Both whites and Negroes can confuse their own roles as being an essential part of themselves. Whites can easily flatter themselves into the conviction that they are in fact "superior"; after all, does not the deferential behavior of the role-playing Negro confirm this "superiority"? And Negroes in turn often accept much of the racists' mythology; for does not the imperious behavior of the role-playing white confirm this "inferiority"?

These are not mere speculations of existentialist philosophy. A large body of psychological research convincingly demonstrates the power of role-playing to change deeply-held attitudes, values, and even conceptions of self.[1] Moreover, these remarkable changes have been rendered by temporary role adoptions of an exceedingly trivial nature when compared to the life-long

[1] Psychotherapists have long utilized this process in "psycho-drama" and other clinical techniques. Recently, social psychologists have subjected the process to intensive laboratory investigation in their study of attitude-change. (107, 239, 252, 273, 277, 450, 451)

role of "Negro." [2] Imagine, then, the depth of the effects of having to play a role which has such vast personal and social significance that it influences virtually all aspects of daily living. Indeed, the resulting confusion of self-identity and lowering of self-esteem are two of the most serious "marks of oppression" upon Negro American personality.

SELF-IDENTITY AND SELF-ESTEEM

The quest for self-identity is the search for answers to the all-important questions: Who am I? What am I like as a person? And how do I fit into the world? These are not easy questions for anyone to answer in our complex, swiftly-changing society. Yet they offer even greater difficulties for Negro Americans.

We learn who we are and what we are like largely by carefully observing how other people react to us. But this process is highly structured for the Negro by the role he is expected to play. When he attempts to gain an image of himself on the basis of his typical contacts with white America and the general culture, he often receives a rude jolt. While he is totally American in every conceivable meaning of the term, he finds that most Americans are white and that somehow the mere color of his skin puts him into a unique and socially-defined inferior category. And when the Negro looks around him—except in the spheres of athletics and entertainment—he discovers very few Americans with his skin color who hold important positions in his society. Save for the mass media expressly tailored for Negro audiences, he sees only white models in advertisements and only whites as heroes of stories. (41, 309, 469, 559) When he does see Negroes in the general mass media, they are likely to be cast in low-status roles and appear

[2] The studies cited in Footnote 1 either required a single public presentation orally of a position counter to that held by the subject or a written essay counter to the subject's opinion. Yet all of them demonstrated significant shifts in opinion.

as "amusingly ignorant." [3] Little wonder, then, that the question, who am I?, raises special difficulties for him.

Identity problems are unusually acute during certain periods in a person's life. These periods, these identity-crises, often occur in the preschool years, later in adolescence, and again in young adulthood. All three of these periods impose additional stress on Negroes. Negro parents confess to great anxiety and ambivalence over telling their preschool children what it means to be a Negro in American society. Should youngsters be shielded from the truth as long as possible? Or should they be prepared early for blows that are sure to come?

The importance of identity problems for young Negro children has been demonstrated by a series of ingenious investigations. Following the classical work of Kenneth and Mamie Clark[4] (85, 87), these researches have utilized a wide assortment of techniques in a variety of segregated Southern and integrated Northern nursery and school settings and have consistently arrived at the same critical conclusions. (198, 295, 369, 493, 516) Racial recognition in both white and Negro children appears by the third year and rapidly sharpens each year thereafter. Of special significance is the tendency found in all of these studies for Negro children to prefer white skin. They are usually slower than white children to make racial distinctions, they frequently prefer white dolls and white friends, and they often identify themselves as white or show a tense reluctance to acknowledge that they are Negro. Moreover, young children of both races soon learn to assign, realistically, poorer houses and less desirable roles to Negro dolls. This early "mark of oppression" is illustrated by the behavior of a small Negro boy who participated in one of these studies con-

[3] Mass media stereotypes of minority group members are currently becoming more favorable. (449)

[4] The Clarks' work was prominently cited in the famous Footnote 11 of the United States Supreme Court 1954 public school desegregation ruling.

ducted in Lynchburg, Virginia. Asked if he were white or colored, he hung his head and hesitated. Then he murmured softly, "I guess I'se kinda colored." (369, p. 137)

Some of this direct manifestation of "self-hate" disappears in later years (291), though similar studies of older Negro children find residual symptoms. (258, 456) One investigation of children aged eight to thirteen years in an interracial summer camp found that Negroes tended at first to be oversensitive to unfavorable behavior of their Negro peers and to avoid choosing other Negroes as friends. (561) A successful experience in an egalitarian, interracial setting, however, can alleviate these inclinations. In this study, a two-week experience in interracial camping is shown to have significantly modified these expressions of self-hate in the young Negro campers.

In the teens, sex becomes an acute issue. This is a period of great strain for most American adolescents, but for the Negro child in the North who has close friendships with white children, it frequently means a sudden parting of paths. After puberty, the Negro child is no longer invited to his white friends' parties, for at this time the deep racist fears of miscegenation harbored by many white parents enter on the scene. For the majority of Negro youth of this age who have no white friends, the early teens introduce their own version of identity-crisis. From his teachers, his peer group, his contacts with the white world beyond his immediate neighborhood, the Negro teenager encounters new shocks. The full awareness of his social devaluation in the larger society in addition to the sharp strains felt by all teenagers in a complex society can assume the dimensions of a severe emotional stress-situation. (363)

If the ambitious Negro has successfully weathered these earlier crises, he must face yet another series of identity-shocks in young adulthood. Employment discrimination may keep him from the job for which he trained, and housing segregation may restrict him from securing the type of housing he wants for his family. Who am I? What am I like as a person? And how do I fit into the world? The old questions from childhood continue to require answers when he is refused a job for which he is qualified and a house for which he has the purchase price.

This confused identity in adulthood even reveals itself among the most militant and articulate Negroes. A careful statistical analysis of Richard Wright's autobiography, *Black Boy*, strongly suggests this famous Negro writer lacked a basic identification with other Negroes. Four-fifths of his descriptions of Negroes are unfavorable and do not at all coincide with his recurrent self-descriptions. "My life at home," wrote Wright, "has cut me off, not only from white people but from Negroes as well." (539, pp. 454-456)

These identity problems are inextricably linked with problems of self-esteem. For years, Negro Americans have had little else by which to judge themselves than the second-class status assigned them in America. And along with this inferior treatment, their ears have been filled with the din of white racists egotistically insisting that Caucasians are innately superior to Negroes. Consequently, many Negroes, consciously or unconsciously, accept in part these assertions of their inferiority. In addition, they accept the American emphases on "status" and "success." But when they employ these standards for judging their own worth, their lowly positions and their relative lack of success lead to further self-disparagement. Competition with successful whites is especially threatening. Laboratory experimentation demonstrates that even when Negroes receive objective evidence of equal mental ability in an interracial situation they typically feel inadequate and respond compliantly. (271)

The sweeping changes of recent years, however, have begun to alter this situation. The old wounds of confused identity and damaged self-esteem have not sufficiently healed, but recent events are potent medicines. Supreme Court decisions, in particular, brought new hope. A 1963 *Newsweek* national poll found that two-thirds of all Negroes credited the Supreme Court for their biggest breakthroughs. "It started the ball rolling," voiced one respondent. And another added, "The Supreme Court gave us heart to fight." (382, p. 27) Moreover, the Negro's own protests and assertion of civil rights (Chapter 7), his increasing educational and economic opportunities, the findings of social science, and the emergence of proud new African nations all have salved the old wounds.

It is difficult for white Americans to grasp the full personal significance of these events for Negro Americans. But imagine how a Negro feels today. All of his life he has been bombarded with white-supremacy ideas and restrictions. Moreover, he has shared much of the naïve conception of Africa as the dark continent of wild and naked savages. Now he is greeted with evidence from all sides that the white supremacists are wrong. On television, he sees segregationists desperately defying his national government in their losing battle to maintain Jim Crow, he sees his President conferring with black chiefs of state with full pomp and circumstance, and he sees his nation's representatives wooing the all-important black delegates to the United Nations. He sees all this, and his wounds begin to heal. The special role of "Negro" remains, but is undergoing drastic change. James Baldwin puts the matter forcefully:

> . . . the American Negro can no longer, nor will he ever again, be controlled by white America's image of him. This fact has everything to do with the rise of Africa in world affairs. At the time that I was growing up, Negroes in this country were taught to be ashamed of Africa. . . . One was always being mercilessly scrubbed and polished, as though in the hope that a stain could thus be washed away. . . . The women were forever straightening and curling their hair, and using bleaching creams. . . . But none of this is so for those who are young now. . . . by the time they were able to react to the world, Africa was

on the stage of history. This could not but have an extraordinary effect on their own morale, for it meant that they were not merely the descendants of slaves in a white, Protestant, and puritan country: they were also related to kings and princes in an ancestral home- land, far away. And this has proved to be a great anti- dote to the poison of self-hatred." (26, pp. 79-81)

The recent rise of Africa is especially important in the changing self-images of very dark Negro Americans. A survey of working-class Negroes in Boston related skin color to attitudes and knowledge of Africa. (401) Fig- ure 1 presents the results. Note that dark Negroes most often agreed that African independence enhanced the self-conceptions of Negro Americans and disagreed that Africans are of no help in the American civil rights struggle. Furthermore, the better-educated dark Negroes were best informed about Africa. Though they identified Negro-American leaders less accurately than other Ne- groes, darker respondents with at least a high school edu- cation more often knew who Haile Selassie I and Kwame Nkrumah were.

THE HOSTILE ENVIRONMENT

Another widespread reaction to racism is a generalized perception of the world as a hostile, threatening place. Horace Cayton considers this a critical feature of the "oppression phobia" experienced by many Negro Ameri- cans: an expectancy of violent mistreatment combined with a feeling of utter helplessness. (76) Negroes ques- tioned in *Newsweek's* national poll groped for words to describe this phobia: "the feeling of being choked," said one; "feels like being punished for something you didn't do," said another. (382, p. 18) Such feelings are also experienced by other minority groups. Many Jews, for instance, have reported a preoccupation with anti-Semit- ism and a vague sense of impending doom, of haunting anxiety, hovering over them. (3)

Psychological studies of young Negro children reveal that this phobia has early roots. One such investigation

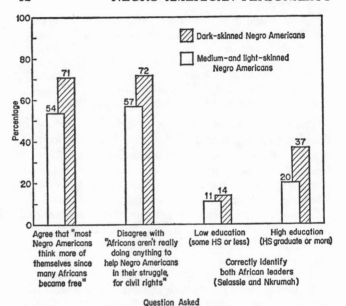

FIGURE 1—SKIN COLOR AND ORIENTATION TOWARD AFRICA

(Data from: T. F. Pettigrew, "Skin Color and Negro American Personality," unpublished paper.)

utilized the Thematic Apperception Test (TAT), a set of imagination-provoking pictures on the basis of which respondents compose brief stories. It found that a sample of nine-to-fourteen-year-old Negro boys viewed the environment as a far more hostile, dangerous entity than comparable white boys.[5] (374) These Negro youths typically told stories in which the hero—presumably themselves—is hated, reprimanded, restricted, or injured. By contrast, the white youths generally fashioned heroes who, unencumbered by environmental barriers, were greatly admired and respected.

[5] A similar perception of the world as a hostile and threatening place has been noted among Arabs who were establishing themselves in cities and who were at the time being treated as an inferior minority group by the French. (124)

Reality testing is involved here, of course, for the world *is* more often a treacherous, threatening place for Negroes. Consider the social scars of discrimination throughout Negro American history that make this true. Slavery cast the longest shadow. Compared with the institution in Latin America, slavery in the United States had an unusually crushing impact upon Negro personality, because it did not recognize the slave as a human being. (143, 508) Spain and Portugal had centuries of experience with slavery prior to the founding of the New World, hence Iberian law had evolved a special place for the slave as a human being with definite, if limited, rights. By contrast, England had no previous involvement with the "peculiar institution," and so its law, adopted by the American colonies, treated the slave as mere property—no different legally from a house, a barn, or an animal. (508)

Recently, one historian ventured a parallel between Southern slavery on the large, cotton plantations and the concentration camps of Nazi Germany. (143) Both were closed systems, with little chance of manumission, emphasis on survival, and a single, omnipresent authority.[6] The profound personality change created by Nazi internment, as independently reported by a number of psychologists and psychiatrists who survived, was toward childishness and total acceptance of the SS guards as father-figures—a syndrome strikingly similar to the "Sambo" caricature of the Southern slave. Nineteenth-century racists readily believed that the "Sambo" personality was simply an inborn racial type. Yet no African anthropological data have ever shown any personality type resembling Sambo; and the concentration camps molded the equivalent personality pattern in a wide variety of Caucasian prisoners. Nor was Sambo merely

[6] One important psychological difference did exist, however, between the two situations. After the first generation of slaves in America, Negroes were born into slavery and had never experienced any other condition of life. Jews, by contrast, had known the life of free men prior to their internment by the Nazis.

a product of "slavery" in the abstract, for the less devastating Latin American system never developed such a type. (143)

Extending this line of reasoning, psychologists point out that slavery in all its forms sharply lowered the need for achievement in slaves. (335, pp. 376-377) Negroes in bondage, stripped of their African heritage, were placed in a completely dependent role. All of their rewards came, not from individual initiative and enterprise, but from absolute obedience—a situation that severely depresses the need for achievement among all peoples. Most important of all, slavery vitiated family life. (32, pp. 240-247; 170) Since many slaveowners neither fostered Christian marriage among their slave couples nor hesitated to separate them on the auction block, the slave household often developed a fatherless, matrifocal (mother-centered) pattern.

Strong traces of these effects of slavery, augmented by racial discrimination, have persisted since Emancipation because of bitter poverty and the uprooted life of migrants far from home. Poverty, is not limited to Negroes, of course, but it takes on a special meaning when due in part to the color of one's skin. Though a substantial number of Negroes have improved their status economically, a much greater percentage of Negroes than whites comprise the nation's most destitute citizens. For these Negroes, poverty means living in the degraded slums of our largest cities in close proximity to the worst centers of the nation's vice and crime. Poverty means less education, less opportunity, and less participation in the general culture. And it means less ability to throw off the effects of past oppression. A Negro drug addict and ex-felon expresses the matter bluntly:

> . . . a young kid growing up in Harlem, the only people he sees who have money are the pimps, the prostitutes, the people in the sporting world. So then maybe he go home and maybe his mother ain't working and he asks her for money and she ain't got none and maybe sometimes there ain't no food. Then he

grows up and gets a job and all his money goes for rent and food and clothes. . . . You ain't got nothing. Then you see the sporting people and they seem always to have it, right in their pockets. A man got to be pretty strong to resist that temptation. (266, pp. 126-127)

Furthermore, Negro Americans are often lonely, recent arrivals to huge metropolitan areas, strangers detached from their home moorings. Between 1950 and 1960, over one-and-a-half million Negroes left the South and came to cities in the North and West; others came to Southern cities from the farms. (Chapter 8) These migrants are frequently ill prepared for the demands of urban life, with only an inferior Southern rural education and few if any job skills. Consequently, they must fit onto the lowest rungs of the occupational ladder and hope for economic survival in an age when automation is dramatically reducing the number of jobs for unskilled workers. Small wonder such individuals come to view the world as a hostile place.

FAMILY DISORGANIZATION AND PERSONALITY

Both poverty and migration also act to maintain the old slave pattern of a mother-centered family. Not only does desperate poverty disturb healthy family life through dilapidated housing, crowded living conditions, restricted recreational facilities, and direct contact with the most corrupting elements of urban disorganization, but it makes the ideal American pattern of household economics practically impossible. Employment discrimination has traditionally made it more difficult for the poorly-educated Negro male to secure steady employment than the poorly-educated Negro female. In many areas of the nation, North as well as South, this is still true, with Negro females always able to obtain jobs as domestics if nothing else is available. When the unskilled Negro male does manage to secure a job, he generally assumes an occupation that pays barely enough to support himself—much less a family. Such conditions obviously limit the ability of lower-class Negroes to follow the typical American pattern—that is, a stable unit with the husband providing a steady income for his family.

The Negro wife in this situation can easily become disgusted with her financially-dependent husband, and her rejection of him further alienates the male from family life. Embittered by their experiences with men, many Negro mothers often act to perpetuate the mother-centered pattern by taking a greater interest in their daughters than their sons. For example, more Negro females graduate from college than Negro males, the reverse of the pattern found among white Americans.

Family stability also suffers from the effects of migration, with its tensions over relocation and its release of the migrant from the sanctions of his home community. When all of these factors are considered, the prevalence of divorce, separation, and illegitimacy among poor Negroes should not come as a surprise. For when American society isolates the lower-class Negro from contact with the general norms and prevents him from sharing in the rewards which follow from abiding by these norms, it guarantees the emergence of a ghetto subculture with different standards of conduct, motivation, and family life.

Census data for 1960 illustrate the depth of this family disorganization among Negroes: over a third (34.3 per cent) of all non-white mothers with children under six years of age hold jobs as compared with less than a fifth (19.5 per cent) of white mothers with children under six[7] (523); only three-fourths (74.9 per cent) of all non-white families have both the husband and the wife present in the household as compared with nine-tenths (89.2 per cent) of white families[8] (523); and

[7] During 1950, 35 per cent of all non-white mothers under forty-five years of age held jobs compared with 19 per cent of similarly-aged white mothers. (189, p. 98)

[8] The vast majority of incomplete Negro households is lacking the husband. Frazier estimated in 1950 that the male parent was missing in roughly 20 per cent of Negro households. (168) In addition to divorce and separation, part of this phenomenon is

only two-thirds (66.3 per cent) of non-whites under eighteen years of age live with both of their parents as compared with nine-tenths (90.2 per cent) of such whites. (523) These data do not cancel out the effects of social class differences between the two groups; rough comparisons between the lower classes of each race, however, still reveal a greater prevalence of father-absence among Negroes. The scar of slavery upon Negro family life, perpetuated through poverty and migration, is still evident.

Recent psychological research vividly demonstrates the personality effects upon children of having been raised in a disorganized home without a father. One such study reveals that eight-and-nine-year-old children whose fathers are absent seek immediate gratification far more than children whose fathers are present in the home. For example, when offered their choice of receiving a tiny candy bar immediately or a large bar a week later, fatherless children typically take the small bar while other children prefer to wait for the larger bar. (366) This hunger for immediate gratification among fatherless children seems to have serious implications. Regardless of race, children manifesting this trait also tend to be less accurate in judging time, less "socially responsible," less oriented toward achievement, and more prone toward delinquency. (364, 365) Indeed, two psychologists maintain that the inability to delay gratification is a critical factor in immature, criminal, and neurotic behavior.[9] (372)

Sex-role adoption is a second personality area which distinguishes children from intact homes from those in

due to a higher Negro male death rate. The percentage of widows among Negro women fifty-four years old or less is roughly twice that of white women. (357)

[9] Contributing to this situation is the fact that where fathers are not present children more often have the additional stigma of being illegitimate. Although illegitimacy is more naturally accepted in lower-class Negro culture (286), careful research reveals better school and personal "adjustment" among legitimate Negro children. (257)

homes without fathers. One study found that five-to-fourteen-year-old Negro youths without fathers experienced unusual difficulty in differentiating between male and female roles. Thus, boys and girls without fathers described themselves in very similar ways, while boys from whole families described themselves in considerably more masculine terms than girls from whole families. (111) Another investigation of high school students reported far sharper differences between the sexes in their values among white than among Negro children. This occurred primarily because the Negro girls revealed interests generally associated with males; compared with the white girls, they valued theoretical and political concerns more and religious and esthetic concerns less. Significantly, these Negro children more often came from families without fathers than did the white children. (312)

Studies of white American boys whose fathers left them during World War II and of Norwegian boys whose sailor-fathers ship out for years at a time report related phenomena. These father-deprived boys are markedly more immature, submissive, dependent, and effeminate than other boys both in their overt behavior and fantasies. (23, 314, 453, 455, 497) Eight-and-nine-year-old, father-absent Norwegian boys, for instance, when playing with self-representative dolls, put them in a crib rather than a bed. (314) As they grow older, this passive behavior may continue, but, more typically, it is vigorously overcompensated for by exaggerated masculinity. Juvenile gangs, white and Negro, classically act out this pseudo-masculinity with leather jackets, harsh language, and physical "toughness." (361)

The reasons for these characteristics of father-absent children seem clear. Negro girls in such families model themselves after their mothers and prepare to assume male as well as female responsibilities. And various investigations have demonstrated the crucial importance of the father in the socialization of boys. (27, 375) Mothers raising their children in homes without fathers are frequently overprotective, sometimes even smothering, in their compensatory attempts to be a combined father and mother. Burton and Whiting persuasively contend that the boys whose fathers are not present have initially identified with their mothers and must later, in America's relatively patrifocal society, develop a conflicting, secondary identification with males. (68) In other words, they must painfully achieve a masculine self-image late in their childhood after having established an original self-image on the basis of the only parental model they have had—their mother.

Several studies point to the applicability of this sex-identity problem to lower-class Negro males. Two objective test assessments of widely different groups—Alabama jail prisoners and Wisconsin working-class veterans with tuberculosis—found that Negro males scored higher than white males on a measure of femininity. (69, 234) This measure is a part of the Minnesota Multiphasic Inventory (MMPI), a well-known psychological instrument that requires the respondent to judge the applicability to himself of over five hundred simple statements. Thus, Negroes in these samples generally agreed more often with such "feminine" choices as "I would like to be a singer" and "I think that I feel more intensely than most people do."

Psychiatrists have noted the prevalence of pseudo-masculine defenses among neurotic Negro male patients. (448) And an investigation employing the personality-probing Thematic Apperception Test (TAT) with a representative national sample revealed Negro males to be unusually high in their need for social power and dominance. This need is apparently a compensatory reaction to their lowly role, for it, too, grows partly out of the broken home situation. The same study demonstrated that a strongly-felt need for power is a typical personality trait among men, Negro and white, raised by only one parent as opposed to men from intact homes. (529) Finally, a survey of working-class Negroes in Boston matched 21 adult males whose fathers had been absent during their early childhoods, with 21 men who possessed similar social characteristics (age, income, education, region of birth, etc.), but whose fathers had been present during their early childhoods. (402) Figure 2 illustrates the differences between these matched groups. The most critical distinction involves marriage; the first group of men was more likely to be either single or divorced—another manifestation of their disturbed sexual identification. They also felt more victimized, less in control of the environment, and more distrustful of others. (Figure 2)

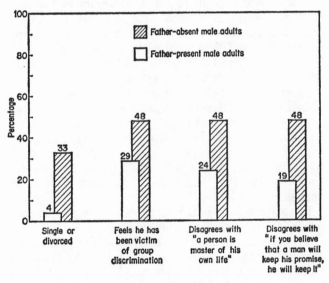

Question Asked

FIGURE 2—FATHER ABSENCE AND ADULT NEGRO PERSONALITY

(Data from: T. F. Pettigrew, "Father Absence and Negro Adult Personality: A research note," unpublished paper.)

These findings reflect not only the effects of family disorganization but also the effeminate aspects of the "Negro" role many of these men must play in adult life. Servility is often required, and most low-paying service occupations typically open to unskilled Negro males—for example, cook, waiter, orderly, dishwasher—generally carry a connotation in American culture of being "women's work." Thus, the sex-identity problems created by the fatherless home are perpetuated in adulthood.

Personality development of children in families without fathers may also be related to three recurrent problems among Negro Americans: juvenile delinquency, crimes against persons, and schizophrenia. More research is necessary to link definitely these symptoms of social disorganization to impaired family structure, but present data are most suggestive. In predicting juvenile crime, Eleanor and Sheldon Glueck find that more delinquent boys, when compared with non-delinquents, come from broken homes. (193, p. 280) Other researchers, focusing upon the "good" boy in high delinquency neighborhoods, note that such non-delinquents typically come from exceptionally stable, intact families. These boys think of themselves as "good" and score favorably on a personality measure of socialization. (445) Family disorganization upsets this normal socializing influence of the home and creates the potential for juvenile delinquency. Community institutions such as the school and the church, which sometimes can help deter delinquent acts, simply do not possess the same meaning for unsocialized children from impaired families as they do for other children. (168) In fact, one investigator finds that Negro delinquents tend to come from homes even more unstable than those of comparable white delinquents. (21)

The findings connecting personal crime and schizophrenia with family structure are more tenuous. One ingenious study of a variety of non-literate societies throughout the world reveals that those with high rates of crime against persons are characterized by: mother-child households with inadequate opportunity to identify with the father; mother-child sleeping arrangements which foster a strong dependent relationship between the child and his mother; an abrupt and anxiety-producing preparation for independence; and a general distrustfulness of others (as in Figure 2). (24) Perhaps personal crime is merely one aspect of the masculine façade which mother-raised boys tend to present as they enter "the man's world." Concerned about their sexual identity, they assert their masculinity through person-directed violence. In any event, this suggestive lead deserves further attention in research among Negro Americans. Likewise, a matrifocal situation, particularly a family composed of a strong mother and a present but weak father, seems to be positively related to schizophrenia. (293) Since this pattern is common even among intact lower-class Negro families and this particular psychosis is especially prevalent among lower-class Negroes, future research along these lines is also indicated.

These considerations have led social scientists to emphasize the stability and structure of the home as crucial factors in counteracting the effects of racism upon Negro personality. A warm, supportive home can effectively compensate for many of the restrictions the Negro child faces outside of the ghetto; consequently, the type of home life a Negro enjoys as a child may be far more crucial for governing the influence of segregation upon his personality than the form the segregation takes— legal or informal, Southern or Northern. (20) One psychologist maintains that full awareness of his social devaluation and role as a "Negro" does not usually impinge upon the individual until early adolescence. (263) Just how the Negro bears up under this severe emotional stress is largely a function of the degree of ego-strength that he has developed in his earlier, family-centered years. The ego-strong Negro, nurtured in a stable and complete family, may come out of this stressful encounter harboring some self-hatred, but he generally manages to dissociate his basic personality from his socially-defined role of "Negro." He maintains his self-respect as a unique and worthwhile human being apart from the position of inferior being that the racists insist he assume. As one elderly Negro candidly expressed it, "Being a Negro is no disgrace, but it sure is an inconvenience." (262)

By contrast, the "psychologically vulnerable" Negro, crippled by weak ego development from earlier family disorganization, is more likely to fall prey to mental illness, drug addiction, or crime, depending on his particular life history. He has few personality resources to withstand the gale winds of discrimination that strike him full force in adolescence. Thus, segregation has its most fundamental influence on Negro personality in the manner in which it affects Negro family functioning. (263)

Case studies bear out these contentions. In their psychoanalytic investigation of 25 Negroes, *The Mark of Oppression,* Kardiner and Ovesey studied "O. D.," a twenty-nine-year-old, lower-class male. (266, pp. 91-98) Although he was a trained automobile mechanic, O. D. had been forced by the usual pattern of employment discrimination to take a series of poorly-paid service jobs with their typically effeminate features—dishwasher, short order cook, and hospital orderly. His mother had been warm yet strict, but he had never known a stable father-figure during his poor, and sometimes hungry, childhood. As an adult, O. D. had substituted an aggressive, educated wife for his mother and had become very dependent upon her. Also consistent with the father-deprived personality pattern were his serious difficulties in adopting a masculine role; he suffered from problems of sexual impotency and an almost complete inability to express anger. The case of O. D. offers an example of a lower-class Negro who, made "psychologically vulnerable" by an impaired family background, expressed his serious personality difficulties in sexual disturbance.

The case studies of New Orleans Negroes conducted by Rohrer and his associates provide further examples. (438) This research consisted of a re-examination of individuals who, as children nearly two decades earlier, had served as subjects for a pioneer study of Negro personality, published as *Children of Bondage.* (115) Again the devastating personality scars rendered by the absence of fathers in matrifocal family life were apparent in many of the lower-class Negroes. Girls raised in such households tended as adults to establish similar households for themselves and to live either with or very close to their mothers. Boys from this background evidenced the familiar pattern of conflict over sexual identity. Many of them as youths had joined gangs of older boys and acted out this conflict within the gang in the form of compulsive masculine behavior. "The gang member," conclude the investigators, "rejects this femininity in every form, and he sees it in women and in effeminate men, in laws and morals and religion, in schools and occupational striving." (438, p. 163) This blanket rejection by gang members of the values and institutions of society is obviously not likely to lead to an ambitious struggle out of the lower class. In fact, such alienation often leads directly into a life of crime, drug addiction, and deep despair.

"THE SELF-FULFILLING PROPHECY"

If, like these gang members, you believe the world to be a hostile place, you will probably act in such a manner as to cause the world to become in fact hostile toward you. In this sense, a person's own beliefs about a social situation can contribute to shaping the situation. Such beliefs, then, are "self-fulfilling prophecies." (348)

This phenomenon of social interaction is often crucially important in the exacerbation of the Negro's "marks of oppression." (222) The compliant Negro's behavior may serve both to "prove" the racists' contentions and to heighten and make more serious the personality scars inflicted by being classified and treated as an "inferior." A vicious circle can thus be established: the deeper the scars from discrimination, the more in keeping with the discrimination is the Negro's behavior, the greater the reinforcement of the discriminatory pattern, and thus the deeper the scars.

This vicious circle can be broken only by "outside" influences. Economic and political forces can restructure the discriminatory situation; new experiences, formal education, and the mass media can change the participants directly. These influences weaken the discriminatory pattern and begin a benign circle of allowing the scars of oppression to heal. And once these scars begin to heal, once the Negro gains a new image of himself and the situation, he can initiate change himself and further accelerate the self-correcting benign circle. (Chapters 7 and 8)

THE ROLE AND ITS BURDENS

"Suffering which falls to our lot in the course of nature, or by chance, or fate," commented Schopenhauer, "does not seem so painful as suffering which is inflicted on us by the arbitrary will of another." (3, p. 142) This sage observation has special force for Negro Americans. And the evidence reviewed in this chapter suggests that much of their "painful suffering" has been mediated through two social processes: the inferior role of "Negro" and severe family disorganization.

Being a Negro in America is less of a racial identity than a necessity to adopt a subordinate social role. The effects of playing this "Negro" role are profound and lasting. Evaluating himself by the way others react to him, the Negro may grow into the servile role; in time, the person and the role become indistinguishable. The personality consequences of this situation can be devastating—confusion of self-identity, lowered self-esteem, perception of the world as a hostile place, and serious sex-role conflicts.

By no means all Negro Americans succumb to these problems. Those reared in stable, accepting families generally develop the psychological resources to withstand the most debilitating aspects of the "Negro" role. But racial discrimination, from the time of slavery to the present, creates a type of family disorganization which causes many Negroes to be especially vulnerable to the role's full effects. The absence of the father in a sizable minority of Negro homes is particularly critical for personality development. Socialization without the agency of the father may be an important contributor to three persistent problems—juvenile delinquency, crime against persons, and schizophrenia. These, then, are the bitter fruits of racial prejudice and discrimination.

2

REACTIONS TO OPPRESSION

"To separate [Negro children] from others of similar age and qualifications solely because of their race," wrote Chief Justice Earl Warren in his 1954 public school desegregation opinion, "generates a feeling of inferiority as to their status in the community that may affect their hearts and minds in a way unlikely ever to be undone." This historic statement raises vital questions: How do Negroes live with feelings of inferiority that "affect their hearts and minds"? How do Negroes react to oppression? No psychological understanding of Negro Americans is possible without an examination of the answers to these queries.

Negroes in the United States have evolved a great variety of responses to the situations in which they find themselves. Broadly speaking, this diversity of reactions to oppression can be subsumed under three categories: moving toward, against, or away from the oppressor. (238) The first of these, moving toward, consists of seeking full acceptance as an equal human being. The other two form the familiar fight or flight pattern; moving against includes the numerous types of aggressive reactions, and moving away, the numerous types of avoidance reactions. In any individual Negro, some aspects of all three of these general alternatives are likely to be present, though one type of response usually predominates.

Moving Toward the Oppressor

Always a minority and long immersed in the national culture, Negro Americans have typically sought acceptance into a racially integrated society. On the social level, this preferred mode has expressed itself in repeated organizations. Today's National Association for the Advancement of Colored People, National Urban League, Congress on Racial Equality, Southern Christian Leadership Conference, and Student Non-Violent Coordinating Committee all strive without reservation for such a goal, all "move toward the oppressor." That these groups reflect, rather than generate, a Negro desire for racial desegregation is suggested by the data from the *Newsweek* 1963 opinion survey of Negroes throughout the nation: three out of four definitely preferred to work in a racially mixed group; two out of three to live in a mixed neighborhood; seven out of ten to send their children to a mixed school. In short, organizations oriented toward the oppressor represent the sentiments of a substantial majority of Negro Americans. (382)

On the individual level, this general type of reaction to discrimination leads to responses ranging from special vigilance to enhanced effort. For example, Negroes who wish to overcome the barriers of race and enter the mainstream of American life often develop an acute protective sensitivity in interracial situations. They learn to "sense" from subtle cues when they are likely to be rejected. One study had Negro and white graduate students make friendship choices and predict the choices of others after 12 meetings together in leaderless group discussions. The Negro subjects proved more attuned to the white social preferences than whites were to Negro preferences. (324) This keen sensitivity also exists among Negro children. Investigators at an interracial camp found that Negro children frequently prefer to observe others in the new situation quite carefully before actively participating themselves. As one eleven-year-old Negro boy phrased it: "I always test [a boy] by the things he does. I watch almost everything he does, to see if he would be nice to be a friend to, and to see if he likes me." (561, p. 43)

Such heightened vigilance and sensitivity are often accompanied by anxiety, hyperactivity, and sometimes mild dissociation. One questionnaire study of fourth, fifth, and sixth graders in the North found that Negroes manifested significantly more anxiety than whites. (388) Another investigation noted that this uneasiness is greater in integrated than segregated high schools, though the Negro students in the integrated schools were more satisfied with their teachers and school administrators. (420) Moreover, Negro adult males, in two separate questionnaire studies using the Minnesota Multiphasic Index (MMPI), scored considerably higher as a group than comparable whites on a standard measure of manic behavior, indicating a tendency toward anxious hyperactivity. (69, 234) Typical items from this MMPI scale are: "I work under a great deal of tension," and "I have long periods of such great restlessness that I cannot sit long in a chair."

Finally, as previously mentioned, Negroes may handle tense interracial situations by attempting to separate their true selves from their role as "Negro." Allport points out that this mechanism actually involves a mild dissociation; one is "himself" with other Negroes but transforms his behavior to meet the expectations of prejudiced whites. (3, p. 58) Some such dissociation occurs in the acting out of many social roles, but the intensity of racial role-playing renders this type of dissociation especially dangerous. Carried to extremes, it culminates in mental disorder.

More commonly, however, Negroes are unable to maintain this split effectively, and their confusion of self and role shapes their personalities into the narrowly prescribed mold of the deferent, shy, dependent human being. Particularly is this true for many Negro Southerners. Three different research projects using the Edwards Personal Preference Schedule on Negro college students in the South provide the relevant data.[1] (58, 211, 212)

[1] Special methodological problems are involved when Negro Southerners are compared directly with white national norms in this fashion (400), so caution must be taken not to overgeneralize from these data.

When compared to white liberal arts college students, the Negro liberal arts students in each of these studies scored distinctly higher on deference and lower on exhibitionism, autonomy, and dominance. Though counter to the stereotype of the "Negro," two other findings replicated by all three projects fit with this pattern. The Negro students were markedly high in organizing their work and lives systematically and low in their interest in the opposite sex.

Yet it should be remembered that shortly after these data were collected, Negro college students in the South began their now-famous sit-in protest movement. Though the non-violent technique of the sit-ins may have some special appeal for those with deferent personalities, this movement strongly suggests that those students who initiate sit-in demonstrations tend to be those who have successfully separated their conceptions of themselves from their racial role. (Chapter 7)

Other Negroes utilize less dramatic ways of moving toward the general culture. They try to overcome racial obstacles through sheer personal effort. An interesting example of Negro American striving comes from World War II. Negroes comprised less than one per cent of the Army's officer corps during the war, and Negro soldiers realistically ranked their chances of promotion as relatively poor. Yet many Negro enlisted men still hoped for and sought officer rank; in fact, at every educational level, they expressed a desire to become officers more often than white enlisted men. (498)

This reaction to discrimination seems to appear in elementary form at a very early age. It has been observed in an integrated kindergarten, for example, that Negro children at the dawn of racial awareness often react with overactivity and special vigor. (198) Yet such attempts at direct compensation do not generally continue unless they meet with some success. And on the lowest rungs of society success is rarely forthcoming. Consequently, a number of studies have shown that lower-class Negro children of school-age typically "give up the fight" and reveal unusually low need for achievement. (312, 347, 374, 440) More fortunate Negroes have their extra effort rewarded and continue to strive valiantly to attain distant goals and a record of excellence. Thus, upper-status Negro youths harbor surprisingly intense needs for achievement and set for themselves very high levels of aspiration. Their needs are more intense and their levels of achievement are higher than comparable white youths. (54, 440)

Such sharp social class differences in striving have assumed major significance in the last few decades. Class differentiation has been rapid within Negro urban communities, and a sizable, stable middle class has formed. The economic and social gains of these materially more secure Negroes, like the gains of other middle-class Americans, lead to better health, smaller families, and altered child rearing practices. (116, 259, 298, 454, 527) A new perspective on race relations also emerges, but its precise character is a matter of debate in social science circles.

Franklin Frazier emphasized the ambivalence of the Negro middle class over moving toward the general society. (169) In their restricted role as the elite of a segregated community, argued Frazier, middle-class Negroes typically find themselves squeezed between several conflicting pressures: the compulsion to demonstrate to whites their equal intelligence, talent, and respectability, the basic lack of identification with the Negro masses, and a desire for white acceptance only possible through desegregation—all encourage movement toward the oppressor; while vested economic and social interests in maintaining segregation influence movement away from the oppressor. As revealing evidence of the resulting ambivalence over desegregation, Frazier pointed to the heated disputes in numerous middle-class groups over the continued use of "Negro," "Colored," or "African" in organizational titles. (169, p. 299) Many of the organizations which maintain such terms are basically oriented to intragroup concerns and problems. Other organizations, such as the National Medical Association, are generally oriented toward universal concerns and usually exist because of exclusion from similar white groups.

The issue is clarified somewhat if a distinction is made between status and welfare goals in desegregation. (545) Those benefits from desegregation which are most attractive to middle-class Negroes generally involve an increase in social status and general acceptance in the wider culture; whereas direct economic benefits are the most attractive to poorer Negroes. For an extreme example, the middle class sometimes concerns itself most with the desegregation of public golf courses and seating at the opera, while the lower class becomes most involved when the desegregation of the building trades or aid-to-dependent-children programs are at issue.

Such generalizations, however, are at best approximate. They apply largely to that segment of the middle class most firmly sealed within the Negro community. But, as Frazier himself recorded (169, p. 301), the Negro middle class is becoming highly diverse. As racial barriers tumble, qualified Negroes are seizing the opportunity to market their job skills on the same basis as whites. Frazier concludes:

> This is resulting in an escape from the segregated Negro community where they have lived in a world of unreality into the world of reality where they can play a more responsible role as salaried professional and white-collar workers. (169, p. 301)

As this trend continues, middle-class persons increasingly predominate among those Negroes who most strongly evince a desire to move toward and gain acceptance in the total society. The Negro middle class usually furnishes the leaders for the major desegregation organizations and the trail blazers, the "first of the race" in newly desegregated institutions. (452, 533) Studies also show that its members have more favorable opinions of whites and are better able to make distinctions among different types of white people. (28, 101,

169, 337, 533, 536) Though sometimes spurned by whites, middle-class Negroes typically refrain from deprecation of those whom they wish to join.

The principal reasons for the increasing identification of middle-class Negroes with similarly-situated whites are the common values they share; personality research on middle-class Negroes and whites repeatedly finds far more similarities than differences. To cite representative examples, Negro medical students have essentially the same interests as white medical students (500); Negro Southern college students apply virtually the same criteria in selecting a marriage partner as white Northern college students[2] (503); Negro female college students in the South have a pattern of basic values quite similar to that of white female college students in the South (139, 206); and Negro grade-school children give the same explanations of physical phenomena as white grade-school children. (263) Research on Negro and white high-school students in Kentucky reveals that by this educational level similarities outweighed differences, although the two groups had been kept apart by segregation and were not equal in socio-economic standing. (312) Religious and social concerns rated highest with both, esthetic lowest. The predominantly lower-class Negroes, however, proved more oriented toward security, while the predominantly middle-class whites were more oriented toward self-expression—a distinction often noted between the social classes.[3] (312)

As desegregation progresses, similarities in interests,

[2] Both groups considered such criteria as mutual attraction, dependability, neatness and refinement, and consideration to be of particular importance, and such criteria as similar education and politics to be least important. Two interesting differences did arise, however. Negroes revealed a special concern over good health in their future mates, while whites emphasized insight and understanding. (503)

[3] Another study of male high-school seniors uncovered a comparable finding. Negro boys especially valued "a job which you are absolutely sure of keeping," and white boys especially valued "a very interesting job." (472)

values, and ideas among Americans of all colors will increase. And any lingering self-hate illusions Negroes still possess about the supposed "superiority" of the white world will also be dispelled. "Now I know there are some stupid white kids, too!" candidly remarked one of the Negro children who first desegregated Little Rock's schools when asked about her new interracial experience. Or, as Negro comedian, Dick Gregory, tells of his hypothetical sit-in experience: "I sat at a lunch counter for nine months, and, when they finally integrated, I suddenly discovered they didn't even have what I wanted!"

Sometimes, however, enhanced personal efforts to move toward the total culture results only in what Allport has termed "symbolic status striving." (3, pp. 157-158) The oppressed seeks the culturally-defined tinsel façade of success and not true success itself. He tries to attain status by conspicuous consumption and ostentatious display—expensive clothing, pretentious use of language, etc. Frazier, in his fiery *Black Bourgeoisie*, contended that conspicuous consumption is a central characteristic of the Negro middle class. Though he clearly overgeneralized his description, Frazier saw this behavior as a desperate attempt to gain within the ghetto the recognition long denied in the larger society. (171)

Symbolic status striving, of course, is by no means limited to members of minority groups. And it can often be a refusal to accept one's "place," an aggressive assertion of personal dignity: "You think I'm contemptible; well, I'll show you!" This trait shades into the second general category of reactions to oppression.

Moving Against the Oppressor

Just as there have been Negro social movements moving toward whites, there have been others moving against. Organized slave revolts presented an early example. And today the Black Muslims preach a vitriolic denunciation of the "blue-eyed devils" in their midst. This movement has not approached in size the mass fol-

lowing of Marcus Garvey in the 1920's, but it nevertheless sounds a resonant note throughout Negro America.
"There will never be many Muslims," muses Murray
Kempton, "but I should be surprised if there were not a
little Muslim in every Negro." (274)

Even at the social-movement level, however, hatred of
whites proves to be a difficult matter. The Negro's fundamental Americanism ensures that his hatred of white
Americans requires that he hate himself. The Muslim
ambivalence toward middle-class whites reveals this
mechanism clearly. The movement's newspaper, *Muhammad Speaks*, often takes unabashed and understandable
pride in the achievements of Negroes in the broader
society,[4] and it constantly exhorts the members to adopt
essentially the Protestant ethic of the white middle class:
"Observe the operations of the white man. He is successful. He makes no excuses for his failures. He works hard
—in a collective manner. You do the same."

The Muslims thus offer a means of mobility out of
the depths of the lower class without the necessity of
"selling out" to whites. In this sense, then, they move
toward as well as against the mainstream of American
society.

Similarly, on the individual level, aggressive, anti-
white reactions to discrimination are generally involved
in highly complex personality dynamics. Apart from
racial considerations, many personality theorists, such as
Erich Fromm, Karen Horney, Carl Rogers, and Harry

[4] In the November 30, 1962, issue of *Muhammad Speaks*, there
is a picture of Liberia's United Nations representative shaking
hands with Adlai Stevenson. The legend reads:

Liberia, though small in the realm of world politics, played a
highly important role in the United Nations' handling of the
explosive Cuban crisis. Here, Nathan Barnes, permanent Liberian
representative to the UN, receives congratulations and thanks
from a representative of a world power, Adlai Stevenson, permanent United States representative to the World Organization.

No damnation of the white man here; and no denunciation of
blacks who do favors for the white man.

Stack Sullivan, have emphasized the intimate connection between acceptance of self and acceptance of others.[5] (174, 237, 436, 502) "The peculiarity exists," declares Sullivan, "that one can find in others only that which is in the self." (502) Considerable empirical evidence supports this contention; repeatedly it is found that persons who think well of themselves tend to think well of others, while those who disapprove of themselves disapprove of others. (42, 43, 158, 159, 408, 464, 495, 565)

Likewise, Negroes who passionately hate whites tend to be those Negroes who most hate and reject themselves. In a study of 202 Negro children, one investigator noted that those children who harbored the most negative attitudes toward both Negroes and whites tended to be among the least self-accepting. (518) Studies of Negro college students reach a similar conclusion. These investigations revealed that those students who exhibited rejection of whites together with self-hate typically had "authoritarian personalities" (210, 489); that is, they exemplify a widely-recognized personality type marked by a lack of personal insight and a projection of aggressive impulses onto others. (1, 3, 79, 403) Finally, a study of 515 Negro adults in the South and Far West found that such authoritarians were generally more prejudiced against both other minority groups and whites as well as less identified with Negroes. (385a) For Negroes of all ages, then, moving against the oppressor is positively related to moving against oneself, a phenomenon also observed among Jews. (232, 562)

Since the playing of the role of "Negro" is likely to lead to low self-esteem, many Negroes also have a low

[5] Fromm argued that the hostility expressed against Jews in Hitler Germany was related to a type of cultural self-rejection. (174) Horney stated the principle in terms of a person who does not believe himself lovable being unable to love others. (237) Rogers has written: "When the individual perceives and accepts into one consistent and integrated system all his sensory and visceral experiences, then he is necessarily more understanding of others and is more accepting of others as separate individuals." (436, p. 520)

regard for others. In addition, there are intimate relationships between hate and love and between frustration
and aggression. The psychoanalytic principle that you
cannot hate that which you do not love is demonstrated
in anti-white feelings among Negroes. Highly organized
minorities with their own cultures, who are neither fully
accepted by the general society nor seeking acceptance,
typically do not disparage the majority; they ignore it, if
possible.[6] (553) It is precisely because Negro Americans
are fully acculturated, desperately want full acceptance,
and are denied this acceptance, that hostility against
whites is generated. (Chapter 6)

Add to these factors the many frustrations Negroes
receive in their role as "Negroes," and one can appreciate
the depth of the motivation to move against the oppressor. The contention of the frustration-aggression hypothesis that *all* aggression is preceded by frustration
means in this case that there is an enormous amount of
potential aggression created by the frustrating situations
in which Negroes find themselves trapped. (131) Naturally, not all frustration is released in aggression; fortunately, there are sublimating alternatives taking the
form of moving toward and away from the frustrator.
Nor is all of the aggression directed at whites; the angry
Negro often displaces his hostility onto safer targets.

Despite these alternatives, researchers have uncovered
empirical evidence of widespread aggression, bitterness,
and anti-white attitudes among Negro Americans. Studying 400 grade-school children in Virginia, one investigator employed a projective test which required the subject to draw a house, tree, and a person (the H-T-P
test). (215) The Negro children in the sample revealed
significantly more aggression in their drawings than the
higher-status white children with whom they were compared. This phenomenon was clarified by determining
with the TAT precisely which types of aggression dif-

---

[6] Also, within a minority, those members most marginal in terms
of appearance and of desire to enter the majority group often
possess the greatest degree of personal insecurity. (276, 325)

ferentiated the fantasies of young Negro and white boys. (374) The whites in this study told significantly more stories expressing "self-defensive aggression" and "killing in anger," while the Negroes told stories with far more "emotional and verbal aggression." Furthermore, the Negro stories contained fewer expressions of admiration and respect and fewer friendly relations.

The relative indirectness of this aggression among Negro youth has also been noted among Negro adults. Tentative data indicate that Negroes, particularly in the South, have special problems created by excessive denial of aggression.[7] (268) The open expression of hostility by Negroes toward whites is fraught with danger. In the South, such outbursts in the past have been punished by lynchings and other violence; so Negroes are naturally fearful of acting out their hostility. This repression of hostility often takes its toll in emotional dullness. However, an inquiry into the racial attitudes of 150 adults residing in an upstate New York community discovered that Southern-born Negroes in the relative safety of the North expressed markedly more anti-white feeling than Northern-born Negroes. (262) While roughly two-fifths of the migrants agreed, "Sometimes I hate white people" and "I would like to get even with the white man for some of the things he has done to Negroes," less than a fifth of the Northern-born Negroes agreed.

Aggressive resentment of whites and discrimination is openly expressed by Negroes in numerous ways. Research on Negro soldiers in World War II showed that they typically defined army situations in racial terms. Though Negroes adjusted to military life as well as whites, they candidly reported their anger over discriminatory treatment and their reluctance to serve in the South and under Southern officers. Many found it difficult to become enthusiastic about a war against racism, while racial

[7] These data are tentative because Southern whites were excluded from the study's analysis, making it impossible to determine whether the differences noted in the denial of aggression were racial, regional, or both. (268)

discrimination continued in the army and the nation at large. Those Negroes exhibiting the highest morale saw a link between their performance and the betterment of race relations; if we fight and die for America, went the reasoning, surely our country will no longer deny us our rights. (498) Repeated disappointment on this score after each war, however, has led a minority of Negroes to reject this expectation. *Newsweek's* 1963 national poll revealed roughly a fifth of the Negro population was at least not sure their nation was worth fighting for; the poorest of the ghetto-dwellers formed the bulk of these alienated respondents. (382)

The same poll extensively explored anti-white feelings among Negroes. The most intense loathing was reserved for white supremacists—the Ku Klux Klan, the White Citizens' Councils, and particular Southern governors. In general, they perceived improvement in white attitudes toward the rights of Negroes. A majority of the respondents felt that white attitudes had become more favorable during the previous five years, and three-fourths believed white attitudes would become increasingly favorable during the next five years.[8] Nevertheless, distrust and resentment of whites were widespread. Each interviewee was asked: "On the whole, do you think most white people want to see Negroes get a better break, or do they want to keep Negroes down, or do you think they don't care one way or the other?" Forty-one per cent of the sample believed most whites want to "keep down" Negroes; only a fourth thought most whites favored a "better break" for Negroes; 17 per cent felt whites did not "care one way or the other"; and the remaining 17 per cent were not sure. Responses varied sharply from group to group. Among a special group of militant Negro leaders, half held that most whites favored a "better break" for Negroes, and less than a tenth regarded most

---

[8] Less than 3 per cent believed white attitudes toward Negroes had become worse in the five previous years, and less than 2 per cent believed white attitudes would grow worse during the next five years. (382)

whites as attempting to "keep down" Negroes. And among middle- and upper-income Negro Southerners, almost three times more thought most whites wanted Negroes to get a "better break" than thought whites wanted to keep Negroes down (45 to 17 per cent). But the starkest bitterness appeared in the most deprived sections of Northern ghettos. Of low-income Negro Northerners, 56 per cent believed most white men were out to keep them down; only 6 per cent felt whites typically wanted to see Negroes have a "better break." (382)

Clinical observations support these data. Harry Stack Sullivan, after interviewing briefly a number of Negro youths in a small town in the Deep South, felt that his subjects suffered from a consuming, "ubiquitous hatred of the white." (501) Two separate psychiatric reports tell of Negro patients being overwhelmed with the problem of handling their aggressive impulses. (266, 448) In fact, Negro children often engage in a ritualistic game of abusive insults called "playing the dozens" which is a preparation for controlling such impulses. A player loses the game when the tormenting insults become more than he can tolerate, and he physically strikes out at his adversary. (40, 130)

Each Negro finds his own idiosyncratic manner of expressing and controlling his rage over racial barriers, of course, but certain broad generalizations are possible. Understandably, Negro males in the South appear as a group to be exceptionally passive, repressing their hostility for fear of retaliation. (268, 333) And Negroes of different social status typically vary in their handling of hostility. Just as moving toward the oppressor is more common among upper-status Negroes, moving against is more favored by lower-status Negroes. (81, 101, 282, 337, 382, 536) Furthermore, recent research suggests that skin color and the psychological problems it entails are factors; the darkest of lower-class Negroes harbor the most intense anti-white feelings of all. (401) To be sure, the open expression of aggressive impulses is more prevalent in lower-class American culture generally. But, in addition, the poorest and darkest of Negroes have the least to lose, have suffered the most severe physical deprivations, and have the fewest opportunities to gain acceptance. Even the desegregation process will not noticeably improve the lots of many of these people. (Chapter 7) Little wonder, then, that these people are susceptible to such movements as the Black Muslims which flaunt explicitly anti-white ideologies.

The means for moving against the oppressor range widely, from raw physical attack to an "aggressive meekness" that outwardly passes for extreme servility. Race riot behavior offers the most public exhibition of physical attack. In 1943, with suddenly elevated aspiration-levels of both whites and Negroes frustrated by war-time and racial restrictions, a series of severe riots exploded in Detroit, New York, and elsewhere. Young persons of both races did most of the fighting, while older, more professional criminals supervised the looting. Both the white and Negro groups attracted largely unskilled, poorly educated, and desperate men. The riots thus served as outlets for mass frustration. Especially for the Negro participants, the violence offered a dramatic, thrilling acting-out of long-smoldering hostility, though their aggression could not be directed at the ultimate causes of Negro frustration and deprivation but only at their immediate agents—such as the policeman and the storekeeper. (2, 81, 86, 296, 386)

A poll conducted a few weeks after the Harlem riot in New York revealed the extent to which the anti-white violence won approval among Negroes who did not themselves participate. (81) Thirty per cent of the sample condoned the riot, a segment differentiated from those who condemned the affair by their greater age, higher percentage of males, and less frequent church attendance. It was not the respondents' general attitudes toward racial matters which seemed to determine their acceptance or rejection of violence as a means of rectifying racial injustice so much as their concern for the observance of the social codes requiring orderly behavior.

Those who approved of the riot were openly emotional over racial discrimination and did not assign primary importance to the wider society's disapproval of disorder.

Apart from riots, violence may be displaced onto other Negroes. Recent crime research in Philadelphia and Cleveland reveals that well over 90 per cent of Negro homicide is intra-racial, with the victims typically being family members or friends of the murderer. (39, 552) The nature of many of these spontaneous, emotional homicides strongly suggests the sudden and diverted release of an enormous amount of pent-up frustration. (Chapter 6)

A more prevalent aggressive response is to return the compliment of anti-Negro prejudice and stereotypes with anti-white prejudice and stereotypes. Though varying somewhat by region and social class, there is considerable agreement among urban Negroes in their conceptions of white people. (100, 101, 337, 428) Whites, they feel, "stick together," evidence more consideration for their women, and are "very businesslike, ambitious, shrewd, deceitful, and tricky." (337, p. 11) The two races, however, are seen to possess equal intellectual and technical potentials. As in the case of most group stereotypes, this image of whites has its favorable aspects, but the overall configuration is critical. In matters concerning motivation, this generalized view seems to accept the racist whites' inflated conception of themselves (ambitious), but in matters concerning genetic endowment it sternly rejects white superiority notions (equal intellectual and technical abilities). A plaintive note reflecting the position of the Negro in America is apparent in the general agreement that whites "underestimate the Negro's ability," "keep the Negro down," "feel superior," "judge Negroes by the worst type," and "do not care to be among Negroes." Even white liberals are widely regarded by these respondents as giving mere "lip service" to racial justice. (102, 337)

These stereotypes of the white are also evident in Negro humor. Consider, for instance, the joke about two

Negro women in domestic service comparing notes. "At my place," complains one, "I have a terrible time; all day it's 'Yes, Ma'am,' 'Yes, Ma'am,' 'Yes, Ma'am.'" "Me, too," comments the other, "but with me it's 'No, Sir,' 'No, Sir,' 'No, Sir.'" (66)

Anti-white prejudice and stereotypes among Negroes are altered in the same manner anti-Negro prejudice and stereotypes among whites are altered: by interracial contact in situations where there is no discrimination, where the participants have equal status and common goals, and where no racial competition exists. (3) One investigation, replicating earlier studies of attitude-change on the part of whites in public housing projects (543), found that Negro couples who lived in an integrated project were markedly more positive in their attitudes toward whites than couples living in a virtually all-Negro project. (557) Another investigation noted that a sample of Negro Southerners who served in World War II and encountered for the first time liberal white Northerners apparently experienced a lessening of anti-white attitudes. (429) Negro veterans from the North, by contrast, encountered for the first time prejudiced white Southerners and apparently became more anti-white. (429) Acceptance invites acceptance; prejudice breeds prejudice.

Negro prejudice against other minorities represents another displaced form of moving against the oppressor. A victim of discrimination, points out Allport, can react in two ways toward other victims: he can sympathize with his fellow underdog and be extremely free from prejudice; or he can direct his frustrations upon these relatively safe targets in an all-out effort to be superior to somebody. (3, 5) Examples of both extremes are readily found among Negro Americans, though considering the marginal status of most Negroes it is easy to understand why the latter type predominates. While a number of researches indicate that the pattern of Negro student prejudices are similar to comparable white groups (34, 35, 345, 489), one Southern college study found that Negro students rate all other out-groups more negatively than white students. (205) Low-income Negroes in Northern cities frequently pick out their nearest competitor for unskilled employment, at present the Puerto Rican, as a target for their pent-up frustration. (382)

Anti-Semitism among many urban Negroes is a special form of this displaced aggression. (82, 205, 465, 471) The Black Muslims single out the Jew—"the brains of the white race"—for particular abuse. (306, pp. 165-169) Richard Wright wrote in his autobiographical *Black Boy*: "To hold an attitude of antagonism or distrust toward Jews was bred in us from childhood; it was not merely racial prejudice, it was a part of our cultural heritage." (558, p. 55) In part, this prejudice represents acceptance of attitudes prevalent in the general culture and a tenuous bond with white anti-Semites. But, more fundamentally, it represents the safest expression of anti-white feelings. In three basic contacts with whites, as tenant, customer, and employee, urban Negroes are likely to encounter Jews. Consequently, the latter can come to symbolize the despised white world, even though Jewish Americans are more likely than other whites to work for Negro rights. Two studies of urban Negroes show that a majority of all classes in both the North and South do not believe that Jews are "more sympathetic" to the Negro's struggle. (337, p. 11) Finally, Negro merchants sometimes find anti-Semitism a useful device in the battle with Jewish competitors for Negro business. (465) The intensity of anti-Semitism among Negroes, however, is frequently exaggerated. National polls reveal it is concentrated among the ghetto poor in the North and is only slightly more pronounced than anti-Semitism among whites of similar backgrounds. (382, 403)

The most constructive means of moving against the oppressor is to repudiate racist claims, take pride in being a Negro, and become aggressively militant. This type of multiple-reaction resembles some of the moving-toward mechanisms, though it also includes a strong positive identification with Negroes as a group and a particularly forceful rejection of the concept of the "proper place" of Negroes.

Aggressive militancy is seen in its clearest form in the social type known as "the race man." Usually the spearhead of organized militancy in the Negro community, the race man "sees the world through race-colored glasses and interprets most events in their racial context—how they will affect the Negro." (262, p. 207) While he is typically hostile toward whites, he is prepared and able to waive this hostility whenever he encounters whites who are willing to join him in militant racial action. His hostility extends as well to compromising Negro leaders and to those elements of the Negro masses who prefer to move away from the oppressor.

More common are milder forms of this type of response. In interviews with 200 Negro industrial workers in Chicago, one sociologist discovered a wide range of reactions to employment discrimination. (439) Some minimized race as a factor, some took a defeatist attitude, some placidly accepted fate, some exaggerated to their family and friends the importance of the lowly jobs they held; but others worked tirelessly through their unions and outside protest groups in an unending and militant search for higher-status occupations. This type of directed and determined militancy is increasing among Negro youth. Earlier research noted that Negro students usually sought unrealistic goals and minimized the obstacles in their path; but more recent work finds high school seniors far more knowledgeable, assertive, and eager in their orientation toward the future. (312)

Positive group identification among Negro Americans is more widespread than generally recognized. Though often fused with self-hatred and great concern over segregation, this group pride has been documented in a series of investigations of Negro students. (241, 248) After studying Little Rock, Arkansas, Negroes, one investigator concluded that there existed a positive norm of "group belongingness." (208, 209) Certainly, such a norm has never become as widespread as it has among such highly organized minorities as Jewish and Japanese Americans, but group pride and group identification among Negroes has recently gained, in direct proportion to the diminution of self-hate.

Less direct and less constructive are numerous sly and cunning means of moving against the oppressor. "Sneaky" traits may develop both for survival values and for taking petty revenge. "The Negro cook who 'totes' from her white mistress's kitchen," observes Allport, "may do so for symbolic as well as gastronomic reasons." [9] (3, p. 150) Working slowly and inefficiently or suddenly leaving a job without notice offer other such alternatives. "The white man may be able to order me around," goes the feeling, "but he doesn't *own* me." Sharp resentment among employers is evidence that whites recognize the aggressiveness of these actions.

Still more indirect is the "aggressive meekness" many older Negroes assume in the presence of whites. The Negro's expression of aggression has been channeled over the years by the situations in which he found himself. (417) "Aggressive meekness" was one of the few modes of hostility-release widely available to slaves, and it has continued to be employed in difficult racial situations. Akin to the masochist's pleasure from pain, self-effacing humility not only helps to control intense hatred but also serves to allay the guilt that arises from harboring this hatred. The meek Negro can even hope to snatch victory from defeat. While deluding whites, he is also acting in the manner that Christianity teaches is the core of moral virtue: the meek shall inherit the earth; suffering will be rewarded; the final victory will be achieved in heaven. (343, 417)

This mechanism is rarely seen in pure form among today's younger Negroes. Their explicit vituperation directed at the servility of the "Uncle Tom" Negro is

[9] Richard Wright in *Black Boy* described instances of such stealing in detail. (558, pp. 160-161, 163-167)

heard everywhere now. But this heated repudiation is suspiciously vigorous, as if they were denying some of it within themselves as well. Suspicious, too, is the hyper-concern that even the most direct interaction with whites may be interpreted as "Tomming." The militant Negro comedian, Dick Gregory, has remarked perceptively:

> You don't see any bitterness in me. . . . It doesn't mean I'm Tomming, either. Most misused word in America today. . . . You smile, some people say you're Tomming; say thank you, you're Tomming. Everybody, be he black, white, pink or purple, one time or another, he is an Uncle Tom. . . . A cop stops you for speeding and to try to talk him out of it, you let him say things to you in a tone and language you'd never let anyone ordinarily. And *that's* a form of Uncle Tomism. You're not doing anything more'n try to get out of that ticket. (362)

In many of its forms, aggressive meekness is more easily described and understood in terms of our final general category of reactions.

MOVING AWAY FROM THE OPPRESSOR

There are at least three distinct types of Negro social movements which exemplify a withdrawal from the white world. One type involves vague and fanciful colonization schemes, as in Marcus Garvey's "Back-to-Africa" appeal of the 1920's and the Black Muslims' declared intention to take over a "few states." A second and more realistic type is the proposal to establish separate all-Negro communities within the United States. Mound Bayou, Mississippi, and Boley, Oklahoma, are perhaps the best known fruits of these experiments, initiated in the last half of the nineteenth century. The third type comprises heaven-centered religious organizations, whose withdrawal is spiritual rather than physical. (170, Chapter 14) Still a potent institution in Negro America, these church movements have in recent years shifted their interests markedly from the future in heaven to the present on earth, from a moving away to a moving toward the oppressor.

On the individual level, a suggestive distinction has been drawn between those Negro patients in psychotherapy who maintain that all of their problems derive from racial discrimination and those who just as strongly maintain that their problems have nothing whatsoever to do with being a Negro. (44) The former response attempts to avoid all personal responsibility, the latter to avoid all considerations of race. This second type of patient—displaying an individual reaction similar to the group reactions of colonization—wants desperately to shed the woes inherent in the role of "Negro," to leave the field of conflict.

There are at least four general categories of such moving away from the oppressor: passivity and withdrawal, social insulation, passing, and extreme escapism. Passivity and withdrawal in Negro children are evident in interview, projective test, and questionnaire data. The first set of data comes from interviews with 150 Negroes from ten-to-twelve-years of age in New York and St. Louis concerning racial discrimination. (194) Fifty-seven per cent of these youths reported having had some urge to fight or argue when confronted with discriminatory experiences, but only 17 per cent had actually carried out these impulses into action. The customary reaction was quiet withdrawal. Consistent with these reports, TAT story-data reveal that a New York sample of lower-status Negro boys of similar ages showed a greater need for passivity when compared with comparable white boys. (374) And 100 upstate New York Negro youths, in answering a race relations questionnaire, provided the following data: 10 per cent agreed that they kept away from white people as much as they could; 29 per cent agreed that it was best to stay away from white people in order "to avoid all embarrassing situations"; 57 per cent agreed that Negroes should not enter business establishments where they think they are not wanted; and 77 per cent agreed that, when a business place refused them service, they should leave without causing any trouble. (262)

There is, however, ambivalence among these Northern youths between moving away and moving toward whites. Thirty-eight per cent of them preferred to live in a racially integrated neighborhood, and 62 per cent of the sample preferred a mixed social club to an all-Negro club. And there was overwhelming agreement that "colored and white people should try to mix together more often," that they would like to know more whites, and that they would not mind having whites in their social groups. A similar ambivalence existed among the Northern adults examined in this research. While 64 per cent of the older respondents believed Negroes should not enter business establishments where they think they are not wanted, 38 per cent preferred living in a racially integrated neighborhood, and 46 per cent preferred a mixed social club to an all-Negro one. (262) What seems to be operating here is a desire to be accepted in the larger society combined with a highly-developed readiness to withdraw passively if confronted by rejection and humiliation.

Negro Southerners are less ambivalent. More accustomed to almost constant rebuffs from whites, they evidence considerably more moving away from the oppressor. (262, pp. 202-203) Indeed, their massive migration from the South since 1915 can be interpreted partly as a means of avoiding whites who are the most openly anti-Negro. Passive withdrawal can also take such minute forms as ordering goods from a catalog or by telephone to eliminate face-to-face contact with whites. Further contacts with the white world are minimized by traveling in automobiles and avoiding public conveyances.

Perhaps the most common mechanism of moving away is the adoption by Negroes of an impervious mask of passive acquiescence when confronted by whites. "Got one mind for white folks to see, 'nother for what I know is me . . ." go the lyrics of an old Negro folksong, and white social scientists have repeatedly learned the truth of these words when conducting research on Negroes of all ages. (12) One study found that Negro children only two years old revealed restricted verbal responsiveness when examined by a white person. (394) Another discovered that Negro kindergarten children reacted differently to a mother-identification test depending upon whether the experimenter was white or Negro. (517) Working with Negro college students, a third investigation recorded immediate reactions to the presentation of racially derogatory terms when the experimenter was Negro, but not when the experimenter was white. (540)

Similarly, public opinion surveys using both Negro and white interviewers have obtained sharply diverse results with equivalent samples of Negro adults, particularly in answer to questions concerning the race issue. The classic example occurred in a 1942 Memphis poll. (71) In response to the question: "Would Negroes be treated better or worse here if the Japanese conquered the U.S.A.," almost twice as many respondents answered "worse" to white interviewers (45 per cent) as to Negro interviewers (25 per cent). A recent survey conducted in North Carolina reported further examples. When questioned by a Negro rather than by a white interrogator, Negroes mentioned higher educational aspirations for their children, more often agreed that changes must be made "in the way our country is run," and more strongly approved of the student sit-in protest demonstrations and school desegregation. (418) This hesitancy to appear militant to a white interviewer is not limited to the South. Figure 3 illustrates the results of a third survey in Boston. (404) Not only did the Negro respondents again evidence less militancy to white interviewers, but they also admitted to fewer feelings of racial victimization.

So effective is this impassive façade, many white Americans have long interpreted it as proof that Negroes are happy and contented with their lot. But sensitive whites know better; thus, William Faulkner remarked:

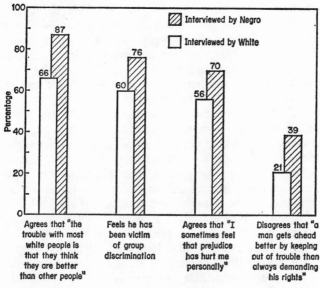

FIGURE 3—RACE OF INTERVIEWER AND NEGRO POLL RESPONSES
(Data from: T. F. Pettigrew, "The Negro Respondent: New data on old problems," unpublished paper.)

"No white man understood Negroes and never would so long as the white man compelled the black man to be first a Negro and only then a man, since this, the impenetrable dividing wall, was the black man's only defense and protection for survival." (151, p. 308)

Beyond passive withdrawal is the attempt to insulate oneself as completely as possible from the broader society. Such social insulation is usually only possible for upper-status Negroes. They have attained an economic and professional position which releases them from dependence upon whites, and have many of the material comforts which consumption-oriented America identifies with "success." Why, some of these people ask, should they risk their privileged situation by challenging whites or championing Negroes? Within a severely restricted existence, a few Negroes are able to achieve protective insulation from the race problem—as some faculty members of all-Negro colleges in the South manage. But this apparent complacency about race is rarely a complete success; many feel guilty over their neglect of the problems which at some level affect all Negro Americans. (506, pp. 44-46)

"Passing" offers the lightest segment of Negro America another alternative for avoiding the race problem. Primarily limited to depersonalized urban centers where people's pasts are less known or traceable, the annual amount of complete passing from Negro to white has. been variously estimated from a mere two thousand five hundred to about twenty-five thousand. (67, 548) Precise calculations are made impossible not only by the secrecy inherent in the phenomenon, but by its frequently opportunistic and temporary character. Apparently only a small fraction of those who pass surrender their Negro identities completely and permanently. Often they act as whites only to secure employment or to engage in cultural and recreational activities which would otherwise be closed to them, while still remaining in the Negro world. Others pass completely while young, but resume their Negro identity in later life. The principal motivations for passing, then, are probably less concerned with relinquishing racial identity than with achieving advantages made impossible by segregation and discrimination. Consequently, as desegregation progresses, there should be less necessity for passing.

Racial passing, of course, is dependent on the curious American definition of a Negro as a person with even the slightest trace of Negroid ancestry. In any biological sense, the "Negroes" who are able to pass have in fact as many or more Caucasian ancestors as they have Negroid ancestors.[10] But the critical issue is the social, not

[10] It is widely believed that a mulatto must have only one-sixteenth, or one-eighth Negro ancestry in order to pass successfully; but there are carefully documented cases of mulattoes with one-half Negro ancestry passing. (548, p. 308)

biological, definition. (Chapter 3) So it is natural that some Negroes pass partly in order to "put something over" on whites and their racist doctrines. James Weldon Johnson, in his quasi-autobiography, described his feelings while passing: "Many a night when I returned to my room after an enjoyable evening, I laughed heartily over what struck me as the capital joke I was playing." (261, p. 133)

The number who actually play this "capital joke," of those light enough to play it, is small. (548, pp. 309-310) The reasons for this are not hard to understand. Those who pass must always be anxiously alert to avoid detection; they must have the training and skills to compete effectively in the white world; and, if they are severing ties completely, they must face painful estrangement from their families and guilt over rejecting their own group for personal gain.

Many Negroes, particularly those harboring self-hate, roundly condemn passing. (210) But the severe color conflict created by discrimination leads to a modified equivalent among Negroes in the widespread use of cosmetics to approximate more nearly the physical appearance of whites. (53, 266, 376) Hair-straighteners and skin-bleachers are as vigorously advertised in Negro newspapers and magazines as their counterparts, hair-curlers and skin-darkeners, are advertised among whites. As comedian "Nipsey" Russell puts it: "We deeply appreciate the efforts of many white Americans to curl their hair and darken their skins, and we Negro Americans want you to know that we are doing the best we can to meet you half-way!"

Competing with the hair and skin advertisements in the Negro mass media are those for alcohol, a symptom of still another means of moving away from the oppressor—extreme escapism. Excessive drinking, like other escape mechanisms, is hardly unique to Negroes. But they have, as a group, more from which to escape. Thus, as one would suspect, large numbers of Negroes, especially lower-status individuals, seek the "big kicks" and engage in escape activities to extreme degrees. (282) In addition to high rates of alcoholism, drug addiction is prevalent among lower-class Negroes in the larger urban ghettos. Approximately 60 per cent of addicts recorded by the Federal Bureau of Narcotics are Negro. (90) Such high rates stem from a basic need to shut out the hostile world and gain a compensatory feeling of superiority. Marijuana, for example, remains popular in the depths of ghetto slums because it offers relief from anxiety and vastly magnifies one's feeling of importance. (160, 326)

Chemical kicks are not the only way to escape harsh reality. Day-dreaming can create a new "reality," one without deflated egos and racial barriers. And this shades into such serious mental difficulties as schizophrenia. (Chapter 4)

REACTIONS TO OPPRESSION

Three general types of responses characterize Negro American reactions to oppression: moving toward, against, or away from the oppressor. But each of these responses is uniquely shaded and shaped by the person-alities of individual Negroes. These general types are only useful abstractions, for no two human beings ever react to the same situation in precisely the same manner. Some may react in entirely opposite ways. Furthermore, Negroes face a wide range of racial situations, differ-ing sharply from region to region and by social-class. Broadly speaking, public opinion poll data suggest that moving-toward orientations are most common among middle-class Negroes, moving-against orientations most common among the poorest and darkest Negroes, and moving-away orientations most common in the South.

Many problems of life which Negro Americans face, of course, are also faced by white Americans. Conse-quently, Negro personality trends will closely resemble white personality trends when there are similar circum-stances. Yet one problem does in fact distinguish the two racial groups in the United States: virtually all Ne-

groes encounter the additional problem of color prejudice. Many of the reactions to this special burden lead
to personality damage and constriction—anxiety, symbolic status striving, self-hate, prejudice against others,
meekness, passivity, social insulation, and extreme escapism. But by no means are all Negro responses to this
common problem of prejudice socially maladaptive.
Many of the world's greatest achievements were born
of suffering, and some of the products of the Negro's
experience in America illustrate this fact. Jazz, for instance, is acclaimed as one of the most original American artistic contributions to the world. Yet jazz is primarily an expression of the Negro's adaptation to suffering and has often been intimately associated with the
most debilitating expressions of the same suffering, such
as drug addiction, crime, and alcoholism.

St. Clair Drake and Horace Cayton, in their classic
study of race relations in Chicago, *Black Metropolis*,
succinctly summarize the Negro's reaction to oppression:

> . . . for most people, wearing their dark skin color is
> like living with a chronic disease. One learns to "take
> it" and not to let it unduly cramp one's style of life.
> And anodynes are always present: religion, the social
> ritual, whiskey, dope . . . (133, p. XXVI)

Part II

RACIAL DIFFERENCES

3

THE CONCEPT OF RACE

Race has been called "man's most dangerous myth." (367) Strange, that a scientific term should develop such lethal political and social implications. Yet the darker pages of Western history relate the story: race has been employed as a popular rationalization for slavery, for colonial domination, for segregation, for gas-chamber extermination. Before any discussion of "racial differences" can begin, then, it is necessary to delimit precisely the scientific meaning of the term from its perilous popular meanings.

RACE AS A BIOLOGICAL CONCEPT

Anthropologists agree that there is only *one* human species, immodestly named *homo sapiens* ("wise man"). But there are many varieties of this one species. These subspecies, or races, began evolving thousands of years ago through reproductive isolation brought about by geographical and cultural barriers. Oceans, mountains, and deserts divided mankind into relatively separate groups, each carrying on its own experiment in evolution. Sometimes cultural taboos against intergroup marriage served essentially the same function, as with the Hungarian gypsies and the Hindu castes of India. Intragroup breeding in time elaborated differences in length of limb and shape of face, in eye color and hair form, in shade of skin. Thus, the many races, though all variations on a common theme, grew more distinct in some physical traits. But these differences are typically quantitative and not qualitative, matters of degree and not of kind. In simplest terms, then, races are genetically isolated mating groups with distinctive gene frequencies. (55)

Especially important for evaluating racial differences is an understanding of the genetic processes which lead to human diversity. (491, Chapter 33) Mutations are the basic source for originating genetic newness, but they are not in themselves a major means for establishing genetic newness. Two principal processes determine change and diversity: "genetic drift" and natural selection. Genetic drift refers to the chance assortment of genes over generations which can lead to the loss or fixation of a particular trait. It is most important in small populations and with traits determined by a single gene; and it can lead to the establishment of non-adaptive, neutral characteristics, or even mildly maladaptive characteristics. As a means of creating racial differences, genetic drift was most operative during prehistoric times when the total human population was small, groups were maximally isolated, and when devastating wars, famines, and epidemics drastically reduced the size of these groups still further.

Natural selection, however, remains the chief agent of evolution. Made popular knowledge by Darwin, this principle holds that the genes responsible for the greater reproductive fitness of certain individuals in each group will be represented in higher proportions in later generations than the genes responsible for the lesser reproductive fitness of other individuals. Note the special features of this process. Like genetic drift, natural selection operates in all groups; but, unlike genetic drift, it is effective in large groups and usually influences traits determined by a multiplicity of genes. "Fitness" is objectively defined as that which relates to reproductivity, without any value connotations of superiority or inferiority. But what is adaptive will vary from one environment to another—a critical factor in generating human diversity.

Skin pigmentation presents a classic example of a conspicuous racial difference rendered by natural selection. Human skin does not differ between races in the number of pigment cells in any one particular body region. Rather, an individual's skin color largely depends on the activity of a single enzyme system within the pigment cells. (300, 301) This enzyme system is apparently influenced by as many as five different genetic components which are genetically independent of other physical characteristics which differentiate Negroes and Caucasians. (491, pp. 351-359, 695) Natural selection for beneficial genes acted differently upon these two groups, for dark pigmentation proved to be an adaptive protection against the intense sunlight of Africa, while light pigmentation proved to be an adaptive means of allowing sufficient penetration of the faint sunlight of Northern Europe for the manufacture of vitamin D. Chapter 4 points out the still-adaptive properties of dark skin and cites similar examples of naturally-selected defenses against malaria. Differences in nose shape between Negroes and Caucasians provide a final example. The long, narrow noses more common among whites are thought to have been adaptive in warming up cold outside air before it enters the lungs, while the shorter, broader noses of Negroes seem more suited to warmer surroundings.

In addition to genetic drift and natural selection, new types of genetic populations are brought about by the widespread interbreeding of already diverse populations. Indeed, Negro Americans constitute an example *par excellence* of such a cross-racial group, different enough from each of its parent races to be considered by some anthropologists as a relatively separate race itself.

FOUR RECURRENT QUESTIONS

This biological conception of race immediately raises four recurrent questions. Are there "pure" races in the world today? Is interracial mixing harmful? How many races can be said to exist? And are some races superior to others?

To begin with, there are no "pure" races. All of the major subspecies of mankind share in their "gene pools" some of the genes once considered racially distinctive. Modern transportation makes geographic isolation almost an impossibility. Indeed, as scholars learn more about prehistoric times, it becomes apparent that man has always been a wanderer. Cultural and genetic interchange has been far more continuous and extensive than previously envisaged. "Nothing can be more certain than that pure races in man never existed and can not exist," assert Dunn and Dobzhansky. "Mankind has always been, and still is, a mongrel lot." (137, p. 115)

Nevertheless, racist theorists assume racial purity has existed into the twentieth century and only now is disintegrating. They maintain that this interracial mixing, or, as they prefer, "mongrelization," will eventually destroy mankind since the "inferior" stock will increasingly dilute the "superior." Their theory is, if you will, a biological Gresham's Law—the bad drives out the good. On the American scene, such racists insist the integrity of the white race is at stake; they fear an "inundation by a black sea" and feel a crusade to save white skin from extinction is in order. Politically, such fears have fostered laws in over twenty states which forbid marriage between Negroes and Caucasians. Genetically, in addition to claims of racial superiority, this reasoning assumes two forms. (491, Chapter 32) Miscegenation is said both to destroy well-adapted racial gene combinations and to originate disharmonious gene combinations.

But modern genetics does not support such thinking. Curt Stern has demonstrated that if panmixis— completely random mating with no regard to racial differences—were to take place in the United States, the darker skin shades of Negroes would be virtually eliminated, but there would be little noticeable effect on the skin color of Caucasians. (490) In other words, the Negro one-tenth of the nation would be "inundated by a white sea" in respect to skin color and other polygenic traits which distinguish the two racial populations. Stern maintains:

> When complete fusion has occurred, there will probably be no more than a few thousand black people in each generation in the entire country, and these are

likely to have straight hair, narrow noses and thin
lips. I suppose that if some person now living could
return at that distant time, he would ask in wonder:
"What became of the Negro?" (490, p. 85)

Stern provides two reasons for believing that disrup-
tion of formerly adaptive racial gene combinations
through miscegenation is "of little concern." (491, pp.
695-697) First, technological developments have so fundamentally altered man's environment and his power
to manipulate it that racial adaptations to older environments are largely obsolete. Second, each human being
possesses an internal adaptiveness, a biological ability
to orchestrate and regulate a wide variety of organic
situations. Consequently, human beings appear perfectly
capable of establishing adaptively balanced internal systems regardless of the diversity of gene combinations
inherited from two racial stocks.

Similarly, there is little reason to believe that miscegenation originates disharmonious gene combinations.
Racists typically cite examples of maladaptive animal
hybrids, such as the grotesque product of a dachshund
and a Saint Bernard. But the dachshund is a dispropor-
tioned animal, corresponding to certain types of human
dwarfs and not to naturally-occurring human races. Distinctive differences between human races are apparently
dependent on polygenic combinations rather than on
single genes which individually shape striking bodily
properties. This more complex configuration allows for
the development of harmonious bodily systems among
interracial hybrids. "This seems to be the explanation,"
concludes Stern, "for the fact that no well-substantiated
examples of disharmonious constitution resulting from
miscegenation have been reported." (491, p. 696)

Indeed, there is the possibility that cross-mating may
often be biologically beneficial. (491, p. 699-701) Miscegenation reduces the potentially harmful effects of
genetic drift by diminishing the degree of isolation and
enlarging the mating population; this process acts to
lessen pathological conditions. And, not unlike the

phenomenon of hybrid vigor in plant life, cross-group
mating may result in especially sturdy human specimens.
One investigation of Swiss villagers discovered that offspring from marriages of persons from different villages
were on the average significantly taller and more robust
than offspring from marriages of members of the same
village. (242) Assuming that the persons who marry
outside the village are not genetically different from
those who marry within the village, this finding suggests an intergroup stimulation that may also operate
for interracial matings.

Because of the impurity of races, anthropologists vary
in their estimates of how many races exist. The number
has ranged from several dozen to three or four. Races
are now delineated from blood group gene frequencies
as well as from morphological characteristics. Boyd, for
example, utilized approximately a dozen blood group
systems to distinguish seven principal races: European,
African, Asian, Indo-Dravidian (the peoples of the In-
dian-Pakistan sub-continent), American Indian, Pacific
(Indonesians, Melanesians, and Polynesians), and the
Australian Aborigine. (56) Most classifications include
some equivalents of three basic subspecies: Caucasoid,
Negroid, and Mongoloid. And all of the schemes stress
the great overlap between the races (e.g., the Negro
American) and the many marginal types that do not fit
neatly into any of these three general categories (e.g.,
Indo-Dravidian, American Indian, and Australian Aborigine). Regardless of which classification is accepted,
race remains a relative, not an absolute, concept.

The biological view of race has been more misused
and distorted than perhaps any other scientific conception. The temptation to believe one's own race biologically superior proves too much for some to resist. Racists
of many skin shades and nationalities have seized upon
the concept and twisted it to their own purposes. In the
United States, white supremacists cite the technological
accomplishments of Western society as positive proof
that Caucasians are vastly superior to all other races.

But it is well to recall Lord Ragland's pointed statement:

> It has been said against the African Negroes that they
> never produced a scientist; but what kind of a scien-
> tist would he be who had no weights and measures, no
> clock or calendar, and no means of recording his ob-
> servations and experiments? And if it be asked why the
> Negroes did not invent these things, the answer is that
> neither did any European, and for the same reason—
> namely, that the rare and perhaps unique conditions
> which made their invention possible were absent!

More sophisticated white supremacists insist that
Caucasians are superior because they evolved first from
homo erectus to *homo sapiens*. The controversial volume
by Carleton Coon, *The Origin of Races*, is cited as the
scholarly source of this argument. (98) Actually, how,
when, and where the very gradual evolution from *homo
erectus* to *homo sapiens* occurred are still matters of
debate and disagreement among anthropologists. And
it seems highly unlikely that this process occurred five
separate times, as Coon's theory postulates. Consequently, many of the professional reviewers of Coon's
volume question the validity of his conclusions.[1] But
even if it were known that one group evolved later than
the others, this has no direct bearing on the present.
"Even if Coon is correct in his paleontological arguments
—and I disagree with many," writes anthropologist

[1] In addition to the two examples cited in the text, these reviews include one by anthropologist Barnicot of University College, London, and another by geneticist Pollitzer of the University
of North Carolina. "It is a pity that, behind a modern look,"
writes Barnicot in the *Observer*, "there lurks the shadow of an
older, less critical anthropology which has already done much to
discredit the subject as a science." (29, p. 24) "A few factual
errors, especially in anatomy," observes Pollitzer in the *American
Journal of Human Genetics*, "creep into the text and may make
one question the over-all accuracy and the thoroughness of scholarship. . . . The obvious danger in this work is that it is subject
to misuse by the racist to be subverted toward an end which the
author probably does not intend." (414, pp. 217-218)

Howells of Harvard University in his *New York Times* review of Coon's work, "it is not possible to use these standards to measure modern racial differences, and anyhow I see no way of using such arguments to disprove the Constitution of the United States." (240, p. 3) In his *Scientific American* review, geneticist Dobzhansky of Columbia University goes further:

> If it were true that the Caucasoids 200,000 years ago attained the state that the Congoids achieved only 40,000 years ago, would it not follow that the rate of evolutionary development of the Congoids was since then about five times faster than that of the Caucasoids? This is surely not a conclusion that white supremacists would embrace with pleasure. (127, pp. 169-172)

One popular version of white supremacy reasoning holds that the Negro is physically closer to the ape than the white man. It is true that Negroes tend to look more simian than Caucasians in facial prognathism, nasal index, eye color, and cranial capacity.[2] (233, p. 140) However, on six other critical traits Caucasians tend to be more simian: cephalic index, body hair, hair form and length, and lip form and color. Those advancing racial superiority ideas exaggerate the importance of certain traits and ignore a basic genetic fact: two individuals within the same race may differ on many times more genes than those which differentiate typical Negroes and Caucasians. (190)

Further complications arise when white supremacists extend their arguments to cultural attainments and such psychological capacities as intelligence. As Lord Ragland implied, the direction any culture takes is complexly shaped by its history and its exchange with other cultures. There is no evidence whatsoever for genetic causation of a culture's attainments. Furthermore, who is to

[2] Incidentally, cranial capacity is not—as racists often assert—significantly related to intelligence and intellectual achievement. (331, p. 18)

judge the achievements of a people? How can an objective scale of values be established? Is sculpture from ancient Rome to be ranked above that of ancient Ghana?

Though no genetic linkage has been detected between such characteristics as skin color and intelligence, white supremacists are convinced sharp psychological disparities exist between the races. Fuller and Thompson counter such beliefs:

> The most diverse human cultures have common features related to the perpetuation of the species. It is difficult to conceive of a society in which intelligence, cooperation, and physical vigor would not have positive survival value. Hence, it is likely that natural selection tends to oppose the establishment of major heritable behavior differences between races. (176, p. 324)

THE UNITED STATES AS A BIOLOGICAL MELTING POT

North and South America are among the most racially heterogeneous regions in the entire world. Today the United States is no exception, for it is as much a biological as a cultural melting pot. In spite of stern sanctions against black-white sexual relations, Negro Americans have been a part of this process. The first result of this centuries-long miscegenation was the spread of Caucasian genes into the Negro American population without any significant reciprocal flow of Negro genes into the white population. This was true because all mulattoes were socially defined as Negro. But in time the process became one of mutual exchange, with the "passing" of light mulattoes (Chapter 2) introducing an appreciable flow of Negro genes into the socially-defined white group. Some of this gene flow from racial passing returns Caucasian genes from the Negro gene pool back to the white. Given further miscegenation over future generations, geneticists predict that the nation's Negro and white populations will become similar for most gene frequencies in which they now differ except for those few genes which contribute to the superficial physical characteristics, such as skin color, employed socially to designate race. (491, p. 694)

A series of investigations over the years provide comparable estimates of the genetic influence of cross-racial mating upon Negro Americans. Early studies lacked modern blood system genetic methods and relied upon morphology and the reconstruction of ancestral lines. This research estimated that the percentage of Negroes with at least one known white forebear ranged between 72 and 83 per cent. (548) With a large sample of fifteen hundred Negroes, Herskovits in 1930 arrived at more detailed figures. (227) He calculated from the reports of his subjects that roughly a seventh (14.8 per cent) had more white than Negro ancestors,[3] a fourth (25.2 per cent) had about the same number of white and Negro ancestors, almost a third (31.7 per cent) had more Negro than white ancestors, and the remainder (28.3 per cent) had no known white ancestor. In addition, a quarter of the sample's Negroes (27.2 per cent) claimed one or more known Indian forebears.

Modern serological techniques yield similar results, though they suggest the incidence of Indian genes is not nearly so high among Negroes as Herskovits and others believed. Glass estimates that between 22 and 29 per cent of the Negro American gene pool consists of non-Negroid genes. (191) And he further calculates from his blood system data that it is unlikely that much of this admixture is Indian in origin. Genetic data on Indians, however, have so far come largely from those tribes who had the least opportunity to mix with Negroes; further research on Indian Southerners may necessitate some readjustment. Caucasian genes have apparently percolated fairly well throughout the Negro population (490), though Pollitzer has recently shown that the Gullahs of coastal South Carolina remain genetically closer to Africans than other Negro Americans. (413) This investigation also reveals that the morpho-

[3] This proportion would be larger, of course, were it not for the fact that many of these persons successfully pass as whites.

logical and serological estimates of Caucasian admixture among Negroes are quite similar.

The ancestry of Negro Americans is complicated further by the fact that both the Negro and Caucasian strains originate from a great variety of African and European peoples. Africans were brought to the shores of North America from areas as far apart as West Africa, Angola, and Madagascar (the present-day Malagasy Republic) and represented a biological range as great as that found in Europe. The Caucasian forefathers of Negroes, though concentrated in the South, nonetheless possessed not only Irish, Scottish, and English stock but French, German, and Spanish as well. Little wonder, then, that Negro Americans today evidence an unusually wide range of physical traits. Their skin color extends from ebony to a shade paler than many "whites"; their nose-shape from extremely flat to aquiline; their stature from basketball giant to dwarf.

Yet, despite this great heterogeneity, a curious social definition of "Negro" has developed in the Unted States, a definition in sharp contrast to that used in Latin America. No matter how Caucasian one's genes may be in origin, one known trace of Negro ancestry makes you "Negro." Bitterly, Negroes joke that "Negro blood" must be powerful stuff if it can overwhelm any amount of "white blood."

A FURTHER COMPLICATION IN "RACIAL DIFFERENCES"

If white supremacists overestimate the biological distinctions between Negro and white Americans, they equally underestimate the social distinctions. Differentials unfavorable to whites are explained away or ignored, while any health, I.Q., or crime differentials unfavorable to Negroes are quickly interpreted as racially determined, without consideration of the vast disparities in opportunity between the groups.

The operation of such conditions as poverty, impaired family life, and limited opportunities illustrate the fallacy involved. These social disabilities tend to result in more disease, lower scores on intelligence tests, and higher rates of crime regardless of race. And, as we have noted in the previous chapters, Negroes as a group are poorer, more often from broken homes, and more likely to be the victims of discrimination than white Americans. Thus, it makes no sense to compare gross white and Negro data as a test of "racial" factors. It is hardly a test of race to contrast, for instance, middle-class whites from intact homes with lower-class Negroes from broken homes. Indeed, the economic floor for Negroes—the group's direst poverty—is so distinctly below the floor of whites that not even comparison of lower-class Negroes with lower-class whites is generally an adequate test of racial factors. The following three chapters will detail the importance of this methodological complication in three specific realms: health, intelligence, and crime.

Further confusion stems from the implications of the term "racial differences," for just because differences are discernible between races does not necessarily mean that these differences are *due* to race.

RACE AND RACIAL DIFFERENCES

The concept of race is dangerous because of its popular and social interpretations. Scientifically, race signifies only subspecies of the one species of mankind; more technically, races are relatively isolated mating groups with distinctive gene frequencies. They derive from three processes which lead to human diversity: mutation, genetic drift, and natural selection. Modern authorities hold that there are no pure races in the world today, that there is little reason to believe that interracial mixing is genetically harmful, that the precise number of races in existence depends on the particular scheme of the classifier, and that there is little support for the ranking of races as genetically superior or inferior.

Extensive racial intermixture has taken place from ancient times to the present. Modern technology has made geographic isolation almost an impossibility and has so altered man's environment as to render racial adaptations to older environments largely obsolete. This means purity of races is even more impossible of achievement than before. Furthermore, miscegenation is not likely to have negative effects even if it disrupts naturally selected racial gene combinations. Nor does miscegenation appear to establish unfortunate gene combinations, for there exist no well-substantiated cases of disharmonious constitutions caused by cross-racial mating.

White supremacy arguments meet an array of difficulties. Caucasians and Negroes are equally simian in morphological characteristics. Moreover, two individuals within the same race may differ on many more genes than do typical Negroes and Caucasians. And no genetic linkage has been found between such a racially-designating physical trait as skin color and such capacities as intelligence. Indeed, the natural selection process undoubtedly has acted to enhance intelligence and physical capacities in the evolution of all races.

On the American scene specifically, miscegenation over the past three centuries has resulted in about one-fourth of the Negro American gene pool's consisting of genes of Caucasian origin. But the United States defines a "Negro" socially as anyone with one known Negro ancestor —regardless of how Caucasian one's genes may be in origin.

In spite of its severe limitations, this social conception of "race" is employed throughout this book for two compelling reasons. First, for reasons of practicality: the pertinent research literature has typically used the concept in this loose fashion. Investigations of "Negroes" cited throughout this volume are actually studies which have utilized samples of socially-defined Negroes. Many of the individuals who participated as subjects in these studies were at least partly Caucasian in ancestry. Second, the real problems of American race relations are posed in these terms. Negro health, Negro intelligence, and Negro crime are less strictly genetic problems than they are the social problems of an especially deprived group.

4

NEGRO AMERICAN HEALTH

WITH ANN HALLMAN PETTIGREW, M.D.

The 1840 Census of the United States proved to be a great revelation to the nation. (121, 308, 488) Right in the midst of the brewing storm over slavery, this census presented truly amazing data on mental illness and feeble-mindedness among Negro Americans. Though there were no appreciable regional differences for whites, the reported ratio for "insane" and "idiotic" Negroes was only one in every 1558 in the South but one in every 144.5 in the North.[1] Even more startling was the near-perfect correlation of rate with geography. In Maine every fourteenth Negro was recorded either "insane" or "idiotic"; in Massachusetts one in every 43; in New Jersey one of every 297; while Virginia had only one in 1229; and Louisiana had only one in 4310. Here were the juicy figures into which a pro-slavery fire-eater could sink his teeth. Obviously, slavery was a benign institution, protecting the Negro from the rigors of competitive society that so quickly drove him either mad or idiotic. Abolition of slavery, argued John Calhoun immediately, would thus prove to be "a curse instead of a blessing." (488, p. 65)

Soon a young physician and statistician, Dr. Edward Jarvis of Massachusetts, challenged the accuracy of the census. Finding such glaring errors as Northern communities with more reported "insane" and "idiotic" Ne-

[1] A recent analysis of the records of pre-Civil War Southern estates as recorded in probate courts of the time indicates that the ratio of slaves suffering from mental illness and retardation was roughly one per 86, a figure over 18 times that cited by the 1840 Census. (416)

groes than their total Negro populations, Jarvis completely refuted the incredible data. "It was the census that was insane," pithily commented a Northern clergyman, "and not the colored people." (308, p. 46)

As in the slavery debate, the desegregation controversy has revived the issue of Negro American health. Surely, argue many segregationists, the Supreme Court could not mean that whites must associate with "diseased Negroes." The Mississippi legislature even resolved to use health criteria as a possible means of preventing public school desegregation. (481a, p. 4) Thus, the matter of health is central to present race relations concerns and to the psychology of the Negro American.[2]

MENTAL ILLNESS

Ever since the census of 1840, the mental illness rates of Negroes have been a subject of considerable interest and debate. But formidable methodological problems must be overcome before any reasonably accurate estimate can be made of the "true" amount of psychosis and neurosis existing in the general population. For many years, investigators merely counted the number of people detained at any one time in mental institutions. This procedure is obviously inadequate. Such a rate not only reflects the number of the mentally ill, but also the duration of confinement, the availability and quality of the treatment facilities, and a host of other factors unrelated to the immediate problem. Consequently, later investigators have employed rates of mental illness over a specified time period. Two distinctly different types of these rates exist—"incidence" and "prevalence."[3] Incidence refers to the number of new cases of a disease occurring in a population during a particular time interval; while prevalence refers to the total number of active cases of a disease present in a particular population dur-

[2] An earlier draft of this chapter by the authors appeared in 1963 in *Phylon*, under the title of "Race, Disease, and Desegregation: A New Look."

[3] These same terms are also applied to rates of physical illness.

ing a particular time interval. Thus, prevalence includes new cases together with old cases who have either continuously remained ill or who have relapsed. This distinction is a vital one, for the two types of rates may lead to diverse conclusions.

Though the use of specified time periods and of both incidence and prevalence rates mark definite improvements in technique, serious problems remain. Generally, only the data from public institutions are secured, causing an underestimation of mental illness among those who can afford private treatment. And even studies which carefully include both public and private patients leave uncounted the many mentally ill people who never receive treatment. Equally serious problems are raised by the absence of a rigorous conception of mental illness and the dependence upon psychiatric diagnoses. Various researches have employed different definitions of mental illness, introducing error that is often compounded by unreliable medical judgments.

Further complications involve the special position and treatment of Negroes in American society. Since Negroes as a group are less educated and less attuned to the mass media than whites, they are less informed about mental disorder. A survey conducted in four Texas communities revealed that the Negro respondents were more likely to believe that the mentally ill "just don't want to face their problems," lack "will power," and look different from other people. (103) Such beliefs together with inadequate financial resources to care for disturbed family members at home often lead to the more rapid institutional commitment of Negroes. In addition, some Southern juries commit Negroes to mental institutions more readily than whites. (173) Once committed, Negro lower-class patients, like lower-class patients in general, are less likely to receive advanced therapy; indeed, they may well receive only custodial care and thus be consigned to lengthy institutionalization. (103, 319, 494) This is especially true in the South, where virtually all private facilities are closed to Negroes, and the few public facilities open to them are symbolic instruments of white-supremacy state governments—segregated, inferior, and grossly overcrowded. These factors operate to elevate spuriously both the incidence and prevalence mental illness rates of Negroes, since they amplify the number of Negroes institutionalized without necessarily representing an actual increase in the amount of mental illness.

Mindful of these sharply limiting qualifications, a few broad generalizations can be tentatively ventured on the basis of available evidence. Consider first the psychoses, the most severe mental aberrations. Repeated studies of first admissions to state hospitals in a variety of areas generally show Negro incidence rates for psychosis to be about twice as large as white rates.[4] (88, 175, 250, 319, 320, 321, 322, 392, 542, 544) Particular psychoses contribute disproportionately to the greater Negro rates. Schizophrenia, the bizarre condition of social withdrawal and personality disorganization, is especially frequent among Negro first admissions.[5] Two organic diagnoses, paresis and alcoholic psychosis, are also overrepresented among Negroes entering state hospitals.

But such state hospital research obviously underestimates the amount of white psychosis. Allowances must be made for the fact that whites are better able to afford private treatment and thus escape enumeration in these studies of public facilities. Investigations which attempt to overcome this difficulty by including private facilities have turned up conflicting results. In one study of prevalence rates in Baltimore, the Negro psychosis rate was roughly twice that of whites for state hospitals alone, but when the predominantly-white private and veterans' hospitals were included the Negro-to-white ratio was lowered to one-and-a-half to one. (392) A Texas study

---

[4] For methodological criticisms of these studies, see Schermerhorn. (446)

[5] One investigation found that Negro schizophrenics are less likely to respond favorably to electroshock therapy (389), a finding that suggests particularly profound disorganization among Negro victims.

of incidence, however, found that the Negro rates were actually below that of "Anglo-Americans" once both private as well as public first admissions were calculated. (251)

Finally, there is the problem of ascertaining how many mentally ill persons remain unhospitalized and untreated. As can be readily imagined, research on this problem is extremely difficult. One preliminary effort, a Baltimore health survey, found that the non-institutionalized prevalence rate for psychosis was roughly ten times higher for whites than Negroes, but serious methodological weaknesses cast doubt upon this remarkable finding.[6] (392)

Obviously, the definitive epidemiological research on this question is yet to be performed. Meanwhile, personality tests confirm a greater tendency among Negroes to report psychotic symptoms. Two investigations independently conducted on diverse populations noted that Negro males scored significantly higher than comparable white males on the Minnesota Multiphasic Inventory (MMPI) scales measuring psychotic trends. (69, 234) Illustrative items from these scales include: "I have had periods in which I carried on activities without knowing later what I had been doing," and "At times I have had fits of laughing and crying that I cannot control." On balance, we can tentatively conclude that Negro psychosis rates, especially for schizophrenia and some organic psychoses, are higher than white rates.

[6] The weaknesses were threefold: (1) the non-institutional prevalence rates were projected from just 17 actual cases of psychosis. (2) The problem of reliable and valid diagnoses was particularly acute, for internists, not psychiatrists, examined the subjects and often diagnosed mental disorders without psychiatric consultation or psychometric testing. Subsequently, one psychiatrist, who had not himself seen the subjects, reviewed the records and assigned the ratings. (3) These difficulties led to a serious sampling bias. Since for lack of information the psychiatrist-rater had to discard "about one third of the cases which had been diagnosed by examining physicians," the final rates for the non-institutionalized were based on an unrepresentative sample of Baltimore's population. (96, p. 96)

If group data on psychosis are difficult to decipher, group data on neurosis are even more confusing. Most of these less serious mental abnormalities do not require institutionalization; particularly among lower-status Negroes, neurotic symptoms may often be ignored. (228) Not surprisingly, then, comparative group data on neurosis are somewhat contradictory. Neurosis incidence rates for first admissions to state hospitals are generally much higher for whites than Negroes (542), though this may merely reflect that only incapacitated Negroes are accepted. In addition, many neurotics receive treatment from private sources, and for economic reasons these individuals are predominantly white.

Service studies from World War II provide inconclusive evidence. Two Navy investigations reported less neuroticism among Negroes than whites (178, 244), whereas an Army investigation reported more frequent "minor psychiatric illness" among Negroes. (427) This discrepancy may be due in large measure to different mental health standards applied by the two services at induction centers, for there is reason to suspect that the Army's wartime requirements for Negro inductees were especially low.

Personality test results on neurotic measures generally do not reveal racial differentials comparable to those obtained on measures of psychotic trends. In fact, two MMPI studies found samples of white males scored significantly higher than comparable Negro males on a character-disorder scale of psychopathic personality trends. (69, 234) Two examples of this scale include: "I have not lived the right kind of life," and "My way of doing things is apt to be misunderstood by others." All told, we can tentatively conclude that the ratio of Negro to white neuroticism is not as great as for the psychoses, and for certain other conditions, like character disorders, the Negro rate may actually be less than the white.

The findings on suicide are more straightforward. Negroes commit suicide far less frequently than whites; the national non-white death rate from suicide, 1949 through

1951, was only 42 per cent of the white rate. (380) Negro
American aggression is more often turned outward in the
form of homicide than inward as suicide. (Chapter 6)

What lies behind these racial differences in mental
illness? Authorities agree that innate racial factors do
not provide an adequate explanation. To be sure, genetic
potential probably interacts with environmental circumstance to produce such severe conditions as schizophrenia. (52, 265) But there is no evidence to suggest that
this genetic potential is differentially distributed among
the races. Instead, it is generally reasoned that the genetic
potential for mental illness is roughly the same among
the world's larger populations (307), but that dissimilar
situations trigger the potential to diverse degrees. This
thinking holds with special force in comparisons between Negro and white Americans, since as noted in
Chapter 3 they possess a considerable proportion of similar genes in their two gene pools. Thus, any distinct differences in mental illness between the two groups should
be traceable to contrasting patterns of environmental
triggering. And these contrasting environmental patterns
are not hard to identify, for distinctions of social class
and poverty, on the one hand, and racial restrictions,
on the other, play critical roles in mental illness.

Witness first the importance of class. Hollingshead
and Redlich, in their research on *Social Class and Mental
Illness*, found the patterns of treated mental illness
among white lower-class patients in New Haven closely
resemble those just described for Negro patients.[7] (235)
Treated psychosis, particularly schizophrenia, has a
higher incidence and prevalence among the poor than
the prosperous. By contrast, neurosis incidence rates do
not vary by class, though neurosis prevalance rates are
actually higher among the economically well-to-do. The
type of neurotic diagnosis also varies by class. Lower-
status patients more often "act out" their problems—in
anti-social and hysterical reactions; while upper-status

[7] Only 6 per cent of the two lowest classes analyzed in the New
Haven study was Negro. (235, p. 202)

patients more often "act in"—in depressive and obses-
sive-compulsive reactions and character disorders.

Chicago data from the 1930's indicated that social
classes within the city's Negro population had markedly
diverse mental disorder rates.[8] (150) The reported incidence of different types of schizophrenia, in particular,
varied; the Negro area nearest the downtown business
district had a rate over 60 per cent greater than that of a
more middle-class Negro area. Not all studies have obtained such clear results with Negroes (251, 283), but a
recent incidence survey of Philadelphia Negroes dis-
closed that schizophrenia and mental illness in general
were much less frequent among upper-status Negroes.
(390) These findings were further confirmed in a study
of first admissions to the state mental hospitals of Ohio.
With each race analyzed separately, it was noted that
higher rates existed for both the white and Negro lower
classes. The investigator concluded that the higher ad-
mission rates of Negroes were "a function of the low
status of the Negro rather than some biological or genetic
difference due to 'race.' " (175)

But social class is only part of the explanation. As
early as 1913, one American psychiatrist had pointed out
how the behavior of three Negro schizophrenics was directly related to their racially restricted experiences. (148)
These observations have often been repeated during the
past half century. For example, a higher incidence of
mental illness noted among Negro enlisted men on an
isolated Pacific island was attributed to, among other
factors, the dissatisfaction of the Negroes with their
white officers and their strong sense of being the vic-

[8] Compared with whites, Negro Americans have significantly
larger rates of schizophrenia than manic-depression. This coin-
cides with the fact that both the New Haven and Chicago investigations found less correlation between class and manic-depression than between class and schizophrenia. In addition, twin
studies reveal a smaller genetic component for schizophrenia than
for manic-depression. (265) In short, environmental factors appear more important for the mental disorder which reveals the
greater racial differential.

tims of racial discrimination. (427) The majority of the
psychotic breakdowns among the Negroes in this situation were diagnosed as "paranoid schizophrenia," a fact
that recalls the admonition of Kardiner and Ovesey
against hasty application of the term "paranoid" to
Negro patients. For Negroes "to see hostility in the environment is a normal perception. Hence, we must guard
against calling the Negro paranoid when he actually
lives in an environment that persecutes him." (266, p.
343)

One of the less direct mechanisms whereby persecution might lead to greater mental illness is the necessity
for persons with few job skills to migrate long distances
to seek employment. There has been considerable controversy over this point; it now seems that previous
waves of particularly poor Negro migrants did have unusually high rates of mental illness (e.g., during the
1930's), but that better-educated recent arrivals to the
North no longer evince this phenomenon. (280, 323)
Another possible mechanism is the perception of relative deprivation, the discrepancy between high aspirations and actual attainments. (Chapter 8) There is a
growing body of research evidence which suggests this
is a critical psychological determinant of mental disorder. (281) And certainly racial discrimination acts to
bar the very achievements which the society encourages
individuals to attempt. (Chapter 1)

The deterioration of mental health through a combination of poverty and persecution is not limited to Negro Americans. The Peruvian *mestizo*, barely managing
to survive on the outskirts of Lima, presents a case in
point. (441) Mental illness, alcoholism, and family disorganization are widespread, as well as the familiar personality syndrome of inferiority feelings, insecurity, and
hostility. The human species reacts to crushing oppression in much the same way the world over.

Also instructive is the comparison of data on Negro
Americans with those on Jewish Americans. Rather than

the near-total rejection long faced by Negroes, Jews have generally faced a more subtle, ambiguous kind of rejection. This more uncertain, shadowy form of discrimination, together with the Jews' higher social status and closer group and family bonds, have contributed to a mental illness pattern strikingly different from that of the Negro. Whereas the Negro suffers from psychosis relatively more than neurosis, Jews in the United States have fairly low psychosis rates but especially high neurosis rates. (377)

These Jewish patterns suggest a laboratory analogy. In his famous conditioning research on dogs, Ivan Pavlov established what appeared to be a type of "experimental neurosis." (396, Chapter 36) First, he trained a dog to distinguish between a circle and an ellipse by presenting food each time the circle appeared and withholding food each time the ellipse appeared. Then Pavlov began gradually altering the shape of the ellipse till it more and more resembled the circle. Suddenly, at a point when the hungry animal could no longer differentiate one object from the other, the dog's behavior changed drastically. To speak anthropomorphically, the dog rejected the whole situation, became aggressive toward the experimenter, and in other ways tried to defend himself from intolerable anxiety. Other investigators, using an assortment of animals ranging from goats to chimpanzees, have replicated Pavlov's results. (305) The "experimental neurosis" created by these researchers often has the long-term effects and stubborn resistance to therapy characteristic of the more serious human neuroses.

The subtleties of anti-Semitic discrimination often blur cues for the victim. Determining whether a cool reception represents bad manners or prejudice can be as difficult as distinguishing the circle from the modified ellipse. With legal desegregation, this kind of anxious uncertainty increases for the Negro. The clear-cut rejection of the past contributed to such conditions as the excessive withdrawal of schizophrenia; the ambiguous, discreet rejection of the future may well lead to an increase of neuroticism among Negroes, as it has among Jews. This possibility along with the Negro's rising economic levels and strengthening group and family bonds suggest an hypothesis for future trends in mental illness: among Negro Americans, psychosis rates will begin to recede as neurosis rates climb steadily.[9]

COMMUNICABLE DISEASE

Poverty, family disorganization, and slum conditions propagate communicable diseases even more than they do mental illness. Four categories of these diseases assume special significance for Negro American health: pulmonary tuberculosis, venereal disease, childhood disease, and parasitic disease.

Exposure to pulmonary tuberculosis was virtually universal in the nineteenth century; it struck members of all "races" and social classes throughout the nation. But a general attack upon the disease, through improved sanitation, nutrition, and treatment, has now localized it among specific groups which have benefited least from these advances. Today, the spread of tuberculosis is largely restricted to crowded, lower-class urban areas, "where the presence of individuals with tuberculosis in communicable form makes the dissemination of infection inevitable." (33) The further eradication of tuberculosis from these pockets is possible with the wider application of the same techniques which have already proven effective: improved standards of living, nutrition, and therapy.

In the meantime, lower-status Negroes are one of the underprivileged groups still evidencing high rates of pulmonary tuberculosis. Compared to whites, death rates for the disease are roughly four times higher for Ne-

[9] Support for this hypothesis can be inferred from the findings of a study which compared the development of neurotics with that of schizophrenics in two social classes. Neurotics had been more rebellious and more often had come from stable homes and had loving and affectionate parents. (378)

groes[10] (380); and incidence rates of active cases are about three times higher for Negroes. (463, pp. 27, 45) Segregationists who employ these data to argue that biracial schools in the South present a health hazard, however, greatly oversimplify the problem. The age group most resistant to the disease is between five and fourteen years old, the age range chiefly affected by educational desegregation. (463, p. 28) Furthermore, the Negro-white differential in the incidence of active cases is smallest in the South. While the ex-Confederate states had a median white incidence slightly above the national white figure for the years 1957-1959, they had a median Negro rate only about half the national non-white rate. (462, 463) Thus, instead of non-white incidence rates four to six times those of whites, as found in such colder, highly urban states as Illinois, Michigan, New Jersey, New York, and Pennsylvania, Negro incidence rates in the South average out less than twice the white rates. Consequently, the threat of the spread of active tuberculosis, a most complex process in itself,[11] offers a feeble argument against the desegregation of Southern schools. If the segregationist were truly frightened by such a prospect, he would not allow Negroes to prepare his food or tend his home and children—situations that potentially raise more realistic threats of tubercle transmission.

Beyond the immediate concerns of desegregation is the question of innate "racial susceptibility" to pulmonary tuberculosis. Group constitutional predispositions to tuberculosis may exist, but they have never been proven; indeed, no definitive answer can be rendered until the various subspecies of mankind attain approximately the

[10] These rates are for the period, 1949-1951; mortality rates cited throughout this chapter for Negroes are actually for non-whites, 95.5 per cent of whom, in 1950, were Negro.

[11] "Thus, while exposure to the tubercle bacillus is one necessary factor for the development of tuberculosis, there are many poorly understood accessory factors which, taken together, determine whether the disease will develop in the exposed person and which might be thought of as etiologic in one sense." (330, p. 132)

same standards of living. Meanwhile, the Negro-white differences in frequency of cases in the United States appear to be largely a function of exposure and socio-economic factors.[12] (33, 331) In 1945, for example, the Negro death rate from the disease in cities with a population of over a million people was almost twice that of Negroes in cities of from one to two hundred thousand people. (397) It is in the most desperate slums of the urban ghettos where overcrowding, wretched sanitation, and inadequate nutrition take their greatest toll. Nonetheless, the improved standard of living and better health facilities enjoyed by many Negroes in recent decades have brought about a dramatic decrease in tuberculosis mortality and incidence. In Manhattan, between 1910 and 1950, the non-white death rate from the infection fell from 445.5 to 62 per 100,000. (249) From 1955 to 1960, the national non-white rates of new active cases dropped almost a third. (462, p. 8)

The incidence of tuberculosis is also found to be unusually high in particular Caucasian groups. Celtic peoples in France, Wales, Ireland, and Scotland long had such elevated mortality rates from the disease that some observers regarded them as inherently more susceptible to the disease. But, as with Negroes, general improvement of living conditions and active efforts to combat the infection have brought declines in recent years. (331, pp. 118-119) And all nations experiencing the onset of industrialization, the devastation of war, or the deprivations of economic depression have suffered sharp increments in deaths from tuberculosis. (330, 331, pp. 132-133) In the United States today, white mortality from the disease is still elevated among workers exposed to toxic dusts (e.g., coal miners), undernourished mountain folk, poor migrants, the institutionalized, and elderly, indigent males. (33, 331, 474)

The importance of sheer exposure in contracting the malady is demonstrated by the high rates of positive

[12] For a similar conclusion in regard to the Indian American, see Morse. (370)

reactions to tuberculin skin tests in white medical students and nurses. (267) And when exposure and social class factors are roughly equal between the racial groups, differences decline. One North Carolina study of lower-status white female hospital employees and Negro student practical nurses noted virtually the same percentages of negative reactions to tuberculin skin tests. (475) Such data lead May to conclude that "cultural factors play a predominant role in the distributional pattern" of pulmonary tuberculosis. (331, p. 131)

If there are true genetic group differences in susceptibility and resistance to diseases such as tuberculosis, they are not confined to any one group or race. For instance, another infectious respiratory disease, histoplasmosis, strikes whites in a fulminant form far more often than Negroes. (177) Of similar interest is the close resemblance between the leprosy bacillus and tubercle bacillus, for some observers believe that Negroes are innately more resistant to leprosy than Caucasians and Mongoloids. (331, p. 144)

Pulmonary tuberculosis death rates, then, are steadily declining in the United States for both races, and there is every reason to expect that this trend will continue as treatment and environmental conditions improve. Negro death and incidence rates from the disease are still considerably higher than white rates; however, evidence from many sources suggest that this is a function not of "race," but of exposure and socio-economic differentials between the two groups. Even if there were a "racial" difference in susceptibility to the infection, it would be virtually irrelevant since the disease can be eliminated and prevented. "Tuberculosis is a totally unnecessary disease," writes Perkins. "It can be prevented. It can be cured . . ." (398)

Venereal disease, particularly syphilis, is another serious communicable infection undermining Negro American health. Unlike tuberculosis, problems of reporting greatly complicate accurate estimates of the Negro-white differential in the incidence of diseases such as syphilis.

Because of the potent connotations of sin and shame surrounding syphilis in middle-class America, most infected individuals do not seek medical aid at all. Other victims who can afford it go to discreet private physicians and are generally not officially recorded. Lower-class victims, disproportionately Negro, typically receive medical assistance at public facilities and are on record. Furthermore, the symptoms of the initial stages of syphilis disappear spontaneously, leading some victims to think they have recovered. Consequently, Maxcy calculates "that more than one-half of the cases of syphilis go into the latent stage undiscovered and unreported." (330, p. 264) And among those reported, lower-status persons are undoubtedly overrepresented.

Additional problems involve the screening blood tests which have often been cited. For instance, racial differences in the results of World War II induction blood tests are still widely quoted, even though penicillin was not introduced as a treatment until 1943, and this drug vastly altered the modern dimensions of the disease. To complicate the statistical picture further, blood screening tests can be falsely negative or falsely positive. Even a truly positive blood test does not mean that an individual is infectious, only that he has or has had syphilis at some time in his life. A positive reaction to a blood test can still occur after adequate treatment, and even without treatment an individual can suffer the ravages of the disease himself without being infectious to others. (162, 330)

Moreover, reported mortality rates due to syphilis are notoriously unreliable. (330) Death results from complications in the latent stage of the disease decades after the initial infection; and the shame surrounding the disease insures that, particularly for high-status persons, syphilis as a direct or contributory cause of death will frequently go unlisted.

Within these severe restrictions, the available data suggest high Negro rates of syphilis and its complications. Public health data for 1960-1961, for instance, indicate a Negro incidence rate ten times greater than the white and a death rate almost four times greater. (419) Research suggests these group differences are inflated through disproportionate underreporting of whites. Various autopsy investigations agree that from 5 to 10 per cent of the general population shows evidence of syphilitic infection, a figure far higher than other reported rates would indicate. (330) But if the Negro-white ratios usually quoted are too high, there is little doubt that Negroes do have elevated rates.

Greater Negro susceptibility to syphilis is not at issue. "There is no evidence," declares Dubos flatly, "that different races or different individuals differ in their susceptibility or resistance to [syphilitic] infection." (136, p. 583) What, then, underlies the difference in group rates? Maxcy declares:

> The social and economic environment—including income, housing, education, medical care and availability, cost and use of medical services and provision of control measures—determine to a considerable extent the occurrence and distribution of the venereal diseases in a particular community. (33, p. 285)

It is therefore not surprising that American groups with the lowest incomes, poorest housing, least education, and most restricted medical facilities have the highest rates of venereal diseases and their sequelae. In addition, the prevalence of family disorganization among lower-class Negroes discussed in Chapter 1 is an especially significant correlate. (119)

The other major venereal disease, gonorrhea, is subject to similar but even more serious recording errors. It is actually much more prevalent than syphilis, with reported Negro rates far exceeding those of whites. (330, 474) Gonorrhea is responsive to the same social factors important in syphilis, and no group distinctions in susceptibility are known. The same general considerations apply to three other minor diseases regarded as venereal in their transfer: chancroid, granuloma inguinale, and lymphogranuloma venereum. The last of these was once thought to be limited to Negroes, but recent studies indicate that it is more widespread. One investigation found Southern Negro college students have a rate approximately that of whites, suggesting that social factors are also important in the incidence of this condition. (313)

Venereal disease has been increasing disproportionately among the nation's youth. (162) These diseases present real problems for public education—though not the problems raised by segregationists. And Southern segregationists who infer "racial immorality" from the reported venereal disease rates of Negroes might modify their "logic" if they realized that the South has the highest white syphilis rate of any region in the United States. (474) Schools might well lead a massive informational campaign against venereal disease, since such education is urgently needed by Americans of both races. Part of this informational campaign should be focused upon the many fear-ridden myths which surround venereal disease and have become part of the desegregation controversy. Typical examples are the mistaken notions that venereal diseases are readily transferred via such objects as toilets (intimate physical contact is necessary) and that venereal disease contracted from a member of another race is especially virulent. (136, p. 569; 162)

Communicable childhood diseases are very important to Negro American health. Compared to white mortality rates, Negro mortality rates are particularly high during early life. This is in part due to diseases, such as whooping cough, meningitis, measles, diphtheria, and scarlet fever, for which there are no known racial susceptibilities. Though the fatal complications of these disorders can be drastically reduced by modern medicine, Negroes have death rates from them at least twice those of whites. (380) Whooping cough, for example, is most likely to be fatal in the first two years of life, and it can be prevented during this critical period by immunization; yet reported Negro death rates from this disease over the nation during 1949-1951 were six times the white rates. Such data dramatize the continuing need for improved medical services for Negro children. The same need applies for adults so long as death rates for such ameliorable diseases as nephritis, influenza, and pneumonia remain high for Negroes. (380)

Two parasitic diseases, hookworm and malaria, offer revealing racial comparisons. Due to climate and poverty, the South has endured a wide variety of enteric infections. Hookworm, in particular, was once the scourge of the region, though in recent decades control measures have sharply decreased its incidence. Since it is concentrated among those who live in deprived, unsanitary conditions, Negro Southerners would be expected to have a greater incidence of hookworm than white Southerners. Yet hookworm is primarily a disease of rural white children (474, p. 247), suggesting a relative immunity to the disease among Negroes. (231, p. 416; 474, p. 247)

While malaria is not a public health threat in the United States today, it affords an instructive lesson in the evolution of racial differences. Malaria has for centuries been a mass killer in many parts of the world. This set the scene for the survival and spread through natural selection of genetic mutations which defended against the disease. (Chapter 3) And because malaria is a blood disease, these defenses all involved changes in the blood. The most studied and best understood of these natural defenses is an inherited ability to change red blood cells into "sickle" shapes under certain conditions. This ability is due to a special blood component, hemoglobin S, in the red blood cells, one of 20 inherited variations in human hemoglobin. By interfering with the life cycle of the malarial parasite (47, p. 157), the sickling property affords special resistance to the most serious forms and complications of the disease.[13] (106, 109, 135, 487)

[13] The sickle-cell gene may also confer some decrease in susceptibility to hookworm infection and leprosy, together with increased susceptibility to typhoid fever. (47, p. 110)

Figure 4 shows the geographical distribution of hemoglobin S, together with a similar malarial defense, thalassemia. Note that some malaria-infested areas have both blood defenses: Iberia, North Africa, Italy, Greece, and Turkey. The largest hemoglobin S area, however, is the malarial belt across West and Central Africa; indeed, the condition was once thought to be almost entirely an African trait until high frequencies were detected among Mediterranean and Indian populations. Thus, hemoglobin S and its accompanying sickling property are not a function of race but of environmental adaptation. For instance, Africans residing in sectors where malaria is uncommon have a low frequency of the blood trait. (109, 347) Similarly, Negro Americans, residing in an almost malaria-free part of the world, now possess the hemoglobin S trait only about half as frequently as Africans presently living in those regions from which slaves were imported to North America.[14] (109, 135, 487) This lower incidence is beneficial, for there are certain health hazards involved with the condition, particularly sickle-cell anemia.

INHERITED DISEASE

Sickle-cell anemia is a favorite disease-exhibit of white supremacists. Though it derives from an adaptive, evolutionary process, they feel the disease is ultimate proof of the innate inferiority of "Negro blood." The sickle-cell trait is inherited from just one parent (heterozygous state). Such individuals are normal human beings, for the trait does not of itself produce ill effects except under unusual conditions. It is only when the sickling gene is inherited from both parents (homozygous state) that sickle-cell anemia results and produces serious symptoms

[14] Some of this decrease is due to the infiltration of Caucasian genes among Negro Americans; but some of it is due to the fact that hemoglobin S is no longer adaptive. One study of the descendants of Gold Coast natives imported to two different New World islands in the seventeenth century reveals a decrease in the trait only for those living on the one island which was free of malaria. (109, p. 250)

and anemia, usually causing death in the first decade of life. (109, 487, 547)

But, as just noted, hereditary alterations in the blood as a defense against malaria are by no means the prerogative of any one race. Thalassemia, for instance, closely parallels the sickling trait, for it, too, is an inherited property involving a variation in hemoglobin production

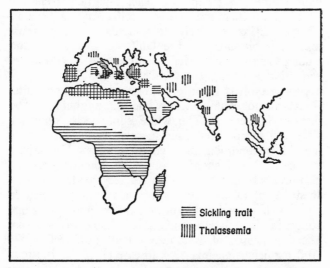

Sickling trait
Thalassemia

FIGURE 4—GEOGRAPHICAL DISTRIBUTION OF SICKLING TRAIT AND THALASSEMIA

(Adapted from: M. M. Wintrobe, *Clinical Hematology*, fifth edition. Philadelphia: Lea & Febiger, 1961. Courtesy of Dr. Herman Lehmann.)

resulting in unusual red cell shapes (target cells). These changes are also believed to have evolved as a protection against the parasite of malaria and perhaps other chronic parasitic anemias. But whereas the sickling defense is concentrated among Africans and descendants of Africans, the thalassemia trait probably originated among Mediterranean peoples, and it is found in the United States primarily among their descendants. (Figure 4)

The heterozygous state (thalassemia minor) varies considerably in its severity, but the homozygous state (thalassemia major), like sickle-cell anemia, is severe, progressive, and usually fatal in early life. (47, 109, 487, 547)

A third alteration in red blood cells believed to protect against malaria is called glucose-6-phosphate dehydrogenase deficiency. Individuals with this deficiency are perfectly healthy except they lack a particular enzyme which makes them sensitive to specific drugs and plants. This condition is widely distributed, especially where malaria is prevalent; in the United States it is found among Caucasians of Mediterranean and Near Eastern extraction and Negroes. (47, Chapter 8; 327)

Just as evolved blood defenses against environmental threats are not confined to any one race, neither are blood diseases in general. The white supremacist dotes on sickle-cell anemia, but conveniently overlooks other innate blood conditions more common among Caucasians.

Like sickle-cell anemia, congenital hemolytic anemia also results from a severe inherited red blood cell defect. It strikes at all ages, but symptoms usually appear in childhood. Though it has been reported among Negroes, congenital hemolytic anemia is best known as a disease affecting people of European origin. (109, 487, 547) And pernicious anemia "is a disease chiefly of the temperate zone and the white race." (547, p. 468; 225) It is a chronic anemia affecting older adults. Genetic factors predispose the individual to the disease, but accessory factors, climate, diet, age, are also involved.

Excessive destruction of blood in newborn babies as a result of the Rh-negative factor in the mother's blood has received considerable popular attention in recent years. There is a lower prevalence of Rh-negatives among Negro Americans, thus this condition is less frequent among Negro babies than white babies. (140) Another innate disorder involves excessive bleeding. Hemophilia, famous as the hereditary inability of the blood to clot among some of Europe's royal families, is quite rare among Negroes. Though not a common condition, it has been recognized for centuries among Europeans. (31, 547)

An additional blood disease, for which the genetic factors have not been completely elucidated, also presents Negro-white differences. Leukemia, considered a type of cancer, has white prevalence rates approximately twice Negro rates for all forms of the disease. (110, p. 30) National death rates for 1949-1951 show a white figure 70 per cent greater than that for Negroes. (380) These large discrepancies do not seem to be a function of reporting error, since statistics for many other cancers do not reveal comparable differences and the elevated white mortality rates for leukemia existed for 1949-1951 in all 32 states reporting racial data.

Three metabolic abnormalities are significant among the genetically-linked diseases revealing racial distinctions: cystic fibrosis, diabetes mellitus, and phenylketonuria (phenylpyruvic oligophrenia). Cystic fibrosis ranks high as a cause of death in childhood. This chronic disorder produces such serious glandular disturbances, especially in the respiratory and digestive systems, that death ensues for 94 per cent of the victims before the age of fifteen. For 1958-1959, the recorded death rate for cystic fibrosis in the United States was over twice as great for whites as Negroes, with an especially large racial differential for females. (352, 432)

Diabetes mellitus, a common chronic abnormality of carbohydrate metabolism, results from a primary inherited predisposition made manifest by a variety of secondary factors. National death rates for 1958-1959 show a 29 per cent higher Negro rate for males and an 88 per cent higher Negro rate for females. (355) The conspicuous over-representation of Negro females reflects the typically greater rate among women of all races who are obese and have borne large numbers of children. (17, 163) Thus, it is unclear whether racial origin is directly related to the condition.

Another hereditary metabolic disease, phenylketonuria,

is caused by an enzyme deficiency and results in severe mental retardation and impaired production of melanin pigments. Ninety per cent of phenylketonuric children are blue-eyed blonds with fair skins, and most cases are of northern European ancestry. Since the disease is estimated to be responsible for one per cent of all of the nation's mental defectives and may be ameliorated by early changes in diet, it has been the focus of mass testing surveys. These surveys indicate the disease is rarely found among Negroes. (422, 487)

DISEASES OF VARIOUS AND UNDETERMINED ETIOLOGIES

Mention of fair skin has a special irony. Dark skin has long symbolized Negro "inferiority" to white supremacists. Yet it is an evolved adaptation still possessing survival value. While the near disappearance of malaria in America renders the sickling trait dysfunctional, the sun and harmful radiation are still with us. And melanin pigmentation "protects the skin against injury by ultraviolet radiation and also enhances the skin's ability to resist other types of trauma. Deeply pigmented skin reacts less readily to chemical irritants, and it is also not so readily sensitized." (411, p. 15) Consequently, all three major types of skin cancer, together the most common of all cancers, occur far more often among Caucasians than Negroes. The most frequent of these, basal cell epithelioma, is concentrated among blond and rufous individuals (85 per cent) and in body areas of greatest exposure to the sun (e.g., the face and neck).[15] (411, 538)

Another physical trait emphasized by white supremacists as inferior, the fuller lip of many Negroes, provokes a similar irony. Negroes have a lower incidence of cancer of the lower lip. (432, p. 636) Cancer of the gall

[15] After injury, some Negroes develop elevated scars called keloids. These reactions arouse cosmetic attention, but are neither contagious nor cancerous.

bladder also offers a racial difference in frequency rates. It is more common in whites probably because Negroes have fewer gallstones, which are thought to be precursors to gall bladder cancer. (432, p. 216) Reporting errors are apparently not responsible for these racial rate differentials, for most other cancers reveal comparable rates for both groups. (303, 380) There is, however, a sex difference in total cancer mortality rates by race. While male rates are similar, Negro females have slightly higher rates than white females. (356, 358, 380) This is true almost entirely because of a higher prevalence among Negro women of cancer of the genital system, an area where cancer has been vastly reduced by preventive measures and advanced medical and surgical techniques more available to the more prosperous segments of the population. (380) Cancer of the cervix serves as an example. Grossly, it is twice as frequent among Negroes, but when white and Negro women from the same socio-economic backgrounds are studied, the incidence is essentially the same. (80) On the other hand, Negro males appear to have significantly lower rates of testicular tumors than white males. (292)

Two conditions with racial differentials are poorly understood as to causative factors. Sarcoidosis is a chronic disorder which resembles such infectious diseases as tuberculosis, leprosy, and syphilis. It is worldwide in distribution, although Scandinavia is the cradle of the disease. Nevertheless, in North America Negroes are more frequently afflicted than whites. (432, 546) Multiple sclerosis is a neurological disease affecting the brain and spinal cord. Although it is more common in colder climates and among whites, further research is needed to determine the importance of race apart from climatic factors. (8, 532)

In recent years, great attention has been focused on the racial differences in cardio-vascular diseases, an area exhaustively reviewed by Phillips and Burch. (409) Total reported Negro death rates for these diseases remain over the years consistently above those of whites, particularly for females. (304, 354, 380) But a breakdown by type is necessary to see the significance of racial differentials. The most critical differential involves hypertension and hypertensive heart disease, with Negro death rates about three times those of whites. (380) One study conducted in Georgia found that the two components of hypertension, elevated diastolic and systolic blood pressures, were more common in a sample of Negroes than in a sample of whites at virtually every adult age-level for both sexes. (97) Genetic predisposition is important in this condition, but many other factors contribute to the development of hypertension, including psycho-social influences. The anxious business executive is a familiar stereotype in this connection. For Negroes, the problem of repressing hostility against whites, discussed in Chapter 2, may be an important factor.

Arteriosclerosis, popularly known as "hardening of the arteries," and arteriosclerotic heart disease accompany the aging process and do not reveal such striking racial differences. Again numerous factors are known to influence this disorder, including heredity, age, sex, diet, blood-cholesterol levels, and life-situation. Although rates for Negroes in general are somewhat lower, sex may be a more crucial variable, with white males the most vulnerable group of all to arteriosclerotic disease. (304, 380, 486)

A third group of cardio-vascular diseases stems from infections and tends to produce Negro mortality rates above those of whites. This largely reflects differential infection rates (e.g., tuberculosis). However, whites are considered probably more susceptible to the development of rheumatic fever and rheumatic heart disease, which figure prominently in this group of diseases. Finally, fewer Negroes than whites are born with congenital heart disease. (409)

Even orthopedic disorders relate to "race" and afford an illustration of the influence of life styles. Negro Americans more often than white Americans suffer from flexible flatfeet. This may be related to inadequate foot support and jobs which typically require standing for prolonged periods. On the other hand, whites, less accustomed to strains of weight-bearing, more often develop march fractures of the feet from their sudden overuse, as in army basic training. (460)

The birth processes introduce still further Negro-white disparities in health standards. Perinatal mortality rates in 1958-1959 were almost twice as high for Negroes and maternal mortality rates in 1959 were four times as high for Negroes, though rapid improvements had been made in both areas over recent decades. (140, 351, 353) Moreover, premature births are roughly 50 per cent more frequent among Negroes. (395, 425) Mortality figures, however, do not adequately reveal the prenatal, perinatal, and postnatal morbidity among Negro infants. Such problems as increased infection, anoxia, and birth trauma may retard Negro infants for life. (Chapter 5) These conditions are the results of the lack of prenatal care, poor family health education, inadequate diet, and inexpert delivery. They are found among the poor of all groups and will only decline as further medical and economic advances are made.

ECONOMICS AND PHYSICAL HEALTH

Repeatedly, as with mental illness, these divergent health rates between Negro and white Americans point up the intimate relationship between physical illness and economics. Three extensive investigations highlight this relationship. The first of these studies conducted a comprehensive health survey which held economic and experiental factors relatively constant. (204) In 1940, the Farm Security Administration studied unselected farm families in eleven rural counties throughout the South; in all, 1714 low-income Negroes and whites were examined at the same clinics. Defective vision, impaired hearing, and deviated nasal septum were far more prominent, and diseased tonsils and dental caries somewhat more prominent, among the poor whites.[16] But hypertension was the particular problem of the poor Negroes. For both sexes at virtually all ages, the Negroes evidenced higher systolic and diastolic blood pressures and a somewhat greater prevalence of heart disease. A last group distinction gives testimony to the inferior medical care long accorded Negroes in such areas. Negro children were less often immunized against smallpox, diphtheria, and typhoid fever.

A second investigation focused upon Negro health in Chicago. (279) The city's non-whites had considerably greater mortality rates in 1950 than the city's whites. Yet careful research revealed that the sharp contrast between the two urban groups in socio-economic standing accounted for virtually all of the "racial differences" in mortality.

A final study related type of occupation to the 1950 death rates of the nation's males aged 20 to 64 years. (213) Differences by occupations were marked, and especially so among non-whites. Urban white laborers had standardized mortality ratios one-quarter larger than those of white skilled and semi-skilled workers; while urban non-white laborers had ratios *twice* as large as those of non-white skilled and semi-skilled workers. This much sharper difference between the laborer and the skilled worker among Negroes is another indication of the Negro's lower economic floor. (Chapter 3) Add to this the far greater percentage of Negroes who hold such unskilled employment as laborers, and the surprising fact is that Negro American morbidity and mortality are not higher than they are.

A FINAL WORD ON HEALTH

This cursory overview of Negro American health underscores the basic fact that serious illness—mental or

---

[16] The disparity in vision may relate to a more general racial difference in visual acuity. Negro Americans on the average have superior visual acuity (269, 270) and are more resistant to a standard optical illusion that in part depends on visual acuity. (405)

physical, communicable or hereditary—is not an exclusive preserve of any one "race" or group of people. As far as inherited disease goes, black supremacists can make a case equal to that of white supremacists; both are wrong. Differences *do* exist between the groups, but they cannot be scientifically adjudged signs of "inferiority" or "superiority." Indeed, such innate conditions as sickle-cell anemia and thalassemia are direct consequences of the evolutionary adaptations various human subspecies have made to their diverse environments.

More crucial medically are the non-genetic threats to life, threats that can be substantially averted through higher living standards and better health care. Tuberculosis, syphilis, whooping cough, perinatal and maternal complications have all been reduced by advances in recent years and can all be reduced further by further advances. The denial of personal dignity is also involved. In particular, mental illness and hypertension appear in part to be direct outgrowths of racial discrimination, to be conspicuous "marks of oppression."

Longevity data tell the story. (359) At the turn of this century, the average non-white American at birth had a life expectancy between 32 and 35 years, 16 years less than that of the average white American. By 1960, this life expectancy had risen to from 61 to 66 years. The many improvements in his situation since 1900 rendered a dramatic increment in the Negro's health, providing solid evidence that corrosive poverty and inadequate medical care were the reasons for his short life span in the past. But while the percentage gain in life expectancy for Negroes over these sixty-odd years has been twice that of whites, there is still a discrepancy of six to eight years. On the basis of the type of data briefly reviewed here, this difference can be traced to the diseases which are treatable, preventable, and unnecessary.

5

NEGRO AMERICAN
INTELLIGENCE

Extending beyond health, white supremacists maintain that Negroes are innately less intelligent than Caucasians. In a statement remarkably comparable to those
made two centuries ago by advocates of the theory of
American degeneration (Introduction), one modern-day
racist phrases the claim in these words:

> Any man with two eyes in his head can observe a
> Negro settlement in the Congo, can study the pure-
> blooded African in his native habitat as he exists
> when left on his own resources, can compare this
> settlement with London or Paris, and can draw his
> own conclusions regarding relative levels of character
> and intelligence. . . . Finally, he can inquire as to
> the number of pure-blooded blacks who have made
> their contributions to great literature or engineering or
> medicine or philosophy or abstract science. (421,
> p. 7)

Such claims assumed special importance among the oppo-
nents of the Supreme Court's school desegregation ruling in 1954. Interracial education simply will not work,
contended many segregationists; Negro children are too
retarded innately to benefit and will only act to drag
down the standards of the white children.

Americans are far less receptive to such reasoning now
than they were a generation ago. Public opinion poll
data reveal that, while only two out of five white Americans regarded Negroes as their intellectual equals in
1942, almost four out of five did by 1956—including a

substantial majority of white Southerners. (247) Much of this change is due to the thorough repudiation of racist assertions by the vast majority of modern psychologists and other behavioral scientists. Indeed, the latest research in this area lends the strongest evidence yet available for this repudiation. This chapter takes a new look at this old controversy and presents a summary of the relevant research.[1]

THE "SCIENTIFIC RACIST" POSITION

The dominant scientific position on this subject has been termed an "equalitarian dogma" and described as "the scientific hoax of the century" by one psychologist, Professor-Emeritus Henry Garrett. (183) He charges that other psychologists have prematurely closed the issue for ideological, not scientific, reasons.

Garrett is publicly joined by two other psychologists, out of the roughly twenty-one thousand who belong to the American Psychological Association. Frank Mc-Gurk, of Villanova University, has conducted research with an unvalidated intelligence test of his own design and concluded that "Negroes as a group do not possess as much [capacity for education] as whites as a group." [2] (341) In 1956 this work gained wide attention when the U. S. News and World Report featured an article under the imposing title of "A Scientist's Report on Race Differences," in which McGurk surveyed six investigations that he claimed to be "the only existing studies that relate to the problem." (341, p. 96)

The crowning production of this small band is Audrey Shuey's The Testing of Negro Intelligence. (468) Shuey, a psychologist at Randolph-Macon Woman's College in Lynchburg, Virginia, provides a large, though carefully selected, review of over two hundred studies bearing on

[1] An earlier draft of this chapter by the author appeared in 1964 in the Journal of Negro Education, under the title of "Negro American Intelligence: A New Look at an Old Controversy."

[2] For a critical discussion of McGurk's work, see Anastasi. (15, pp. 557-558 and 562-563)

racial differences in intelligence.[3] She ignores the newer
conceptions of intelligence and instead relies heavily
upon the earlier, less sophisticated investigations, with
over half of her references dated prior to World War II.
She also concentrates on research performed in the
South, with three-fourths of her studies on students
coming from tightly segregated Southern and border
communities. The great bulk of this research found
most Negroes scoring lower on I.Q. tests than most
whites. Shuey unhesitatingly interprets this fact as point-
ing "to the presence of some native differences between
Negroes and whites as determined by intelligence tests."
(468, p. 318)

In addition to this "sheer weight of uncontrolled data"
argument, these three psychologists attempt to show that
the impoverished environment of the typical Negro cannot account for the observed test differences. One favorite example, prominently cited by all three, is H. A.
Tanser's 1939 investigation of intelligence among the
Negro and white children of Kent County, Ontario,
Canada. (509) Tanser found that his white sample obtained a higher average I.Q. than his Negro sample; and
the "scientific racists" maintain that this is convincing
evidence for their position, since in Kent County "the
social and economic conditions of the whites and Negroes were substantially the same." (185)

The Modern Psychological Position

These arguments have not altered the dominant opinion of modern psychology on this topic. In the first
place, the studies repeatedly cited by the "scientific
racists" in defense of their position are not, upon closer

[3] Garrett claims that Shuey's book examined "*all* of the comparative studies of Negro-white performance on mental tests over
the past 40 years." (184, p. 1) This is not the case. Even papers
by Garrett and McGurk are missing. (180, 339) But more critical
is the exclusion of numerous and important publications which
appeared prior to Shuey's work and run directly counter to its
conclusion. (84, 120, 188, 221, 255, 287, 391, 394, 430, 485,
510, 551)

scrutiny, critical tests of their contentions. Consider the Tanser work in Canada.[4] As in investigations in the United States, the "social and economic conditions" of the two groups were *not* equal. One psychologist, Mollie Smart, was born and raised in Kent County at approximately the time Tanser conducted his study there. She candidly describes the condition of the Negroes in this period:

> . . . Nearly all of [the Negroes'] houses were small wood buildings, often lacking paint and tending towards delapidation. The theaters had a policy of seating Negroes in certain areas. The all-Negro school had been abandoned by my day. My elementary school classes always included Negro children, but I remember none during the last 3 years of high school. My Negro classmates were usually poorly clothed and badly groomed. Negroes held the low-status jobs. They were the servants, garbage collectors, and odd-job men. People called them "Nigger" more often than "Negro." I did not know until I grew up that a Negro could be a doctor, lawyer, teacher, member of Parliament, or even a clerk in a store. . . . I cannot conceive of any social advantages which Negroes enjoyed in Kent County at the time of the Tanser study. (473, p. 621)

Tanser himself admitted that his sample of Negro children had not attended school as regularly as the white children. Moreover, it cannot be said that Southern Ontario is free of racial prejudice and discrimination. Ever since the close of the American Civil War, the position of the Negro Canadian has steadily declined, with violent outbursts against Negroes occurring in Kent County itself. (77, 167, 340) The racial differences in I.Q. observed by Tanser, then, cannot be interpreted apart from the area's racial situation.

These difficulties point up the severely limiting methodological problems which confront this research realm.

[4] For similar analyses of other investigations of so-called "equal groups" commonly cited by white supremacists see Anastasi. (15, pp. 556-558)

Any test of native intelligence must of necessity assume equivalent backgrounds of the individuals and groups under study. But until conditions entirely free from segregation and discrimination are achieved and the floor of Negro poverty is raised to the level of whites, the definitive research on racial differences in intelligence cannot be performed. Meanwhile, psychologists must conduct their work in a culture where training and opportunity for the two groups are never completely equal.

Other fundamental problems raised in Chapter 3 complicate the issue. The very concept of "race" injects special issues. Since Negro Americans do not even approach the status of a genetically pure "race," they are a singularly inappropriate group upon whom to test racist theories of inherent intellectual inferiority of the Negroid subspecies. In addition, confusion is introduced by the ambiguity of the phrase "race differences." To find that many descriptive investigations using intelligence tests elicit differences between the "races" does not necessarily mean that these differences *result* from race.

Empirical efforts are also hampered by the operation of selective factors in sampling. That is, Negroes and whites in the same situation—such as those inducted into the armed forces—may have been selected differently on intelligence, thus biasing the comparison of test scores between the two groups. For instance, Hunt found that the Navy during World War II did not employ the same screening and selection standards for the two groups, permitting a far higher proportion of mental defectives among Negro than among white acceptances. (245) Such a finding renders any comparisons in test scores between Negro and white sailors of dubious value. Much has been made of the intelligence test performances of the two "races" in both World Wars I and II, but such selective factors make these data difficult to interpret.

Despite these limitations, however, modern psychology has managed to achieve significant theoretical and empirical advances in this realm. These advances strongly favor a non-genetic interpretation of the typically lower intelligence test score averages of Negro groups. This work can be conveniently summarized under four general rubrics: (1) new theoretical conceptions; (2) the mediators of intellectual underdevelopment; (3) varying opportunities and group results; and (4) the individual versus the group.

NEW THEORETICAL CONCEPTIONS

Since World War II, psychologists and other scientists have seriously reviewed earlier notions about such basic concepts as "the environment," "heredity," and "intelligence." Instead of the older nature versus nurture conception, the emphasis is placed on nature and nurture.[5] Rather than asking which set of factors—environmental or hereditary—contributes more to a particular trait or ability like intelligence, investigators ask how the environment and heredity combine to form the observed characteristic. Genes not only set broad limits on the range of development, but also enter into highly complex interactions with the environment, interactions which have not been emphasized enough in the past.

An ingenious animal experiment by Cooper and Zubek illustrates this genetic-environmental interaction. (99) These investigators employed two genetically distinct strains of rats, carefully bred for 13 generations as either "bright" or "dull." Separate groups of the two strains grew up after weaning in three contrasting environments: a restricted environment, consisting of only a food box, water pan, and otherwise barren cage; a natural environment, consisting of the usual habitat of a laboratory rat; and an enriched environment, consisting of such objects as ramps, swings, slides, polished balls, tunnels, and teeter-totters plus a decorated wall beside their cages. Figure 5 shows the maze learning performances of the six groups of rats (the fewer the errors, the more "intelligent" the behavior). Note that the two genetically

[5] Much of the following discussion is based on Gottesman's review. (202)

diverse groups did almost equally well in the enriched and restricted environments, sharply differing only in the natural situation. In fact, the environment masks genetic potential to the point where it is impossible to distinguish the enriched dulls from the natural brights or the natural dulls from the restricted brights.

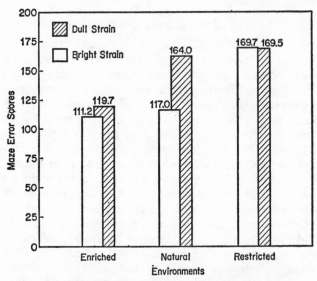

FIGURE 5—MAZE ERROR SCORES FOR GENETICALLY BRIGHT AND DULL RATS REARED IN THREE CONTRASTING ENVIRONMENTS

(Data from: R. M. Cooper and J. P. Zubek, "Effects of enriched and restricted early environments on the learning ability of bright and dull rats," *Canadian Journal of Psychology*, 1958, 12, 159-164.)

The data of Figure 5 bear important implications. "Genotypes," the true genetic potential, often do not coincide with "phenotypes," the actual, expressed trait. Similar genotypes may have different phenotypes (e.g., the bright rats in the restricted and enriched environments), and similar phenotypes may have different genotypes (e.g., the restricted bright and dull rats). Any phenotype is the composite product of the genotype and the environment in which the genetic potential must be realized. Relevant nature-nurture questions thus become: how environmentally modifiable is the phenotypic intelligence of each genotype? And what is the contribution of heredity to the intelligence score differences among a group of individuals on a specific test in a specified environment?

This newer view of the nature-nurture controversy and a mounting accumulation of new developmental evidence has resulted in a revised conception of the nature of intelligence. J. McV. Hunt presents this modern thinking in his volume, *Intelligence and Experience.* (243) Taking his cue from the strategies for information-processing that are currently programmed for electronic computers, Hunt defines intelligence as central neural processes which develop in the brain to mediate between the information coming into the individual via the senses and the return signals for motor reaction. Moreover, he maintains that the initial establishment and subsequent capacity of these processes are probably rooted in the child's earliest encounters with the world around him. Intelligence, then, is not merely an inherited capacity, genetically fixed and destined to unfold in a biologically predetermined manner. It is a dynamic, on-going set of processes that within wide hereditary limits is subject to innumerable experiential factors.

Hunt's view upsets two long-unquestioned dogmas about intelligence, dogmas critical in the area of race differences. He terms them the assumptions of "fixed intelligence" and "predetermined development." The first of these has its roots in Darwin's theory of natural selection. It accepts intelligence as a static, innately-given quantity, and it long influenced psychological thought and the design of I.Q. tests. Indeed, the assumption of fixed intelligence became so established before World War II that many psychologists regarded all evidence of substantial shifts in I.Q. as merely the product of poor testing procedures. But, objected Stoddard in 1943, "to regard all changes in mental status as an artifact is to shut one's eyes to the most significant and dramatic phenomenon in human growth." (496, p. 281)

The second assumption of "predetermined development" refers to the idea that, barring extreme interference from the environment, intelligence will unfold "naturally" with gene-determined anatomical maturation. Classic work on salamanders and Hopi Indian children was cited to demonstrate this maturational effect and that prior experience was unnecessary for normal development. (72, 91, 117) In this era, mothers were told to avoid overstimulating their children, to allow their children simply to grow "on their own." Hunt considers such advice "highly unfortunate," for it now appears that a proper matching of a child's development with challenging encounters with his environment is a critical requisite for increasing ability.

Notice this new outlook in no way denies an hereditary influence on intelligence, an influence well established by twin studies. (202) Rather, it views intelligence in much the same way longevity is now regarded. A strong hereditary component is recognized in longevity; consistently long or short life spans typify many families. Yet, despite this component, the life expectancies at birth of Americans have almost doubled in the past century. (359) Better medical care, better diets, and a host of other environmental factors converge to enable Americans to make fuller use of their longevity potential. Likewise, the modern view of intelligence holds that we have not begun to expand our phenotypic intelligences even close to our genotypic potentials. From this vantage point, it appears our society has placed too much emphasis on personnel selection and eugenics at the expense of effective training programs and euthenics.

Some of the most imaginative experimentation behind this new thinking is that of the eminent Swiss psychologist, Jean Piaget. (243, 410) His ingenious and detailed studies with children of all ages provide abundant evidence that intelligence is the very antithesis of a fixed, predetermined capacity. And a wide range of other types of investigations amply bears out this conclusion. Even animal intelligence seems to be importantly affected by environmental opportunities. The previously-cited rat work of Cooper and Zubek shows how diverse cage environments affect later learning. In addition, pet-reared rats and dogs, with backgrounds of richly variegated experience, later evidence considerably more intelligent behavior than their cage-reared counterparts. (511, 512) And Harlow has demonstrated that monkeys can "learn to learn"; that is, they can develop learning sets which enable them to solve general classes of problems almost at a glance. (219)

Similar effects of early environmental enrichment on the intelligence of young children have been noted. Kirk has shown that early educational procedures can often produce sharp increments in intellectual functioning among mentally retarded children, sometimes even among those diagnosed as organically impaired. (278) Other studies on normal children, both white and Negro, suggest that preschool training in nursery and kindergarten classes may act to raise I.Q.'s. (123; 15, pp. 200-205; 243, pp. 27-34; 297) Among criticisms of this research is the contention that a selection factor could be operating. The natively brighter children may be those who tend to have preschool education. But among deprived children in an orphanage, the beneficial results of early schooling have been noted in a situation where selection factors did not operate. (535) Also relevant is the tendency for orphans to gain in I.Q. after adoption into superior foster homes, the gain being greatest for those adopted youngest. (172)

After reviewing research on cognitive learning in these early years, Fowler concludes that this is the period of human "apprenticeship." (164) The infant is acquiring the most elementary and basic discriminations needed for later learning; like Harlow's monkeys, the infant is "learning to learn." Fowler speculates that conceptual learning sets, interest areas, and habit patterns may be more favorably established at these early stages than at later stages of the developmental cycle. Indeed, emphasis on "practical," concrete, gross motor learning in these early years may even inhibit later abstract learning.

In any event, research has documented the intellectually damaging consequences of deprived environments. An English study found that the children of such isolated groups as canal-boat and gypsy families achieved exceptionally low intelligence test scores, scores considerably below those typically found among Negro American children. (199) Interesting, too, is the fact that as these children grow older their I.Q.'s generally decline, though this is not the case for children of more privileged groups. In a similar fashion, children in orphanages and other institutions tend to have lower I.Q.'s and more retarded motor and linguistic development than children in stimulating home environments. Once again selection factors may operate, with the brighter, more developed children being more often chosen for adoption. However, studies which overcome much of this difficulty still note this institutional retardation. (63, 118, 187, 196)

A related finding concerns the trend toward lower I.Q.'s of children raised in large families. (14) One common explanation of this phenomenon is simply that parents who have large families are natively less intelligent. Yet, as Hunt points out, other findings strongly suggest that it is partly because parents of large families have less time to spend with each child. (243) Thus, twins and doubles born close together in otherwise small families reveal a similar tendency toward lower I.Q.'s. And the negative relationship between family size and intelligence does not appear among wealthy families who can afford servants to provide stimulating attention for each child.

Finally, the extreme effects that can ensue from an impoverished environment are dramatically illustrated in a series of sensory-deprivation experiments. (45) These investigations reveal that normal people respond with marked psychological disturbances when severely restricted in activity and stimulation. They typically experience temporal and spatial distortions and pronounced hallucinations; and they evidence sharply impaired thinking and reasoning both during and after their isolation.

THE MEDIATORS OF INTELLECTUAL UNDERDEVELOPMENT

Within this new perspective on intelligence as a relatively plastic quality, a series of environmental mediators of the individual Negro child's intellectual underdevelopment has been determined. In fact, these mediators exert their effects even upon the Negro fetus. One study found that dietary supplementation by vitamins supplied during the last half of pregnancy had directly beneficial effects on I.Q. scores of the children later. (221) In a sample of mothers from the lowest socio-economic level, 80 per cent of whom were Negro, the group fortified with iron and vitamin B complex had children whose mean I.Q. at three years of age averaged five full points above the children of the unfortified control group, 103.4 to 98.4. One year later, the mean difference had enlarged to eight points, 101.7 to 93.6. The same researchers failed to find a similar effect among white mothers and their children from a mountain area. Presumably, the largely Negro sample was even poorer and more malnourished than the white sample from the mountains. Dire poverty, through the mother's inadequate diet, can thus impair intelligence before the lower-class Negro child is born.

Economic problems also hamper intelligence through the mediation of premature births. (289, 395) Premature children of all races reveal not only a heightened incidence of neurologic abnormalities and greater susceptibility to disease, but also a considerably larger percentage of mental defectives. (220, 290) A further organic factor in intelligence is brain injury in the newborn. And both of these conditions have higher incidences among Negroes because of their greater frequency in the most economically depressed sectors of the population. (Chapter 4)

Later complications are introduced by the impoverished environments in which most Negro children grow

up. At the youngest, preschool ages, race differences in
I.Q. means are minimal. Repeated research shows that in
the first two years of life there are no significant racial
differences in either psychomotor development or intelligence. (188, 287, 391) Racist theorists discount these
findings on two conflicting grounds. (182, 468) They
either claim that infant tests have no predictive value
whatsoever for later I.Q. scores, or cite an older study
by McGraw that found Negro infants retarded in comparison with white infants. Neither argument is adequate. Three recent investigations provide convincing
evidence that properly administered infant tests *do* predict later scores. (134, 246, 288) And the 1931 McGraw
study is no longer regarded as a decisive experiment—
not even by Myrtle McGraw herself. (338, 338a, 393)
It was a pioneer effort that compared white infants with
Negro infants of markedly smaller stature on an unvalidated adaptation of a European test. Furthermore,
later Northern investigations show little or no Negro lag
in intellectual development through kindergarten and
five years of age when thorough socio-economic controls
are applied. (16, 65)

It is only after a few years of inferior schooling have
passed that many Negro children drop noticeably in
measured I.Q. (387, 515) Part of this drop is due to the
heavier reliance placed by intelligence tests at these ages
upon verbal skills, skills that are particularly influenced
by a constricted environment. One Southern study of
"verbal destitution" discovered that those Negro college
students most retarded in a reading clinic came from
small, segregated high schools and exhibited language
patterns typical of the only adult models they had encountered—poorly educated parents, teachers, and min-
isters. (384)

Another factor in the declining test averages over the
school years is simply the nature of the schools themselves. Deutsch gives the example of an assignment to
write a page on 'The Trip I Took,' given to lower-class
youngsters in a ghetto school who had never been more

than twenty-five city blocks from home. Psychologist Deutsch maintains: "The school represents a foreign outpost in an encapsulated community which is surrounded by what, for the child, is unknown and foreign." (122, p. 3)

This tendency of the measured I.Q.'s of Negro children to diminish with increasing age is interpreted by racists not as evidence of the eroding effects of ghetto living, but as proof that Negroes mature more rapidly and begin to decline earlier than whites. (182, 468, 421) Such an idea, based on the belief that Negroes as a "race" are less evolved, is seriously challenged by the often demonstrated fact that environmentally-deprived Caucasian groups reveal precisely the same phenomenon —mountain and other rural children in America and the canal-boat and gypsy children in England. (15) Furthermore, the positive relationship between socio-economic status and tested I.Q. among Negroes increases with age, again suggesting that environmental factors become evermore vital as the child matures. (515)

The nature of the disrupted family life of many lower-status Negro youths decreases further the slum's environmental stimulation. Most of these youngsters are reared in large families, with reduced parental contact. And, as noted in Chapter 1, many of them are in fatherless homes. Deutsch and Stetler have both demonstrated that Negro children raised in such broken homes score significantly below comparable Negro children from intact homes on intelligence measures. (122, 123, 492)

Other research pinpoints the tasks tested by intelligence tests which are most impaired by this restriction of stimulation. Woods and Toal matched two groups of Negro and white adolescents on I.Q. and noted sub-test differences. (554) While superior to the whites on some tests, the Negroes were noticeably deficient on tasks such as detection of errors and drawing pictorial completions which required spatial visualization. And other similar studies reach the same conclusion. (36, 89, 114, 120, 165, 216, 229, 316, 381) One demonstrated that this difficulty with perceptual and spatial relations was considerably more marked in a Southern-reared Negro sample than in an I.Q.-matched Northern-reared Negro sample. (316) This breakdown of spatial performance among otherwise intelligent Negro children, especially in the more restrictive South, offers a suggestive parallel with the comparable spatial breakdown noted in the sensory-deprivation research. In any event, two additional studies provide evidence that this disability is correctable. (48, 138) Both studies gave groups of Negro and white children special training in spatial perception and found that the Negro subjects benefited more from the practice. I.Q. test scores were markedly higher for the Negro subjects five months after the training.(48) Test authority Anne Anastasi believes this work supports the idea that the Negroes tested suffered from an unusually barren perceptual experience in early life. (15)

Organic complications and environmental impoverishment are not the only mediators depressing Negro American intelligence. Both the "functioning intelligence" and the measured I.Q. of an individual are inseparably intertwined with his personality. (203, 264, 478, 499, 519, 534) Edith Weisskopf has given case evidence of the great variety of ways personality problems can deter normal intellectual development. (534) A child may do poorly in learning situations in a conscious or unconscious desire to punish his parents, to inflict self-punishment, or to avoid self-evaluation. And Roen has demonstrated that such personality problems are more highly related to intelligence test scores among Negroes than among whites. (435) He equated two racial groups of soldiers on a wide range of social variables and found that a series of personality measures were more closely correlated with intelligence for the Negroes than for the whites. In particular, he noted that Negro soldiers who had low intelligence scores rated especially low on a self-confidence questionnaire.

Racist claims of Caucasian superiority contribute to the Negro's lack of intellectual self-confidence. This insecurity is especially provoked by any direct comparison with white performance. One investigation administered a task to Southern Negro college students with two different sets of instructions. (272) One set told how other students at their college did on the task, while the second told how whites throughout the nation did. Those subjects who anticipated white comparison performed significantly more poorly on the task and indicated stronger concern and anxiety about their performance.

The role of "Negro" is again a critical factor. (Chapter 1) Put simply, the Negro is not expected to be bright. To reveal high intelligence is to risk seeming "uppity" to a white supremacist. And once more the self-fulfilling prophecy begins to operate, for the Negro who assumes a façade of stupidity as a defense mechanism against oppression is very likely to grow into the role. He will not be eager to learn, and he will not strive to do well in the testing situation. After all, an intelligence test is a middle-class white man's instrument; it is a device whites use to prove their capacities and get ahead in the white world. Achieving a high test score does not have the same meaning for a lower-status Negro child, and it may even carry a definite connotation of personal threat. In this sense, scoring low on intelligence measures may for some talented Negro children be a rational response to perceived danger.

In addition to stupidity, the role of "Negro" prescribes both passivity and lack of ambition as central traits. And these traits are crucial personality correlates of I.Q. changes in white children. The Fels Research Institute found that aggressiveness and intense need for achievement differentiate those children whose scores rise between six and ten years of age from those whose scores recede. (264)

Another protective device is slowness. This trait assumes major importance in the speed instruments typically employed to estimate intelligence. In the Negro lower class there is no premium on speed, for work is generally paid by the hour and there are realistically few goals that fast, hard endeavor can attain. One experiment noted that differences in speed of response are primarily responsible for racial differences in I.Q. estimated by timed performance tests. (114)

Playing "Negro" is made especially critical when the examiner is white. Even two-year-old Negroes, as mentioned in Chapter 2, seem verbally inhibited when tested by a white.[6] (394) In fact, this verbal inhibition may be the principal factor underlying the common observation that Negro children generally evidence verbal comprehension superior to their verbal communication. (74) One investigation had students of both races tested alternately by Negro and white examiners. (70) For both groups, the mean I.Q. was approximately six points higher when the test was administered by an examiner of their own race.

Adult Negroes evidence a similar reaction. A public opinion poll in North Carolina asked Negro respondents for the names of the men who had just run for governor in a primary election. (418) Three out of five Negroes questioned by Negro interviewers knew at least two correct names and gave no incorrect names, compared with only two out of five of a similar sample questioned by whites. A Boston survey replicated these results with two measures tapping intelligence. (404) The first consisted of six informational items; each respondent was asked to identify six famous men: two Africans (Kwame Nkrumah and Haile Selassie) and the rest Negro Americans (Louis Armstrong, Martin Luther King, Adam Clayton Powell, and Elijah Muhammad). The other test required synonyms for ten words, ranging in difficulty from "space" to "emanate." Negro interviewers questioned half of the respondents, and white interviewers the other half. The two samples were equivalent in income, age, education, and region of birth. Figure 6 presents the results. Note that on both tests the Boston

[6] Shuey (468, p. 316) concludes that race of examiner is not important by omitting this key investigation (394) and not mentioning the full results of another (70).

Negro adults rendered more correct answers when interviewed by a Negro.

Apart from the role of "Negro," the middle-class bias of intelligence testing situations operates to hinder a disproportionate share of Negro examinees. Children per-

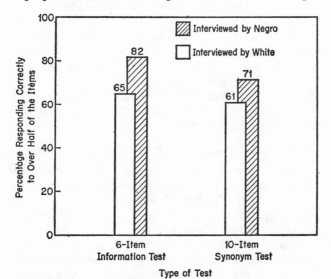

FIGURE 6—RACE OF INTERVIEWER AND NEGRO TEST
PERFORMANCE

(Data from: T. F. Pettigrew, "The Negro Respondent: New data on old problems," unpublished paper.)

form best in situations familiar to them, but the conditions best suited for lower-status children are seldom attained. Most I.Q. tests are strictly urban middle-class instruments, with numerous references to objects and situations unfamiliar to rural and lower-class people. Haggard showed that a less middle-class-oriented test led to significant increases in the performances of lower-class children. (214)

Tests are only one aspect of class bias, however. Middle-class students have generally internalized their need to excel at such tasks; a high test score is itself a reward.

Moreover, they perform most competently in silent testing atmospheres that place heavy reliance upon reading skills. By contrast, lower-class students frequently require tangible, external rewards for motivation. And their typically restricted home environments are overwhelmingly dominated by the spoken, rather than the written, word. It is not surprising, then, that Haggard discovered notable increments in intelligence test scores of lower-class children when there was extra motivation for doing well (e.g., a prize of movie tickets) and when the questions were read aloud as well as written. (214) Sophisticated testing in ghetto schools should follow such guidelines for more adequate estimates of the abilities of disadvantaged children. (477)

Varying Opportunities and Group Results

If all of these mechanisms are operating to mediate the influence of a lean, hostile, and constricted environment upon the individual Negro's tested intelligence, certain group trends under conditions of varying opportunities can be predicted. These testable hypotheses are: (a) in environments which approach being equally restrictive for children of both races, the intelligence test means of both will be low and will approach equality; (b) in environments which approach being equally stimulating for children of both races, the intelligence test means of both will be high and will approach equality; and (c) when any racial group moves from a restrictive to a comparatively stimulating environment, its measured I.Q. mean will rise.

The first of these hypotheses was tested on an isolated Caribbean island, offering little stimulation to its youth. It had:

> no regular steamship service, no railroad, motion picture theater, or newspaper. There were very few automobiles and very few telephones. The roads were generally poor. There were no government schools above the elementary level and no private schools above the secondary level. . . . People of all colors,

then, were restricted to a rather narrow range of occupational opportunity. (108, p. 14)

Even here, however, complete equality of status between whites and Negroes was not achieved. White skin was "highly respected," whites typically held the better jobs, and, while almost half of the white students attended private schools, nine-tenths of the Negroes attended government schools. Nevertheless, there were no significant color differences on nine of the fourteen intelligence measures. The Negroes did best on tests which were less class-linked, less threatening, and less dependent on uncommon words. Thus, socio-economic status was a more important factor than race on four of the five instruments which did yield racial discrepancies, and "lack of confidence," as rated independently by teachers, was highly related to three of them. In general, the island youngsters scored rather low on the tests, with race a relatively insignificant consideration. And the selective migration possibility that the brighter whites were leaving the island is not an explanation for these findings, since there was apparently little emigration or immigration. These data, gathered in a locality which approached being equally restrictive for both races, do "not lend support to the conclusion that colored inferiority in intelligence tests has a racial basis." (108, p. 26)

The second hypothesis has also received support from a number of studies. Three investigations, testing young children in Minneapolis, grade-school students in a Nevada city, and adolescents in the Boston area, revealed that, once social-class factors are rigorously controlled, there are only minor black-white mean I.Q. differences. (65, 336, 344) In these relatively stimulating, educationally-desegregated urban communities, both racial groups secured test averages equal to the national norms.

An additional study was conducted in West Germany. (149) A representative sample of 51 *neger-mischlingskinder*—the mulatto children of Negro American soldiers and German women—was administered a number of intelligence tests and their performance contrasted with a comparable group of 25 white German children. There were no significant differences. Two counter-balancing factors complicate the interpretation of this research. The Negro fathers of these children are undoubtedly an intelligent, highly selected group, selected not only in terms of being chosen to serve in the United States Army in Germany but also in terms of having become acculturated enough to establish an intimate relationship with a German woman. But this factor is balanced by the fact that the children are mostly illegitimate and viewed as such in the German culture, almost by virtue of their color. Furthermore, most of their mothers are probably of lower-status backgrounds and as such have not been able to provide them with the cultural enrichment of the typical German home. And, finally, German culture, even in this post-Hitler era, can hardly be described as totally free of racist thinking. All in all, the satisfactory test performance of these mulatto Germans appears quite remarkable.

Thus, I.Q. means of groups are retarded where there are constrictive environmental conditions and elevated where there are at least average conditions. Three ecological projects provide further evidence for this generalization. One project correlated home rentals with the I.Q. averages of the school children in 300 New York City neighborhoods. (318) Moderately high and positive relationships were found; the more expensive the neighborhood, the higher the test scores. Another noted very close and positive associations between such variables as per capita income and the mean I.Q. level of sixth-grade pupils in 30 American cities. (513) The third project discovered that these ecological correlations tend to be higher for intelligence scores than for scholastic achievement, demonstrating again the extreme sensitivity of the measured I.Q. to the total social environment. (514)

This research is confirmed by further investigations conducted exclusively among Negroes. (123, 373, 430, 433) Especially since World War II and its attendant expansion of social class differentiation among Negro Americans, socio-economic variables correlate highly and

positively with I.Q. means in Negro samples. For example, the I.Q. means of groups of Negro third-graders
in Washington, D.C. tended to be highest in areas
where radios were most often present in the homes and
where rents were highest.

These results suggest the third hypothesis: when any
group moves from a restrictive to a comparatively stimulating environment, its measured I.Q. mean will rise.
Dramatic evidence for this proposition comes from the
unique situation of the Osage Indians. Like many other
Indian groups, the Osage were granted land for the establishment of a reservation. Oil was later discovered on
their land, and the Osage became relatively prosperous.
Since the Osage had not chosen their land, the oil dis-
covery was not an indication of native ingenuity beyond
that of Indian groups in general. But now they could
afford living standards vastly superior to other Indians,
and on both performance and language tests they were
found to meet the national norms and to have achieved
the level of comparable whites in the area. (437) This
finding is all the more impressive when it is remembered
that Indian children generally perform considerably below Negro children in I.Q. tests.

Similar improvements are recorded among white mountain children in East Tennessee, public school students
in Honolulu, and white enlisted men in World War II.
Wheeler gave tests to over three thousand mountain
children in 1940, and compared their performance to that
of children in the same areas and from virtually the same
families in 1930. (537) This ten-year span had witnessed
broad economic, social, and educational changes in East
Tennessee, and the median I.Q.'s reflected these changes
in an increment of 11 points, from 82 to 93. Equally remarkable gains are reported for children of many racial
groups in Honolulu after a 14-year period of steady improvement in the city's schools. (476) And, finally, 768
soldiers, representative of white enlisted men in World
War II, took the old Army Alpha verbal test of World
War I and provided striking evidence of the nation's

rising intelligence between the two wars. Tuddenham shows that the typical white World War II enlisted man did better on the test than 83 per cent of the enlisted men of the first war. (520)

This last study, incidentally, refutes reasoning put forward by Frank McGurk concerning the intelligence test performances of Negroes in the two world wars. He has argued that if environmental factors are responsible for racial differences in intelligence scores, then Negro scores should have steadily approached the white scores between the two wars; yet "the various differences in socioeconomic environments of the Negroes, between 1918 and 1950, have not altered the Negro-white test score relationship." (342) Such "logic" assumes that the socioeconomic standards of whites have not changed over these same years. But in fact the prosperity of whites throughout the nation has been increasing in many ways faster than that of Negro Americans. (Chapter 8) If the old Alpha test had been administered to World War II Negroes, they would have most certainly done significantly better than World War I Negroes. "The Negro-white test score relationship," McGurk refers to, has only remained constant because Negroes have made giant strides in intellectual growth where environmental improvements allowed it. Meanwhile, as the Tuddenham data demonstrate, the white median intelligence has also been climbing with environmental improvements. Intelligence, like longevity, is not a fixed capacity for either Negroes or whites.

Another curious assumption made by racist theorists arises from interpreting regional as well as racial results on the World War I Alpha. A number of social scientists noted that Negro recruits in World War I from such states as Ohio and Illinois had higher median scores than white recruits from such states as Arkansas and Mississippi. (368) These extreme comparisons revealed that the environmental deprivations of some Southern whites clearly exceeded even those of some Northern Negroes. Garrett hesitated to apply his usual explanation for low

scores: namely, to conclude that whites in these Southern
states were innately inferior intellectually. (181) Instead,
he emphasized that Negroes scored below whites within
each state; he argued that the low white scores in the
South were environmentally induced, but that the even
lower Negro scores in the South were a combination of
environmental factors and genetic inferiority. To advance
this argument, Garrett had to assume that Negroes and
whites in the South were *equally* deprived—even before
World War I. This assumption, of course, is absurd. The
period between 1890 and the First World War was the
lowest ebb of Negro fortunes since slavery. Today the
last traces of that era insure that Negro Southerners as
a group are the most environmentally impoverished of all
Southerners. And while there were often no public schools
at all for Negroes in some rural areas of the South before
World War I, the belatedly-improved facilities of today
still lag behind those of the whites. (19, 334, 481n)

Once the Negro American escapes from these inferior
conditions, however, his improved performance parallels
that of the Osage Indians and the East Tennessee mountain children. Service in the armed forces is one of the
most important sources of wider experience and opportunities for Negroes, including those who are illiterate.
The Army in the Second World War operated Special
Training Units and provided a basic fourth-grade education in eight weeks for 254,000 previously illiterate soldiers—roughly half of them Negroes and the great
majority Southerners. A slightly higher percentage of the
Negroes than whites successfully completed the intensive
course, though how this bears on larger questions of
Negro intelligence is a matter of debate, since the men
given this special training were selected. There is no
debate, however, over the fact that the success of these
units proves the educability of many apparently retarded
men of both races. (18, 57, 146, 549, 550)

Another mode of improvement for many Negroes is
migrating North. Negro Northerners routinely achieve
higher test medians than comparable Negro Southern-

ers. (6, 113, 399, 424, 430) And Negro children born in the North achieve higher medians than those who come to the North from the South.[7] (285, 297, 311, 443, 492) But do the Negro children who migrate improve their group performance as they remain in the North? This was the central question the eminent psychologist, Otto Klineberg, set out to answer in 1935; and it led to perhaps the best known research in the field of race differences. (285) Over three thousand ten-to-twelve-year-old Harlem Negroes took an array of individual and group intelligence instruments. These data clearly indicate that the longer the Southern-born children had resided in New York City, the higher their intelligence scores. Those who had been in the North for a number of years approached the levels attained by the Northern-born Negroes. Smaller studies with less elaborate designs obtained parallel results in Cleveland and Washington, D.C. (132, 311)

More recently, Lee replicated these findings in Philadelphia with the most rigorous research on the topic to date. (297) Employing large samples in a variety of different schools, Lee analyzed the test scores of the same children as they progressed through the city's school system. Though never quite catching up with the Philadelphia-born Negro students, the Southern Negro migrants as a group regularly gained in I.Q. with each grade completed in Northern schools. And the younger they were when they entered the Philadelphia school system, the greater their mean increase and final I.Q. The effects of the more stimulating and somewhat less discriminatory North, then, are directly reflected in the measured intelligence of the youngest of Negro migrants.

The major complication in interpreting the Klineberg and Lee work is again introduced by possible selection biases. Those Negro Southerners who migrate North in

[7] In a re-analysis of her New Haven I.Q. data (443), Nancy St. John found that the presence of at least one Northern-born parent was an even more critical variable than the region of birth of the child. (Private communication)

search of a better life may be selectively brighter and rear brighter children. Such a possibility is emphasized by the "scientific racists," though Shuey concedes this factor could reasonably account for only one-third to one-half of the I.Q. increases observed. (468) But other possibilities also exist. Many of the more intelligent Negroes in the South gain some measure of success and establish roots that are more difficult to break than those of the less intelligent. This phenomenon would operate to make the Klineberg and Lee data all the more impressive. Or, perhaps, intelligence has little or nothing to do with the decision to migrate; personality traits, such as aggressiveness or inability to control hostility over racial frustrations, may be more decisive. In any event, Klineberg found the Southern school grades of 562 Negro youths who had since gone North were typical of the entire Negro school populations from which they migrated. (285) More research is needed, but it seems that selective migration cannot begin to account for the dramatic improvement in test performance demonstrated by Negro children who move to the North.

Further evidence that Negro ability goes up when environmental opportunities expand derives from the many diverse educational-enrichment programs current in our major cities. The best known of these is New York City's "Higher Horizons" project. (332) This effort provides a selected and largely Negro student body with an expensive saturation of skilled specialists: remedial-reading teachers, guidance counselors, psychologists, and social workers. Its results have been striking; in the first year, the program cut third graders' retardation in reading from six months down to a single month. Backed by major foundation grants, other cities have also begun to experiment. Detroit and Philadelphia tried sending "school-community agents" into ghetto schools in an attempt to win parental support for education. Kansas City's Central High School and Tucson's Pueblo High School initiated imaginative new programs. (332) And Washington, D.C., launched in 1959 a "talent search" project for

200 deprived seventh graders, 92 per cent of whom were Negro. (481j) Similar to Higher Horizons in its concentration of staff and exposure of students to new cultural experiences, the "talent search" was soon declared a success. Contrasted with a matched control group, the students of the program showed a sharply reduced scholastic failure rate and notable instances of I.Q. increments.

Perhaps, the most remarkable demonstration of all is Samuel Shepard's "Banneker Group" work in St. Louis. (30, 470, 481b, 481e, 481h, 481i, 481m, 481n, 481p) A forceful educator, Shepard performs his "miracles" on the most underprivileged school children in the city without the vast expenditures of other efforts. The Banneker group consists of 23 elementary schools with over sixteen thousand slum and public housing children, more than 95 per cent of them Negro. A Negro who overcame serious economic disadvantages himself, Shepard adamantly rejects the old dogma that sub-standard school work is all you can realistically expect from ghetto children. He bluntly challenges the pupils, parents, principals, and teachers of the district to perform up to national standards; he appeals to race pride and resorts to continuous exhortations, rallies, contests, posters, and meetings with teachers and parents. Students who make good grades are asked to stand in assemblies for the applause of their classmates. Teachers are asked to visit the homes of their charges. And parents are asked to provide their offspring with encouragement, study space, a library card, a dictionary, and other books as gifts. As a concrete incentive, Shepard points out the new and better jobs now open to Negroes in St. Louis and the lack of qualified Negroes to fill them.

The results of the Banneker effort speak for themselves. Despite an unending stream of poorly educated migrants into the area from the South, all test indicators have risen. In the first four years of the program, the median I.Q. increased from the middle 80's to the 90's; median reading, language, and arithmetic levels all climbed; and the percentage of Banneker graduates accepted for the top-ability program in St. Louis's desegregated high schools tripled.

The striking results of these imaginative demonstrations may not be due directly to the exact procedures introduced. Given their vast variety of techniques and their uniform success, the demonstrations probably achieve most of their gains because of the sheer fact of intervention—any kind of thoughtful intervention. Often the rate of initial progress slows once the beginning enthusiasm cools. But this is irrelevant to the larger issue of Negro American intelligence. Dramatic improvement in Negro performance for whatever reason is evidence of the underlying potential for learning heretofore stiffled by lack of opportunity and attention. This potential for learning is also evident in the findings of a recent experiment at the University of Texas. (459) Negro children learned series of paired material as rapidly and well as white children, even though they came from lower socio-economic backgrounds and had significantly lower I.Q.'s.

Such demonstrations arouse speculation concerning the effects of desegregation of public school systems. Segregationists have long voiced the unsubstantiated opinion that "school mixing" would mean educational chaos, with the Negroes dragging down the higher white standards. But the experience of a great diversity of communities indicates that these fears are unjustified. Administrators of 17 desegregated school systems appeared before the United States Civil Rights Commission in March, 1959, and candidly discussed their problems. (480) Twelve of the educators dealt with the question of academic standards. Ranging from Logan County, Kentucky, and Muskogee, Oklahoma, to Baltimore and Nashville, all twelve reported unequivocally that their academic standards had not been lowered—in fact, many maintained that their standards had improved for both races.

Washington, D.C. provided the acid test. It embarked upon a sweeping process of educational desegregation in 1954 with Negroes comprising three-fifths of the students, many of them from the South with limited backgrounds.

The *U. S. News and World Report* soon published articles claiming that the District of Columbia's public school system was well on its way to ruin, and these tracts were widely quoted by segregationists. (525a, 525b, 525c, 525d) But such dire consequences never materialized. A four-track system of ability grouping and other innovations were adopted. Five years later, in 1959, a factual assessment of the changes was made. (217, 481c, 481d, 481f, 481g, 481k, 481l, 484) Though Negro students, swelled by migrants, now comprised three-fourths of the student body, achievement test scores had risen significantly for each grade level sampled and each subject area tested approached or equaled national norms. Furthermore, both Negro and white students shared in these increments.[8] Such results are not unique to Washington. Louisville reported substantial gains in Negro performance and slight gains in white performance after only one year of desegregation. (479, 483)

Clearly, desegregation *per se* does not accomplish these feats. The Banneker demonstration in St. Louis took place in virtually all-Negro schools; Washington and Louisville witnessed sharply improved test medians among their Negro students, whether in biracial or uniracial schools. The principal factor seems to be the new and healthier self-image Negroes acquire in the process. The act of community desegregation bolsters and encourages Negro pupils, parents, and teachers alike. Combining with this heightening of morale is the entrenched Negro desire for education. (Chapter 8) *Newsweek's* 1963 national poll revealed that 97 per cent of the nation's Negroes wants their children at least to graduate from high school. (382)

Also important is the sudden interest Negro education finally wins from the whole community. As long as Ne-

[8] This is not to say that school difficulties no longer exist in Washington. They continue not because of desegregation, however, but because certain Southern members of the House of Representatives insist on treating the District's "children as pawns in a wicked game designed to prove that desegregation cannot succeed." (*Washington Post* editorial, March 2, 1963)

gro education is a racially-separate system, dominant
white interests can and do forget it. But once desegregation forces the community to handle the education of its
youth in one package, to consider Negro education as an
integral part of the whole process, new attention is given
to the schools. Indeed, the rise in white test scores after
desegregation suggests that public education as a whole
benefits from the greater public interest. Washington
offers an illustration. Prior to desegregation, survey testing was only done with the white pupils; Negroes were
ignored. (480) But immediately after desegregation,
testing throughout the system was instituted, and the
same standards were applied at last to both races. Certainly, desegregation is no panacea for the immense
problems faced by public school systems with large percentages of environmentally impoverished children, but
it does prepare the way for tackling the *real* problems
of modern education.

Thus, an array of stimulating circumstances—service
in the armed forces, migration to the North, and participation in revitalized school systems—all act to lift
substantially the intelligence and achievement levels of
Negroes. Often these improvements still do not bring
the average Negro performance completely up to white
norms, but this cannot be considered as evidence for
genetic racial differences until *all* racial discrimination
is abolished.

The Individual versus the Group

The discussion so far has concentrated on group results, yet many of the most important considerations
involving Negro American intelligence concern the individual. Not even racists deny the existence of out-
standing Negro Americans. Usually, however, the same
individuals are cited—Marian Anderson, Ralph Bunche,
George Washington Carver—and are considered "ex-
ceptions" and special "credits to their race." The truth
is that a surprising number of such "exceptional" Negroes have somehow managed to overcome the formida-

ble obstacles of discrimination. Many have naturally entered the struggle for equal rights. But others achieve such stature in non-stereotyped work that they are no longer thought of as Negro. For instance, the originator of the Hinton test for syphilis, the late Professor William A. Hinton, was well known as a bacteriologist and immunologist at Harvard Medical School but not as a Negro.

Superior intelligence comes in all skin colors. While the intelligence test means of the two races are still divergent, the range of performance—from the most retarded idiot to the most brilliant genius—is much the same in the two groups. Some Negro children score I.Q.'s into the gifted range (130 or over) and right up to the testable limit of 200. (254, 255, 510, 551) To be sure, the frequency of such bright Negroes is less than that of whites, but this, too, can be explained by differential environmental factors. The great majority of these superior Negroes are located in biracial schools in the urban North and West, which suggests that many potentially gifted Negroes go either undiscovered or undeveloped in the segregated schools of the South. (254, 256) Proof that such children do exist in the South comes from programs which intensively seek talented Negro Southerners. (84, 485) Once found, they receive scholarships and attend a variety of desegregated high schools and colleges in the North, and the great majority of them accommodate well to their new and challenging situations. Indeed, a recent study of Negro scholarship applicants from the South who have attended integrated colleges reveals that they have a far smaller drop-out rate than white students at the same colleges. (87a)

A further embarrassment to racist theories is created by the fact that the degree of white ancestry does not relate to Negro I.Q. scores. (226, 284, 399, 551) Among intellectually superior Negroes, for example, the proportions of those with varying degrees of white ancestry correspond closely with those of the total Negro American population. (551) Indeed, the brightest Negro child yet reported—with a tested I.Q. of 200—had no traceable Caucasian heritage whatsoever. (510, 551) "Race *per se*," concludes Martin Jenkins, "is not a limiting factor in psychometric intelligence." (254, p. 401)

There exists, then, a considerable overlap in the I.Q. distributions of the two groups. A few Negroes will score higher than almost all Caucasians, and many Negroes will score higher than most Caucasians. Figure 7 shows two typical intelligence test distributions with an overlap of 25 per cent, that is, 25 per cent of the Negroes tested (shaded area) surpass the performance of half of the whites tested. Notice how the ranges of the two distributions are virtually the same, even though the means are somewhat different. This figure illustrates one of the most important facts about "race" and measured intelligence: individual differences in I.Q. *within* any one race greatly exceed differences *between* races.

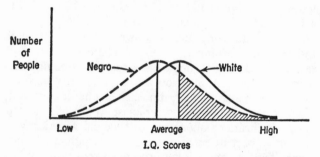

FIGURE 7—TYPICAL TEST DISTRIBUTIONS WITH "25 PER CENT OVERLAP"

There are two practical consequences of this phenomenon for desegregated education. First, when a school system institutes a track program of ability grouping, there will be Negroes and whites at all levels. Second, some gifted Negroes will actually lead their biracial classes even during the initial stages of desegregation. Thus, Janice Bell, a seventeen-year-old Negro girl, led the first graduating class of superior students at Beau-

mount High in St. Louis (481q); Julius Chambers, a
twenty-four-year-old Negro Southerner, became the
1961-1962 editor of the University of North Carolina's
Law Review in recognition of his leadership of his law
school class (481o); and Charles Christian, a thirty-
seven-year-old Negro Virginian, led his Medical College
of Virginia senior class academically in 1962. (481r) "In
the study of individuals," summarizes Anastasi, "the
only proper unit is the individual." (15, p. 50)

The Current Conclusion

Intelligence is a plastic product of inherited structure
developed by environmental stimulation and opportunity, an alloy of endowment and experience. It can be
measured and studied only by inference, through observing behavior defined as "intelligent" in terms of
particular cultural content and values. Thus, the severely
deprived surroundings of the average Negro child can
lower his measured I.Q. in two basic ways. First, it can
act to deter his actual intellectual development by
presenting him with such a constricted encounter with
the world that his innate potential is barely tapped. And,
second, it can act to mask his actual functioning intelligence in the test situation by not preparing him culturally and motivationally for such a middle-class task.
"Only a very uncritical psychologist would offer sweeping generalizations about the intellectual superiority or
inferiority of particular racial or ethnic groups," comments Tuddenham, "despite the not very surprising fact
that members of the dominant racial and cultural group
in our society ordinarily score higher than others on tests
of socially relevant accomplishments invented by and
for members of that group." (521, pp. 499-500)

The principal mechanisms for mediating these environmental effects vary from the poor nutrition of the
pregnant mother to meeting the expectations of the
social role of "Negro." Some of these mechanisms, like
fetal brain injuries, can leave permanent intellectual

impairments. Consequently, the permanency and irreversibility of these effects are not, as some claim, certain indicators of genetically low capacity. Fortunately, many of these effects are correctable. Moving North to better schools, taking part in special programs of environmental enrichment, and benefiting from challenging new situations of educational desegregation can all stimulate Negro children to raise their I.Q. levels dramatically.

From this array of data, the overwhelming opinion of modern psychology concludes that the mean differences often observed between Negro and white children are largely the result of environmental, rather than genetic, factors. This is *not* to assert that psychologists deny altogether the possibility of inherited racial differences in intellectual structure. There may be a small residual mean difference—small not only because of the demonstrably sweeping influence of experience, but also because the two "races" are by no means genetically "pure" and separate. (Chapter 3)

Psychology is joined in this conclusion by its sister behavioral sciences: sociology and anthropology. Witness the following professional statements.

The Society for the Psychological Study of Social Issues, a division of the American Psychological Association, concluded in 1961:

> There are differences in intelligence test scores when one compares a random sample of whites and Negroes. What is equally clear is that no evidence exists that leads to the conclusion that such differences are innate. Quite to the contrary, the evidence points overwhelmingly to the fact that when one compares Negroes and whites of comparable cultural and educational background, differences in intelligence diminish markedly; the more comparable the background, the less the difference. There is no direct evidence that supports the view that there is an innate difference between members of different racial groups. . . . We regret that Professor Garrett feels that his colleagues are foisting an "equalitarian dogma" on the public.

There is no question of dogma involved. Evidence speaks for itself and it casts serious doubt on the conclusion that there is any innate inequality in intelligence in different racial groups . . .

The Society for the Study of Social Problems, a section of the American Sociological Association, concurred in the same year:

> . . . the great preponderance of scientific opinion has favored the conclusion that there is little or no ground on which to assume that the racial groups in question are innately different in any important human capacity . . . the conclusion of scientists is that the differences in test performance by members of so-called racial groups are due not to racial but to environmental factors. This is the operating assumption today of the vast majority of the competent scientists in the field . . .

The American Anthropological Association passed a resolution by an unanimous vote (192 to 0) in 1961:

> The American Anthropological Association repudiates statements now appearing in the United States that Negroes are biologically and in innate mental ability inferior to whites, and reaffirms the fact that there is no scientifically established evidence to justify the exclusion of any race from the rights guaranteed by the Constitution of the United States. The basic principles of equality of opportunity and equality before the law are compatible with all that is known about human biology. All races possess the abilities needed to participate fully in the democratic way of life and in modern technological civilization.

The final, definitive research must await a racially integrated America in which opportunities are the same for both races. But, ironically, by that future time the question of racial differences in intelligence will have lost its salience; scholars will wonder why we generated so much heat over such an irrelevant topic. Yet the results of this belated research should prove interesting.

Even if small inherent differences are found, their direction cannot be taken for granted. Racists have never considered the possibility that the "true" Negro capacity might actually average somewhat above that of the white. Certainly, there are enough environmental barriers operating in the present situation to mask any such Negro superiority. If this possibility should actually be demonstrated, one wonders if white racists would be thoroughly consistent and insist that white children be given separate and inferior education.

The important conclusion for the present, however, is that if there are any inherent distinctions they are inconsequential. Even now, differences in I.Q. within any one race greatly exceed differences between races. Race as such is simply not an accurate way to judge an individual's intelligence. The *real* problems in this area concern ways to overcome the many serious environmental deprivations that handicap Negro youth. To return to the analogy with longevity, the problem is akin to that which faced medicine in the nineteenth century. Automatized America needs to expand the intelligence level of its underprivileged citizens in much the same way it has expanded the life potential of its citizens in the past one hundred years. The success of such programs as "the Banneker group" in St. Louis demonstrates this job can be accomplished when American society decides to put enough of its resources into it. "The U. S. must learn," writes Charles Silberman in *Fortune*, "to look upon the Negro community as if it were an undeveloped country." (470, p. 151)

6

NEGRO AMERICAN CRIME

Crime *is* prevalent among Negro Americans. Once again, white supremacists maintain this indicates the Negro is innately more prone to criminal acts than Caucasians. Asserts one such writer authoritatively: "Students are of the opinion that, with the possible exception of the Aztec, the earth has never known a bloodier race than the African Negro." (421, p. 44)

Alternatively, high Negro crime rates may be—like communicable disease and low I.Q. scores—another handmaiden of oppression. Indeed, the evidence points strongly to the explanation that racial discrimination and social class factors do in fact account for the group differential in crime.

APPARENT RACIAL CRIME RATES IN THE UNITED STATES

There is no pure index of crime. Measurement must be limited to those criminals apprehended—undoubtedly not a representative sample of all criminals. Even measurement of apprehended criminals is crude and approximate at best because of the lack of uniformity in laws and in crime-reporting over the United States. (37, 38, 458) Furthermore, any index of Negro crime runs the risk of being inflated by discriminatory practices of the police, the courts, and penal systems. To begin with, the laws themselves may be discriminatory; segregation legislation makes many acts a "crime" for Negroes but not for whites.[1] For these reasons, the indices which

[1] For example, thousands of Negro Southerners have been arrested during the 1960's for seeking service at "white" lunch-counters; yet white Southerners can typically seek service if they wish at "Negro" lunch-counters with legal immunity.

have to be used are best thought of as measures of apparent crime, not crime *per se*.

One such index relies on reported arrest data, provided annually by the Federal Bureau of Investigation in its *Uniform Crime Reports*. In 1960-61, for example, Negroes were arrested two-and-a-half to three times more frequently than other Americans, proportionate to their percentage of the population. (152) For some crimes, like forgery and counterfeiting, embezzlement and fraud, and driving while intoxicated, Negro arrest rates were approximately the same as white rates. But for other crimes, like murder and non-negligent manslaughter, aggravated assault, and gambling, Negro arrest rates were roughly five to seven times those of whites.

Arrests provide tenuous data, however. The police frequently pick up numerous suspects in connection with a single crime; and, in communities where Negroes lack political influence, the police are often more prone to arrest Negroes than whites. Sociologist Guy Johnson contends:

> The Negro is more exposed to the misuse of police power than any other group. The police custom of arresting Negroes on slight suspicion or of staging mass "roundups" of Negroes is definitely related to the Negro's lack of security and his inability to exert pressure against such abuses. . . . In some places in the South, law officers and magistrates are engaged in a sort of "racket" which involves the rounding up of Negroes on trivial charges for the sake of earning fees. (260, p. 97)

In short, arrests do not offer an accurate estimate of Negro crime.

Prison commitment data furnish another index. Again, over the past few decades, Negro prison rates are high for many types of crime. Von Hentig, analyzing male felony commitments to state and federal prisons from 1930 through 1936, found Negro rates roughly three times the white rates. (531) Imprisonment for criminal homicide and aggravated assault was especially high among Negroes. And these same differences have continued. In 1950 and 1960, Negro felony commitment rates for both state and federal prisons were still about three times the white rates. (153, 156) The federal Negro commitment rate tends to remain slightly lower than the state rate, but it is particularly high among drug law felons. From 1950 to 1960, Negro drug violators constituted half of all such offenders sent to federal prisons and a fifth of all Negro commitments. (156)

But even with convictions and commitments, the exposed position of the Negro is likely to increase his rates. When compared with white defendants, the accused Negro typically has less access to bail, astute legal counsel, cash fines rather than imprisonment, appeals, and other legal protections. He is more likely to be poorly educated and unaware of his full rights. And, in many communities, he must face "a white man's court"— white judge, white clerk, white guards, white jurors. Such conditions set the stage for impaired justice, even when honest efforts are made by officials to prevent bald racial discrimination. The "legal lynching" dramatized by Harper Lee in To Kill a Mockingbird can still occur in some Southern courts. (299) Little wonder that accused Negroes are more often found guilty than accused whites, especially when the alleged crime is perpetrated against a white victim. (60, 179, 260, 552)

This racial difference in conviction percentage occurs not because of, but in spite of, the types of crime most frequently committed by each group. That is, fewer people accused of murder and assault—offenses with especially high Negro rates—are generally convicted than those accused of forgery, counterfeiting, and drunken driving—offenses with especially high white rates. (152, Table 10)

Negro youth likewise suffer discrimination before the law. Mary Diggs studied the disposal of juvenile cases in Philadelphia during 1948. (125) She discovered that a comparatively smaller proportion of the Negro offenders was dismissed or discharged, while a larger proportion of the Negroes was institutionalized or referred to criminal courts. Moreover, the Negro child was more likely to be referred to public rather than private agencies for treatment. Axelrad conducted a similar study of 300 of New York City's institutionalized male delinquents. (21) He noted that Negro youth, when compared to white youth, were committed younger, for less serious offenses, and with fewer previous court appearances. Not all such differences, however, can be attributed purely to racial prejudice. These practices are also consistent with a long-established juvenile court philosophy of intervening earlier in cases from socially disorganized areas. (94)

Discrimination is also evident in the sentencing and paroling of convicted Negroes. During the middle 1930's, Von Hentig noted that among males over 17 years of age Negroes were eleven times more likely to be executed and five-and-a-half times more likely to be given life sentences than whites, probabilities in excess of the arrest and commitment rates of Negroes. (531) For the 32-year period, 1930-1961, 53.9 per cent of the prisoners executed under civil authority were Negro. (157, Table 4) Statistics for armed robbery, burglary, and rape are the most revealing. Indeed, death sentences for these crimes are largely exacted in the South for Negroes convicted of crimes against whites. Of the 34 robbers and burglars put to death during this period, 29 (85 per cent) were Negro and all but one were executed in a Southern or border state; of the 442 rapists put to death, 397 (90 per cent) were Negro and all but two were executed in a Southern or border state. (157, Table 4) The rape data are all the more striking when it is remembered that over half of all convicted rapists are white. Together with anti-miscegenation laws, this record of executions for rape dramatizes the special role of sexual fears on the Southern racial scene.

Even when execution is avoided, convicted Negro felons are likely to remain in prison longer and be paroled less often than whites. Among the felons released from state prisons from 1951 through 1953, the

typical Negro had served two years compared to the typical white's 21 months. (154, 155) Again the greatest
difference involves rape; the median Negro rapist released during this period had served eight more months
than the median white rapist.

Available evidence suggests that Negro felons adjust
to prison somewhat better than whites. At Central
Prison in Raleigh, North Carolina, for example, Negro
felons incur fewer rule infractions than white prisoners.
(407) Furthermore, throughout the country, they less
often attempt to escape than white felons. (156, 1954,
p. 38) Nevertheless, Negro prisoners have less chance of
parole. Von Hentig discovered that 58.2 per cent of the
white prisoners discharged from 1933 through 1936 were
paroled compared to only 38.1 per cent of the discharged Negroes. (531) Thus, the racial composition of
prison populations is the poorest index of Negro crime.
The longer sentences and fewer paroles for Negro inmates cause them to increase the percentage of Negro
prisoners after whites convicted of similar crimes have
been released.

Negro rates of apparent crime, then, are high; though
just how high in comparison with white apparent crime
is difficult to determine by possible racial discrimination
at every stage—arrest, conviction, sentencing, and parole.
A detailed look at criminal homicide is indicated, since
it has particularly high Negro rates and better data are
available for analysis.

CRIMINAL HOMICIDE AMONG NEGROES

Negroes comprised 54 per cent of the reported arrests
during 1961 for murder and non-negligent manslaughter.
(152, Tables 23 and 29) While constituting less than 5
per cent of the area's population, Negroes made up over
half of the inmates incarcerated in Pennsylvania's Western State Penitentiary for murder from 1906 through
1935. (482) Even among those admitted to Pennsylvania state prisons in 1941-1942 who were over forty-
nine years of age, Negroes were more frequently charged

with criminal homicide and aggressive assault than were whites. (412) For the nation as a whole in 1950, slightly over half of the male felons committed to prison for murder were Negro, though Negroes were but a tenth of the population. (153, p. 65) And from 1930 through 1961, 49 per cent of those executed for murder were Negro. (157, Table 4)

But, as just noted, these arrest, commitment, and execution data are inflated by racially discriminatory legal processes. In fact, several investigations reveal a dual code of convicting and sentencing in cases of criminal homicide. Analyzing 1931 data, Thorsten Sellin discovered that Southern states tended to give shorter sentences for homicide to Negroes, while other states tended to give shorter minimum but longer maximum homicide sentences to Negroes. (457) Johnson and Garfinkel later demonstrated that Southern courts usually give lenient sentences to Negroes who have killed other Negroes, but almost invariably give their most severe sentences to Negroes who have killed whites. (179, 260) Furthermore, Negroes accused of killing whites have the highest probability of being convicted.

To illustrate Southern judicial discrimination, Johnson provides data for Richmond, Virginia, for 1930 through 1939. Seventy-three per cent of the Negroes indicted for killing Negroes were convicted and only 6 per cent of these received life sentences; 75 per cent of the whites indicted for killing whites were convicted and only 27 per cent of these received life imprisonment or were executed; the only white indicted for killing a Negro was convicted but sentenced to less than two years; yet the five Negroes indicted for killing whites were *all* convicted and *all* given life sentences. (260) Garfinkel presents similar data for ten North Carolina counties. He shows that for each type of indictment— first degree murder, second degree murder, and manslaughter—Negroes accused of killing whites were the most likely to be convicted and given severe punishment. (179) Recent years have brought improvements in many Southern areas, but this general pattern still exists.

Equally dramatic racial differences were found by Wolfgang in his examination of criminal homicide in Philadelphia from 1948 through 1952. (552, pp. 299-307) Of those receiving a court trial, 81 per cent of the Negroes were found guilty as opposed to 62 per cent of the whites. And for each level of charge, Negroes received more severe sentences in spite of the fact that they had been more often provoked by their victims and were less likely to possess a previous police record. These data strongly suggest that racial discrimination exists in both the South and North in the convicting and sentencing of those accused of criminal homicide.

One index of homicide less subject to discriminatory practices is the cause-of-death data provided by the National Office of Vital Statistics. Instead of counting the perpetrators of the crime, it counts the victims. This procedure avoids the many pitfalls of crime statistics but involves an important assumption: namely, that whites kill whites and Negroes kill Negroes. Since this assumption is verified by recent research (39, 552), cause-of-death data provide a reasonably reliable estimate of racial differences in homicide. Since 1940, these data have shown the relative number of non-white deaths by homicide each year to be roughly ten times the white figure. (380, pp. 934,937) Thus, 27.3 non-whites were killed per 100,000 non-whites annually from 1949 through 1951 compared to 2.6 whites. Negro homicide rates, then, remain extremely high regardless of the index chosen.

WHY IS NEGRO CRIME SO PREVALENT?

The racist argument of innate criminality rests solely on the sheer magnitude of Negro crime. A number of both logical and empirical considerations, however, conflict with this view. To begin with, the "reasoning" is circular: Negro Americans supposedly have high crime rates because they are innately criminal, and are presumed innately criminal because of their high rates. Moreover, crime must be socially, not biologically, defined. By its very nature it cannot have direct racial or genetic causation.

Even if the racist's invalid assumptions concerning the existence of relatively pure white and Negro "races" in America were correct (Chapter 3), three different lines of evidence cast serious doubts upon his position. First, discrepancies in crime rates far larger than racial crime-rate differences in the United States are not uncommon between groups of the same race and nationality. Bonger gives an illustration from German conviction data during the years 1894-1896. (51, pp. 47-48) Compared with German domestics, German workers in manufacturing had rates 50 times higher for rape and 40 times higher for felonious assault. Modern French data provide a further example. (78) Children of domestic servants have 22 times the delinquency rate of the children of farm owners. Large group differences in apparent crime rates are not in themselves proof of a racial factor; social factors can and do cause vast differences within the same race.

Second, Negro American crime rates are by no means uniformly high. Brinton noted that the crime rate in Durham, North Carolina may vary between Negro neighborhoods as much as 500 per cent. (62) Further data are provided by the Negro communities relatively free from white control that seem to have sharply reduced rates. During the 1920's all-Negro Mound Bayor, Mississippi, was said not to have had a single murder in twenty years (59), and in 1943 all-Negro Boley, Oklahoma, was reported to have the lowest crime rate in the state. (230) St. Helena Island, near Beaufort, South Carolina, has traditionally had very little violence and crime. (555) Significantly, the island is composed largely of Negro farm owners and has been blessed with a unique history of interracial harmony.

Consider, too, the low homicide rates of East African peoples. Seventy-one per cent of the 41 tribal groups

studied by Bohannan and his associates had lower
homicide rates than the whites of either South Carolina
or Texas in 1949-1951. (50) In fact, the median Southern state's white homicide rate for this period, 4.4 per
100,000, ranges from four to six times higher than the
rates of such tribes as the Wanga and the Bukayo.
Bohannan concludes: "If it needed stressing, here is
overwhelming evidence that it is cultural and not biological factors which make for a high homicide rate among
Negro Americans." (50, p. 237)

If there is no racial predisposition to crime, what,
then, lies behind Negro American crime? The same class
and discrimination considerations so vital to an understanding of health and intelligence variations again provide an explanation which can be supported by data.
Negroes, when compared with other Americans, are
more often lower class and poor, slum residents of the
largest cities, victims of family disorganization, Southern in origin, young and unemployed, and objects of
extensive discrimination—each an important social correlate of crime apart from race.

Think of the class factor. Though "white collar"
crime is prevalent in the United States (504), the great
bulk of recorded crime is concentrated in the lower socio-
economic segments of all groups. (310, 447) In the
Nashville area, for instance, white delinquents from the
lower stratum commit more serious crimes and are more
often oriented toward a life of crime than white delinquents from higher strata. (423) And in Philadelphia,
over 90 per cent of the homicides are perpetrated by
either the unemployed or those holding the least skilled
occupations. (552)

This close association between economics and recorded crime involves race insomuch as the lower socio-
economic class encompasses a segment of the Negro
population roughly two to three times larger than that
of the white population. Thus, almost half of all non-
white families, but only one-sixth of white families, had
annual incomes under $2500 in 1956. (49, pp. 656-657)

Yet research suggests that white-black crime differentials are not totally eliminated if socio-economic factors are held approximately constant. (46; 552, pp. 36-39) One reason for this is simply that the floor of Negro privation frequently goes below the most indigent of whites. (Chapter 3) Thus, Earl Moses attempted to examine the crime rates of Negroes and whites in four socio-economically equated areas in Baltimore; but he could not find two white districts actually as destitute as the two Negro districts. (371) He finally settled for two white areas with a greater rate of home ownership, thus vitiating his finding of greater crime rates in the Negro areas.

The special role of extreme penury in Negro crime was demonstrated during the Depression. Compared to previous decades, Spirer found that white commitments to Pennsylvania's Western State Penitentiary increased sharply during this period, but Negro commitments actually decreased. (482) These diverse trends were particularly marked for predatory crimes—robbery, burglary, larceny. Governmental aid during these lean years was apparently a significant contributor to this situation. Even with relief, bad times found many whites living below the economic levels to which they were accustomed; while relief schedules lifted impecunious Negroes above their pre-Depression income levels. Two other investigators more recently have demonstrated this phenomenon in Louisiana. (126)

Criminologists offer a number of reasons for lower-class crime. Living in the world's richest nation, surrounded by mass consumption of luxury items, and bombarded by advertisements directed primarily at the middle and upper classes, is it any wonder many lower-class persons are tempted to enter crime? Indeed, delinquent sub-cultures create a situation where law-breaking is expected behavior. (92, 93, 361, 541) In addition, the lower class, both Negro and white, has more direct association with criminal patterns. (104, 505) "Not all Negroes. working-class persons, etc., become criminals because some are presented with an excess of anti-criminal behavior patterns," explains Cressey, "but the *chances* of being presented with an excess of criminal behavior patterns are better if one is a Negro, a member of the working class, a young male, an urban dweller, and a native American than they are if one is white, middle-class, old, a rural resident or an immigrant." (105, p. 59)

This "differential association" factor assumes special importance for the poor who reside in the bleakest slums of the nation's largest urban centers, areas where criminal patterns are most conspicuous. And Negroes are disproportionately overrepresented in such big-city slums. The past two generations of constant migration have led to a significantly larger percentage of Negroes than whites residing in cities of more than a million people. The black ghettos of these metropolises are generally deep within the central city, marked by both physical and social deterioration, and witness to the most severe forms of vice and corruption.

High crime districts are characterized by a loss of any sense of community. One survey compared the opinions and actions of residents of two urban areas of similar economic standing but contrasting rates of delinquency. Figure 8 presents the results. Respondents in the high delinquency area liked their neighbors less, and felt they had fewer "interests and ideas" in common with them. Also, persons in the high crime area less often reported taking corrective measures when they saw delinquent acts in which they were not involved. (315)

Family disorganization is similarly characteristic of such districts. As discussed in Chapter 1, there may be a direct personality relationship between violent crime and the absence of the father. In any event, there is little question that broken families are one of the agents of crime in general. Mary Diggs found that three-fourths, twice the expected ratio, of Philadelphia's Negro delinquents who came before the law during 1948 did not have both of their natural parents living at home. (125)

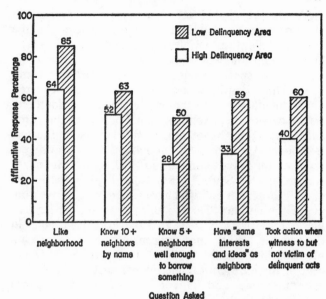

FIGURE 8—DELINQUENCY AND SENSE OF COMMUNITY
(Data from: Eleanor Maccoby, J. P. Johnson, and R. M. Church, "Community integration and the social control of juvenile delinquency," *Journal of Social Issues*, 1958, *14*, 38-51.)

The armed robber seems to spring most often from a background of severely impaired family life. Research on Negro offenders at the District of Columbia reformatory reveals that 84 per cent of the armed robbers came from "demoralized families," 78 per cent were reared in more than one home, and 84 per cent had histories as boys of running away from home—all percentages roughly twice those of other Negro offenders. (434)

The murderer raises additional considerations. Homicide is an intrinsic part of the South's "violent tradition." This tradition is a direct legacy from the frontier with its reliance on firearms and its distrust of formal legal processes; poverty and the Civil War caused the tradition to persist in the South even longer than in the West. (61, 75, 144, 166) There are many expressions of this regional tradition: lynching, esteem for the "hell-of-a-fellow" as a violent personality-type (75), the highest homicide rates for both races in the nation (415, 461), and a special fondness for the armed forces and guns. Thus, despite a system of nationwide congressional appointments to the service academies, Southerners are overrepresented among chief officers of the Army and Navy—though not among the leaders of the less traditional Air Force. Almost half of the Army's generals and the Navy's admirals, in 1950, were born and/or educated in the South.[2] (253) Consider, too, the results of a 1959 opinion poll which asked a representative sample of the nation: "Do you think it should be legal or illegal for private citizens to have loaded weapons in their homes?" Fifty-three per cent of the Southern sample thought it should be "legal," compared with 42 per cent of the Western sample, 35 per cent of the Northeastern sample, and 33 per cent of the Midwestern sample. (9)

Negro Americans are primarily a Southern people, and their homicide is another manifestation of this violent tradition. Consequently, Negro homicide rates vary tremendously by state; during the period 1949-1951, Texas and Florida had relatively four times the Negro homicide rate of Massachusetts and two-and-a-half times that of Connecticut and New Jersey. (406) These differences correlate highly with the state variations in the number of homicides committed by whites. Southern states, particularly those undergoing the most rapid social change, tend to have the highest rates of Negro homi-

[2] Southern esteem for armed service careers is also revealed by a 1947 national opinion poll. Thirty-four per cent of the Southern sample rated a regular Army captain as having an "excellent general standing" in society, compared with 25 to 27 per cent of the other regional samples. (Private communication from Professor Albert J. Reiss, Jr., of the University of Michigan) Though the sampling errors in such a survey are large for regional differences, these data combined with other consistent evidence suggest that the "violent tradition" still lingers in the South.

cide, followed by the Northern states which have received large numbers of Negro migrants from the South. (406) The greater proclivity to commit homicide among Negroes, then, is partly because most Negroes are Southerners or the children of Southerners.[8]

The relevance of migration to crime is not clear. Much as with the migration and mental illness relationship (Chapter 4), Southern-born Negroes in the North had far higher crime rates, particularly for homicide, than Northern-born Negroes prior to World War II. (482, 522) Recent work, however, casts doubt on this relationship (444), suggesting again that post-World War II Negro migrants out of the South are better prepared and qualitatively different from those of earlier years.

The widespread unemployment of ghetto youth also contributes to Negro crime rates. The greatest recent increases in American crime have occurred among the sixteen- to eighteen-year-old group. (145) This age range includes the teenagers who drop out of school and fail to find jobs. They lack money, skills, and societal acceptance; they have time on their hands and a local gang with which to affiliate. Delinquency is the natural result. James B. Conant calls this "the most dangerous social condition in America," latent with "social dynamite." (379, p. 26)

This factor assumes added importance for Negro crime rates, because Negro youth are more likely than white youth to be in this situation.[4] U. S. Department of Labor statistics show that since 1954 there has been a wide discrepancy in the racial unemployment rates of

[8] Roughly two-thirds of all Negroes residing in the North in 1963 were born and reared in the South. (382)

[4] There is also an age difference between the races. A younger group on the average, Negro Americans constitute a larger percentage of youngsters and adults in the heaviest crime-committing years of 15 through 39 than they do of the total population. Though not a critical factor, this age variable can, in certain situations, explain a considerable amount of the Negro-white crime differential. (482)

fourteen-to-nineteen-year-old teenagers. In 1962, for
example, when only one in eight (12 per cent) young
white males out of school were unemployed, the ratio
for young non-white males was over one in five (21 per
cent). In specific ghettos, the figures are much larger.
In the early 1960's, in a Detroit slum with one hundred
twenty-five thousand inhabitants, mostly Negro, 70 per
cent of its youths between the ages of sixteen and
twenty-one were out of school and out of work; in a
similar Chicago slum, the figure for young Negro males
was 60 per cent. (302, pp. 2-3) Even among those young
men who complete high school, the racial difference remains. A 1962 survey of the 1960 graduates of a virtually
all-Negro high school in Louisville, Kentucky, revealed
an unemployment rate two and a half times that of predominantly white high schools, over 25 per cent to 10
per cent. (524, p. 31)

Mention of unemployment introduces racial discrimination as a factor in Negro crime. Discrimination *per se*
need not always lead to high crime rates; witness the relatively low crime rates of Japanese Americans. (505, p.
142) But the unique type of discrimination long practiced against Negro Americans, from slavery to enforced
segregation, has been different in kind as well as degree
from that practiced against other minorities, and of a
type especially likely to produce crime. (260, p. 94) Job
discrimination offers a case in point. In Louisville, for
instance, "only a handful of Negroes" are admitted
among a thousand young men enrolled in the area's apprenticeship programs. (524, p. 31) It is no accident,
then, that the city's Negro high school graduates are disproportionately represented among the unemployed.
The strong need to move away from such racial barriers
results in unusually high Negro rates of escape crimes:
gambling, drug addiction, and drunkenness. These in
turn, especially drugs and alcohol, lead to other crimes,
either to secure money to support the habit or to act out
the less-inhibited impulses released by these agents.

The loss of inhibition resulting from the use of drugs and alcohol contributes to another characteristic of Negro crime—personal violence.[5] This tendency, too, is a direct result of the Negro's oppressed status. (129, 224) Deeply frustrated by his ego-deflating role and unable to express his hostility toward the white man, the lower-status Negro often vents his aggressions in violence directed against other Negroes, especially after drinking during leisure hours. Support for this interpretation comes from Philadelphia data that indicate Negro and white homicide are quite different phenomena in several respects. (552) Thus, alcohol was involved in over two-thirds of Negro killings, but in less than half of the white killings. Negro homicides were more likely than white homicides to occur in the evening and on the weekend. They were also more likely than white killings to have been provoked by the victim and to have involved stabbing rather than a beating. Finally, the motivational and situational patterns tended to be different. Homicides triggered by jealousy or altercations over money were more common among Negroes, as were homicides involving husband and wife. Moreover, a smaller proportion of Negro killings, compared to white homicides, took place outside the home or between strangers. In short, the Negro homicide tends to be a sudden, unpremeditated, alcohol-induced outburst between inti-

[5] While alcohol releases inhibitions, it does not determine whether any expression of aggression will be directed outwardly or inwardly. As mentioned in Chapter 4, Negroes are much more likely to direct aggression outward, as in homicide, rather than inward, as in suicide. Part of the explanation for this lies in the "violent tradition" of the South. And a clue to a further explanation is provided by a nationwide study of fourteen-to-sixteen-year-old American school children. Negro children, particularly boys, reported receiving physical punishment from their parents so much more often than white children that socio-economic differences between the groups alone cannot account for the disparity. Such physical punishment, as opposed to verbal and self-blame forms, is believed to be an important socialization determinant of outward aggression. (195)

mates in familiar surroundings, a pattern consistent with
both the racial-frustration and Southern-origin explanations.

Not all Negro frustration expressed in criminal form
is directed at other Negroes. Armed robbery of whites
may often be motivated as much by hostility toward
whites as other needs. For example, a young English
scholar was accosted by several Negro youths while
visiting the University of Chicago. (95, p. 598) They
demanded his wallet and, when he objected, a knife was
brandished. After they again insisted he yield his wallet,
he argued, "Look here, I don't want to give up my
wallet to you. Besides, I've just arrived from England,
and I don't think this is the way to treat someone who's
a visitor here." The boys looked at one another, and
then one replied, "Oh. We thought you were one of
those white guys," and they fled. "White guys," for these
youngsters, apparently included only those whites who
discriminated against them, not a white guest to their
country.

Negro violence may also be encouraged by police discrimination. Johnson details the process:

> In the interplay of behavior between the police and
> Negro suspects, there is a reciprocal expectation of
> violence. The police too quickly use gun or club, and
> Negroes—especially those with reputations as "bad
> niggers"—are keyed to a desperate shoot-first-or-you'll-
> get-shot psychology. Thus, what starts out to be merely
> a questioning or an arrest for a misdemeanor may
> suddenly turn into violence and a charge of murder
> against the Negro. (260, p. 97)

The too-quick use of firearms by the police was illustrated in the 1943 Detroit race riot. In fact, Negro distrust of the city's all-white police force gave a major
impetus to the spread of the riot. (296) And this distrust was justified. Fifteen Negroes but no whites were
shot to death by the police in the riot, though only three
of the victims had fired on the police. (296, p. 85)

Further insight into this problem is provided by

Kephart's extensive research on the Philadelphia police. (275) More than half of the city's district patrolmen found it "necessary" to be more strict with Negro than white offenders. Figure 9 shows that these men harbored the most unfavorable attitudes toward Negro policemen; they more often objected to riding with a Negro patrolman, resented taking orders from a "well qualified" Ne-

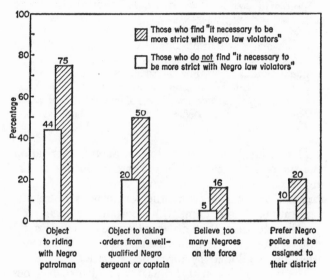

FIGURE 9—STRICTNESS OF WHITE POLICE AND THEIR ATTITUDES TOWARD NEGRO POLICE

(Data from: W. M. Kephart, *Racial Factors and Urban Law Enforcement*. Philadelphia: University of Pennsylvania Press, 1957; Tables 23, 25, 27, and 29.)

gro sergeant or captain, thought there were too many Negroes on the force, and preferred that Negro police not be assigned to their districts. These findings imply that stern handling of Negroes by such white policemen may be as much or more a function of their own bigotry as it is anything unique about Negro suspects.

In a broader, societal context, Merton and other social

theorists suggest how racial discrimination feeds Negro crime. They view this as simply another instance of our society's formally encouraging high aspirations and upward mobility, but at the same time effectively blocking the goals of such striving. The non-criminal "rules of the game" may be quite familiar to Negro offenders, but the supports for obeying the law are outweighed by the emphasis placed by American culture on attaining success. As Merton phrases it:

> . . . when a system of cultural values extols, virtually above all else, certain *common* success-goals for the population at large while the social structure rigorously restricts or completely closes access to approved modes of reaching these goals *for a considerable part of the population*, deviant behavior ensues on a large scale. (349, p. 180)

Thus, crime, too, is a symptom of relative deprivation. (Chapters 4 and 8) And Negro rates need not decline just because the absolute living standards of Negroes improve. Indeed, as with other expressions of relative deprivation, Negro crime will continue to occur at a greater rate than that of white crime as long as the group's aspirations remain far in advance of the modest attainments allowed by token desegregation.

There is nothing in this situation peculiar to Negroes. Daniel Bell highlights the fact that, repeatedly in American history, many members of ethnic groups, imbued with the success ethic but restrained from legitimate means of attainment by various types of barriers, have entered into illicit activity. (38, Chapter 7) Immigrant groups such as the Irish, Jews from Eastern Europe, and Italians have produced their "Shotgun" Kelleys, Arnold Rothsteins, and "Big Al" Capones, just as earlier Protestant groups produced their Jessie Jameses and their "robber barons." In this sense, crime is an institutionalized means for upward mobility in America, and Negroes are presently following the ascent of other groups up the ladder.

If Negroes had not become such an integral part of American society, if they had remained an isolated group refusing to share in the dominant values and aspirations of the general culture, racial discrimination would not be such a potent factor in Negro crime. Economically disadvantaged and persecuted minority groups can maintain low crime rates as long as they remain socially and culturally integrated within their own groups. (553) But as they depart from their sheltered status and begin to enter the mainstream of American life, their crime rates rise rapidly.

A RECAPITULATION

Apparent Negro American crime rates, as measured by a variety of available indices, are high. They are particularly elevated for crimes involving aggression, such as aggravated assault and homicide, and for escapist crimes, such as gambling, drug addiction, and drunkenness. And although racial discrimination still exists throughout much of the United States at each stage of the judicial process, this discrimination alone cannot account for all of the discrepancy. White supremacists are quick to interpret these data as further evidence for their theories of the genetic inferiority of Negroes as a "race." There is, however, no scientific evidence to support such claims. But there are considerable data which indicate that a multiplicity of social factors produce these criminal patterns among Negroes.

One broad set of factors is socio-economic in character. When compared with white Americans, Negroes are concentrated in those social sectors which exhibit high crime rates regardless of race. Thus, Negroes are more often lower class and poor, slum residents of the nation's largest metropolitan areas, victims of severe family disorganization, Southern in origin, young, and unemployed. Note that each of these characteristics is an important social correlate of crime apart from race—and especially for those violations with the highest Negro rates.

The other, closely related set of factors involves the special type of discrimination inflicted upon Negroes. As with other minority g~oups who find discriminatory barriers blocking their path toward the mainstream of success-oriented America, many Negroes turn to crime. Crime may thus be utilized as a means of escape, ego-enhancement, expression of aggression, or upward mobility. The salient feature of Negro Americans is that they have accepted and internalized American culture, but are generally denied the chief rewards and privileges of that culture. High crime rates are but one consequence of this situation.

Part III

NEGRO AMERICAN PROTEST

7

CLOSING THE GAP

If an American, because his skin is dark, cannot eat lunch in a restaurant open to the public, if he cannot send his children to the best public school available, if he cannot vote for the public officials who represent him, if, in short, he cannot enjoy the full and free life which all of us want, then who among us would be content to have the color of his skin changed and stand in his place? Who among us would then be content with the counsels of patience and delay?

These pointed questions were put to the American people by the late President Kennedy in a nationally televised address in June of 1963. They deserve answers. Who, indeed, among white Americans would willingly stand in the Negro's place? The query begs the question, for Americans have historically been a restless people, seldom satisfied with second-best or "content with the counsels of patience and delay." The question thus becomes one of means, of how to close the gap which now separates white and Negro Americans.

The Problem

The dimensions of the problem have been sketched in the previous chapters. Repeatedly, regardless of the realm under discussion, the data point to the same conclusions: (1) "racial differences" do exist, but they are not a matter of innate group "superiority" or "inferiority"; (2) persistent patterns of segregation and discrimination help to create and perpetuate these racial disparities; and (3) even if discrimination were totally abolished tomorrow, the impoverished economic and social resources of the majority of Negroes would act to maintain these racial disparities.

Racial differences do exist; on the preceding pages, these differences have been delineated in personality, health, intelligence, and crime. The basic tenet of the white supremacist is that these data offer proof of the genetic inferiority of Negroes as a race and hence demonstrate the need for racial separation. Such a view encounters several serious obstacles. First, it is irrelevant to democratic principles. Even if Negro Americans actually constituted a relatively pure "race" and tended to be genetically diseased, stupid, and criminal, these facts would not alter the justice of civil rights. A true democracy, according to the nation's most fundamental documents, attempts to provide all of its citizens with equal opportunities so that they may achieve to the best of their abilities. Segregation, whether in its blatant Southern form or more subtle Northern form, thwarts this ideal.

Second, as noted in detail throughout this volume, the assertions of genetic inferiority almost certainly have *no* scientific validity. Such contentions spring from a distorted view of just what constitutes a "race." They also do not allow for the considerable penetration of Caucasian genes throughout the Negro American population, a penetration that renders any discussion of pure races invalid and any suspicion of massive genetic distinctions between Negro and white Americans improbable.

Third, inferiority claims fail to recognize the critical role of environmental factors in interaction with genetic potential. In particular, such claims ignore the corrosive effects of discrimination and poverty. Indeed, the segregationist creates Negro disorganization with his creed, then turns around and justifies his creed in terms of Negro disorganization. In this sense, the segregationist resembles the young boy who in cold blood grabbed a double-barreled shotgun, killed his father with one blast, then whirled the gun around and killed his mother with the other. When brought to trial for the double murder, he pleaded for mercy on the grounds that he was an orphan.

Southern segregationists, in particular, should understand the sweeping effects of environment and the dangers of inferring group inferiority from statistics alone. Elevated rates of many communicable diseases, lower average intelligence test scores, and a higher incidence of violent crimes distinguish white Southerners from other white Americans. Yet these data have not been utilized as proof of the genetic inferiority of white Southerners. Indeed, such findings are correctly interpreted as the bitter fruits of the region's economic retardation, of its unique and tragic history.

Not all racial disparities, however, are traceable to discrimination alone. Inseparably interwoven with racial rejection is debilitating privation. In personality development, mental and physical health, intellectual growth, and criminal behavior, each of the previous chapters has demonstrated the warping role of indigence. And since poverty feeds upon poverty and prevents many Negroes from preparing themselves for the opportunities now opening up, the issue is more than just clearing away discriminatory barriers. The basic problem becomes one of not merely allowing Negroes to enter the mainstream of American life but of *enabling* them to enter. "Even when advancing at the same speed," observes the director of the National Urban League, Whitney Young, "the back wheels can never catch up with the front wheels without special acceleration."

There is, then, an enormous gap yet to close between Negro and white Americans. Remedial efforts must proceed on two interrelated fronts—the personal and the societal.

The New Role of Equal Citizen

Life in one sense is like a game of billiards; the winning player gets a continuous opportunity for practice, while the losing player stands aside and watches. So it is with the role of equal citizen. People who lead the full and free lives alluded to by the late president essentially "learn by doing." They receive, if you will, on-the-job-training in performing as successful citizens, accustomed to exercising their rights and meeting their responsibilities. But for those whose lives are neither full nor free, the role of equal citizen is not so easily assumed. Especially is this true for Negro Americans, who previously have been expected to play only the lowly role of social inferior. (Chapter 1) Thus, on the personal level, remedial steps call for the systematic shedding of the degraded role of "Negro" and the adoption of the upgraded role of equal citizen.

The problem is well-illustrated by the typical reaction of Negro communities toward newly desegregated public facilities. Many of the South's lunch-counters, after their desegregation, do not receive the Negro patronage one might reasonably expect. Some segregationists immediately assume that this is proof "their Negroes" do not want an end to segregation after all; it is only the agitators from outside who come in and stir everybody up. Actually, as a symbol of their dignity, the desegregation process is overwhelmingly supported by Negroes, North and South. (Chapter 2) The reluctance to take advantage of the new opportunity does not stem from disapproval of the change, but from an uneasiness and uncertainty about the new situation. Lingering fears from the past lead many Negroes, particularly the older people, to expect that they will be humiliated and mistreated by whites even at an officially desegregated facility. "Besides," goes a typical remark, "how do I know how the white folks behave at such a place?" The bitter Negro jibe—"you ain't ready yet"—points up their fears and uncertainties over taking on the new role. And the hard fact remains that the only way to learn "how the white folks behave" and "how to be ready" is to enter the strange and threatening situation.[1]

This vicious circle is analogous to what psychologists describe as "avoidance learning." Suppose in an experi-

[1] The principal thing learned by both Negroes and whites in the desegregation situation, of course, is the many values, ideas, and aspirations the two groups have in common. (Chapter 2)

mental setting, a subject's forefinger is repeatedly shocked electrically immediately after the flashing of a light. Very quickly he learns to avoid the painful shock by lifting his finger as soon as he sees the light flash on; in other words, the subject is conditioned in the classic Pavlovian paradigm. But consider what happens when the electric shock is no longer applied. How can the subject acquire knowledge of the change? As long as he withdraws his finger at the light, he can never discover that the light is no longer associated with a shock. This is the critical feature of avoidance learning. Negroes have learned to withdraw from interracial situations where they experience pain and indignity. (Chapter 2) And even though these situations change and the pain and indignity are removed, most Negroes are naturally reluctant to test them and discover the alterations. Avoidance learning, then, is self-perpetuating.

Avoidance learning can only be broken by intervention. By accident or design, the Negro is introduced to new interracial situations that prove rewarding and ego-enhancing. He unlearns previous avoidance responses and fashions new responses and a new role. Though grossly oversimplified, these are the outlines of the problem at the personal level. The nature of the remedial experiences best suited for overcoming past fears and establishing the role of equal citizen is fairly well understood by social psychologists. Since the new learning is social in nature, it is best mastered in particular group settings. Briefly stated, the most striking changes in personality and role adoption are achieved through participation in highly cohesive groups in which the new role behavior is: (1) the chief group focus, (2) expected and emphasized, (3) strongly rewarded, with group status dependent upon it, and (4) actively advocated by the members themselves. (294, Chapter 7; 530)

For maximal effectiveness, such groups must be both cohesive and intensively directed toward change. The people who join must value the groups and their objectives; thus, participants must be open to change. Furthermore, the groups cannot be multipurpose organizations, scattering their efforts in many directions. In this case, Negroes who have still to shed the last vestiges of the "Negro" role must want to adopt the equal citizen role, must want to acquire a heightened self-image. And the groups they need must command respect among Negroes and focus primarily on erasing the personality and behavior traces of the past.

The new qualities—ambition, group pride, assertiveness, in short, all the features of the "Negro" role turned inside out—have to be routinely expected and repeatedly rewarded in the remedial groups. Success and status in the group must be totally a function of how well the member meets group expectations. Any slipping back to the old ways has to be frowned upon and discouraged. The importance of reward in role adoption has been demonstrated by ingenious experiments. (450, 451) Pairs of students debated an issue before a college class, with each member required to argue for the position contrary to the one he preferred. The winner of each debate was apparently determined by the vote of the class (actually, the announced results were manipulated in favor of a predetermined member of each pair). Strong and relatively lasting attitude change in the direction of the debated position and against the subject's initial opinion occurred only for those who had "won" their debates. The adoption of a new role alone is not sufficient; the new behavior needs reinforcement for lasting effects to occur.

Finally, maximal change is achieved when group members themselves actively aid others in acquiring the new role. Alcoholics Anonymous, an unusually effective group meeting all of these criteria, utilizes this principle when it sends out ex-alcoholics to help current alcoholics overcome addiction. Though this process may often be useful to the new recruit as a first step toward joining the group, its principal value lies in the opportunity it provides the ex-alcoholics to act out their new roles. This, together with the individual's candid discussions of his personal problems before a sympathetic audience of fellow sufferers, commits the member publicly. And public commitment is particularly important in permanently establishing altered responses. One study changed the attitudes of high-school-aged subjects toward lowering the voting age by presenting special propaganda on the subject. (239) A portion of the children did not sign their written statements which revealed their new position. Others, however, signed their names and thought the statements would appear in their school newspaper. Later the children read a counterpropaganda message. Two-fifths of the uncommitted group shifted their opinions back in the direction of the counterpropaganda, in contrast to only one-seventh of the publicly committed group. Exposure to novel ideas and behavior alone is not sufficient; deeply-rooted change often requires public commitment.

From this vantage point, the remedial powers of Negro protest organizations can be easily recognized. Most or all of these criteria for profound and lasting personal change are met by these organizations. Consider the Student Non-Violent Coordinating Committee (SNICK), the college-led organization that evolved out of the sit-in campaign of 1960. The group is cohesive, highly regarded by Negro youth, and dedicated entirely to achieving both personal and societal racial change. Recruits willingly and eagerly devote themselves to the group's goals. And they find themselves systematically rewarded by Snick for violating the "Negro" role in every particular. They are expected to evince strong racial pride, to assert their full rights as citizens, to face jail and police brutality unhesitatingly for the cause. Indeed, high status within Snick is in part dependent upon having gone to jail for "freedom." [2] Note, too,

[2] An additional, though not incompatible, explanation for the value placed on going to jail by protesting Negroes has been advanced by one observer. (528) That is, the guilt produced by the conflict between genuine hatred of the white segregationist and the religiously-sanctioned belief in loving even your enemy, actually causes some protesters to seek punishment.

that these expected and rewarded actions all publicly commit the member to the group and its aims.

This insight enables us to solve a riddle posed in Chapter 2. Recall that three independent investigations found Negro college students in the South, in comparison with white college students, unusually deferent, shy, dependent, and passive. (58, 211, 212) Yet these students, shortly after these data were collected, began their sit-in protest movement that culminated in Snick. Earlier it was suggested that the protest initiators were deviants from this prevailing personality pattern so fitting to the "Negro" role. Research supports this contention. One ingenious experiment performed at a Negro state college in the Deep South early in the history of the student protest asked students in actual classroom settings to volunteer for a "Students for Freedom Movement." (200) Each subject indicated his willingness to participate in a variety of protest actions. Those students eager to take part in the more militant activities differed sharply from those less willing in the degree to which they felt their fate was in their own hands. These students had clearly shaken off the effects of the "Negro" role; they preferred direct action in moving toward their oppressor, because they considered themselves determiners of their own destiny, rather than pawns of a hostile, unmoving environment.

Other studies also bear out this conclusion. Although the activists do not differ from non-activists on a variety of standard questionnaire measures (73, 431, 452), they more often come from higher-status backgrounds, participate in extracurricular college affairs, and perceive support for the sit-ins from both whites and Negroes. (452) Similarly, among those Negro parents initially given the opportunity, it was the better-educated, higher-status parents who enrolled their children in Nashville's first biracial schools. (533) Presumably, middle-class Negroes have previously had some of the on-the-job-training in equal citizenship generally denied lower-status Negroes; thus, they are better prepared to lead the way in shedding the "Negro" role and asserting their full rights.

But this explains only the initiation of the movement. After the activists have led, how does local Negro protest become a genuine social movement? The answer at the psychological level lies in the process just described. Reticent Negroes, anxious to throw off their racial role of inferiority but inexperienced in aggressive action, enter the fray gingerly. Soon, however, they are caught up in the movement. The remedial powers of the movements themselves alter their followers in the process. Critics of Negro protest are fond of advising Negroes to stop demanding their rights and to start preparing themselves to utilize these rights. But such advice ignores the growth potential of the protest itself. Negro Americans are learning how to be first-class citizens at the same time they are winning first-class citizenship.

The Snick students working to increase the Negro vote in Mississippi offer a dramatic illustration of this process. This project has faced determined segregationist opposition and cannot as yet point to a significant rise in Negro registration. Yet these workers have brought the protest to the most deprived elements of the Negro population in the United States. But most important, the experience of having to risk life and safety to secure the Constitutionally-guaranteed franchise is leaving an indelible impression upon the Snick students themselves. It is difficult to imagine these young Negroes ever being apathetic about voting the rest of their lives; the vote takes on a fresh significance under such circumstances.

The role shift from designated inferior to recognized equal need not take such dangerous forms as political activity in Mississippi. Nor need it take place within the context of protest movements at all. Any group situation fulfilling most or all of the necessary conditions can be effective. This suggests the structure that desegregated situations should assume to maximize interracial acceptance. Parenthetically, most white Americans require a shift in roles, too, in preparation for the race relations of the future. The imperious role of the social superior must also give way to that of equal citizen. Effective desegregation can and does achieve these needed changes for both races.

Social psychologists have amassed considerable research evidence concerning the factors which comprise successful desegregation. As mentioned in Chapter 2, prejudice declines and new racial roles develop in desegregated situations where the two groups: (1) possess approximately equal status, (2) seek common goals, (3) are cooperatively dependent upon one another, and (4) interact with the positive support of authorities, law, or custom. (3, Chapter 16; 466) Wherever these conditions are attained, in schools, at work, in neighborhoods, or in the armed forces, remarkable alterations occur in the attitudes and behavior of both Negroes and whites. (64, 83, 218, 317, 442, 498, 543, 557) As one Negro officer, who served on a desegregated ship throughout the Korean War, candidly confessed: "After a while you start thinking of whites as people."

SOME NEEDED SOCIETAL REFORMS

To insist Negroes themselves "earn" their first-class citizenship by first eliminating the social disorganization of the ghetto is sheer sophistry.[3] It is analogous to the segregationist claim that Negroes should pay more taxes if they wish improved public services, while simultaneously denying Negroes the better jobs necessary for the income out of which to pay more taxes. Of course, many Negroes like Samuel Sheppard *do* devote their lives to repairing the damage of the past. (Chapter 5) But the immense task of significantly improving the life styles and opportunities of many millions of people requires not only remedial efforts on the personal level but major structural reforms in American society.

[3] This type of argument is even heard from white Northerners who profess to have "the best interests of the Negro American at heart." For a particularly naïve example, see Fischer. (161)

Too often the problems of race relations are placed solely in the context of discrimination and segregation. Throughout this volume, however, caste restrictions are found to be only one of the major contributors to the Negro's present plight. Hand in hand with caste are considerations of class and economic deprivation. In personality development, health, intelligence, and crime, economic factors join with racial rejection to form the pattern of meager and undeveloped lives for most Negroes. Consequently, if all racial prejudice and discrimination miraculously vanished from the national scene tomorrow, the Negro's problems would not be solved. Most white people would still be comfortably prosperous; most Negroes still precariously close to the ragged edge of bitter poverty.

The fundamental bottleneck to Negro economic progress exists in the employment area. This hard societal fact of life will become painfully more obvious over the next decade. The massive occupational upgrading of Negroes—and many whites, too—just when the full effects of automation are starting to hit the labor force will require major societal surgery, not the aspirin-type palliatives so far considered by the United States Congress. Such surgery will be resisted by forces more powerful and entrenched than those which have opposed desegregation; but it will become increasingly necessary for national development and for the resolution of racial conflict as well.

The broad dimensions of the Negro's employment problems are shown in Figures 10 and 11. At a time when automation is already eliminating roughly forty thousand unskilled jobs a week, the Negro is concentrated in the unskilled sectors of the labor force. Figure 10 shows the occupational distribution of non-whites in 1950 and 1960, relative to whites. The overconcentration of non-whites in the three least skilled and most poorly paid areas—farm workers (mostly laborers), urban laborers, and service workers—is apparent. Non-whites are proportionately represented only in the semi-skilled, operative category. And in all other employment categories—from craftsman to professional—non-whites comprise half or less the representation that would be expected if there were no racial distinctions. Also note the failure of non-whites to achieve sizable gains in the better job areas during the 1950's. (Chapter 8)

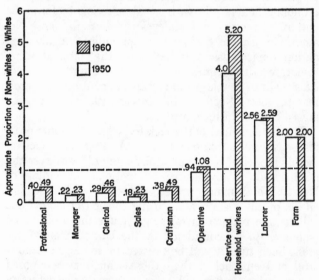

FIGURE 10—PROPORTIONS OF EMPLOYED NON-WHITE TO WHITE WORKERS BY OCCUPATION

(Adapted from: Norval D. Glenn, "Some changes in the relative status of American non-whites, 1940 to 1960," *Phylon*, 1963, 24, p. 110.)

The seriousness of this low occupational status is highlighted by the projected composition and size of the labor force in 1970 (Figure 11). The important expansions in the American labor force during the 1960's are expected to come in the professional and clerical ranks (combined projection of six and one-fifth million more positions by 1970). But these are two areas in which Negroes are severely underrepresented. Moreover, due to automation, farming employment will continue to decline, and no expansion is predicted in jobs for urban laborers. Clearly, a massive Negro occupational upgrading is an economic necessity for the nation apart from its effects upon race relations.

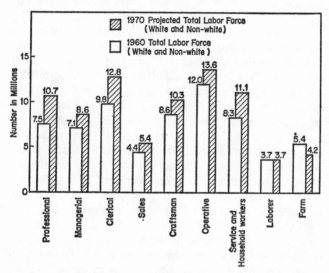

FIGURE 11—TOTAL EMPLOYMENT BY MAJOR OCCUPATIONAL
GROUPS

(Adapted from: William E. Amos, and Jane Perry, "Negro youth and employment opportunities." *J. Negro Education*, 1963 Yearbook, 32(4), 358-366.)

Figure 11 suggests in broad outline the forms this upgrading must take. Negroes need to aim for and be accepted in a wide range of jobs within the rapidly developing professional and clerical fields. Service work is also anticipated to increase rapidly (projected two and two-thirds million more positions by 1970) and can, hopefully, absorb a portion of the unskilled Negroes just off the farm, laid off from employment as laborers, or new to the labor market. This absorption has already been occurring at a rapid rate, as revealed in the growth of the proportion of non-whites to whites in service occupations between 1950 and 1960.

The operative category, also cut by automation, is expected to accommodate only slightly more than a million and a half more workers by 1970, and therefore will not be a major source of new jobs. Skilled crafts employment will probably not expand during the 1960's much faster than operative employment. Only a projected one and two-thirds million more jobs will become available in this realm, and this fact underlies the brewing storm over the Negro's demand for entrance into the building trade unions. Breaking open the nepotistic, medieval-guild-like unions of the building trades is made especially difficult by the slow growth of employment in this area. As the Negro demand for these unions to end their blatantly discriminatory practices sweeps across the country, bitter resistance is likely to be encountered from entrenched white workers fearful of their own jobs.

On the basis of these projections for 1970, the economic future for many Negroes is not bright. The lone answer is a general expansion of the entire economy with a resultant increase in the labor force well in excess of these projections. Negro employment gains have always come fastest during times of rapid growth—as in World War II; significant gains in the 1960's and early 1970's are in large part dependent upon another period of major development. All types of structural reforms necessary to induce economic expansion responsibly are prerequisites, then, not just for national prosperity but for improved race relations as well.

More specific examples of required structural reforms include broadening minimum wage legislation, exempting the poor from federal income taxes, and mounting a crash program of job training and retraining. All three of these reforms are desperately needed by many white Americans, but each has a special relevance to Negro Americans and the problems outlined in this volume.

For those poorly-skilled Negroes who are employed, an extensive broadening of minimum wage legislation could afford considerable relief. Many of the job categories in which Negroes are concentrated—service occupations, in particular—are not covered in the wage provisions of the Fair Labor Standards Act. Thus, the act as it now stands excludes those very people who most require its protection. Chapter 1 indicated how low wages for Negro males act to perpetuate family disorganization; Chapter 4 discussed the direct relationship between severe poverty and disease; and Chapter 6 showed the intimate connection between economic deprivation and crime. A broadening of minimum wage legislation could aid in all of these concerns.[4] Some observers insist that such legislation is more crucial than many of the proposed anti-discrimination laws, though both are essential.

Another reform involves federal income taxes. Major cuts must be made at the bottom, rather than at the top, of the income scale. At the very least, single persons with annual incomes below $2000 and families with annual incomes below $4000 should be exempt from federal income taxes (they will still bear a disproportionate burden from sales taxes).[5] These are levels

[4] It can be argued that broadening minimum wage coverage to include service workers is self-defeating in so much as it would act as an incentive for employers to automatize their operations and eliminate jobs. Yet this argument is not wholly convincing. A great many service jobs are not readily supplanted by machines (e.g., barbers); others are replaceable only by a basic alteration of the character and appeal of the business (e.g., waiters and waitresses replaced by automats). Furthermore, many service employers now pay whites the minimum $1.25 per hour or more, but continue to pay Negroes doing the same work substantially less. To be sure, one certain effect would be a rise in final costs to the customer, but this would largely increase the flow of money from the prosperous to the poor in a more dignified manner than welfare programs have ever devised.

[5] Some maintain that it is vital to tax the poverty-stricken members of the population to give them a true sense of participation in the general society. Such an argument is at best questionable. Everyone can still well-up with honest pride when he pays his state and local taxes; he need not pay federal income taxes to gain this feeling of participation. More importantly, tax-paying is not com-

widely regarded by economists as poverty-stricken according to modern American standards, and these are
the only realistic standards by which to judge the income of Americans. (Chapter 8)

Such a taxation reform would bring immediate help
to a majority of Negro Americans. Sixty per cent of all
Negro families had an annual total monetary income
below $4000 in 1961, compared with only 28 per cent
of white families. (223) In the South, 80 per cent of all
Negro families had such incomes in 1961, compared
with 39 per cent of white families. Tax relief for these
people could in some cases mean a substantial saving.
Under 1963 tax regulations, a married couple with no
dependents and using the standard deductions paid
$480 on a $4000 annual income. Tax-cut revisions for
1964 improve this situation somewhat, but are not extensive enough.[6]

Finally, a great variety of federally-sponsored training
and retraining programs are urgent necessities, for the
economic progress of Negroes depends not only on the
availability of jobs but also on the acquisition of skills
to take advantage of the enlarged opportunities. Compared with present minuscule efforts, however, these
future programs must be daringly new in both concep-

monly viewed as an exciting privilege. Indeed, the payment of
taxes out of meager funds severely restricts the poor's participation in America's expensive society. Voting, by contrast, is viewed
as direct participation in democratic government. Consequently,
observers who are truly concerned about engaging the disadvantaged might better work to modify our electoral processes in
order to maximize lower-class use of the ballot (e.g., shifting
election day from Tuesday to the weekend).

[6] Under 1964 tax regulations, the same married couple with no
dependents and using the standard deductions pays $354, rather
than $480, on their $4000 annual income. To be exempt, such a
couple has to have an annual income no larger than $1500 (for-
merly, the figure was $1000). The new regulations, however,
liberalize the minimum standard deduction, a provision which
removes roughly one and a half million of the poorest taxpayers
from the Federal tax rolls.

tion and magnitude. Automation requires more imaginative and flexible training than has typically been true in the past. The many boys now being taught cabinetmaking, to choose an extreme but actual example, should instead be taught the basic technological skills prerequisite for the jobs in greatest demand. Modern teaching methods must be applied, methods which ease rather than magnify the special problems of disadvantaged individuals. (30, 332, 426, 470)

The size and complexity of this educational task invites attack from many directions—thoroughly revamped vocational training programs for the public schools, the domestic equivalent of the Peace Corps, the Manpower Retraining programs, and a wider use of the educational potential of the armed forces. But if the unemployment and alienation among the inhabitants of the depths of urban ghettos today are to be remedied, a new conception of selection procedures will have to be adopted by these programs. As in the case of the minimum wage legislation, these programs are currently rejecting those unskilled persons who most desperately need the training.

Consider the armed forces. Ever since World War II, the services have been an important institution for social mobility and occupational upgrading among lower-status Negroes. Advantages previously unobtainable are made available, such as travel and training in an interracial environment, superior medical facilities, responsible work, and a stable life situation with specific expectations and rewards. The armed forces intervene in a Negro's life in his late teens or early adulthood, and reverse many of the vicious circles of defeat and despair otherwise established during these years. James Meredith, the son of a tenant cotton farmer, could not have become a trail blazer for Negro Mississippians had he not benefited from extensive Air Force experience. But the Merediths are highly selected. Those young Negroes most defeated in life are least likely to be acceptable to the services. Poor health, a low intelligence-test score, or a criminal record prevent an applicant from meeting the minimum selection standards. Yet these are precisely the youth who most need the advantages and special experience the armed forces can provide.

Another approach, however, is for the services to accept many of those now rejected and to furnish these young Americans with special remedial training. A precedent was established in World War II with the Special Training Units. (Chapter 5) These units had considerable success in giving an intensive and basic fourth-grade education in eight weeks to illiterate soldiers; a similar plan today could provide an intensive and basic ninth- or tenth-grade education, complete with fundamental machine skills, in about one year. For lower-class boys of both races, particularly those raised in fatherless families, such training would have a number of psychological advantages over the "sissy" public school training. No longer would education be seen as an impractical feminine institution; courses would be given in the context of service in the armed forces, the instructors would all be males, and pay and promotion could be employed as direct and immediate rewards for achievement.

Together with other approaches, this fuller utilization of the armed forces' educational potential could make a vital contribution to training the most disadvantaged members of our society. As with all effective and broad-gauged programs, such an approach would require considerable financial support. But such funds would have the political advantage of coming under defense appropriations, a category apparently more acceptable to many legislators. And the fact remains that no matter how the task is tackled, preparing the most deprived segments of the American population for an automated and technological age will be expensive and difficult; but unless this is attempted, the fundamental educational problems of our time will go neglected.

CLOSING THE GAP

Efforts to close the gap in life styles and opportunities which still persist between Negro and white Americans take place at two interrelated levels. On the personal level, the problem is one of shifting from the role of social inferior to that of social equal. Such a shift appears easiest in a cohesive group context where the altered role behavior is the principal focus, expected and emphasized, constantly rewarded with group status dependent upon it, and actively advocated by the members themselves. Successfully desegregated situations often meet these criteria, and produce dramatic personality changes.

On the societal level, closing the racial gap requires structural reform. Examples range from an extension of public health services in the large urban ghettos to judicial and penal reforms designed to eliminate racial injustice. But the present discussion has focused upon especially key areas for further Negro progress: economics and employment. All responsible measures for rapidly expanding the American economy and enlarging the labor force are as important for the resolution of racial conflict as they are for the nation's general prosperity. In addition, extension of minimum wage coverage, elimination of federal income taxes for the poor, and massive retraining programs are urgently required in race relations.

Organized Negro protest looms as an important feature in both these realms. On the one hand, protest pressure is essential for obtaining the needed societal reforms; on the other hand, organized protest groups often furnish an ideal learning situation for their members to cast aside the lowly role of "Negro" in favor of the new role of equal citizen.

8

ACTUAL GAINS
AND PSYCHOLOGICAL LOSSES

The late Samuel Stouffer, one of America's greatest sociologists, always became incensed when a layman blithely reacted to a finding of behavioral science with, "Who didn't know that?" He countered with a simple true-false test of ten items, the "obvious, common sense" answers to which had all been demonstrated to be incorrect by rigorous social research. Most of those who take Stouffer's test miss every item. The moral is clear: many behavioral science findings appear obvious only after the fact.

Stouffer's favorite illustration involved the relative morale of the Air Corps and the Military Police in World War II. Promotions were rapid and widespread in the Air Corps, but slow and piecemeal in the Military Police. Conventional wisdom predicts that the Air Corpsmen should have been more satisfied with their chances for promotion, for the "obvious" reason that they were in absolute terms moving ahead faster in their careers. But, as a matter of empirical fact, Stouffer found in his famous studies of *The American Soldier* that the Air Corpsmen were considerably more frustrated over promotions than the Military Police. (350, 498) What was not so obvious was that the fliers' wide-open system of promotions led them to assume exceedingly high aspirations; most of them expected such swift elevation that even the generous promotions of their service left them *relatively* dissatisfied. By contrast, morale was reasonably high among the Military Police. The MP's did not expect rapid promotions and learned to be content with what few advances they did achieve. It was not the

absolute level of attainment that made for poor morale
so much as relative deprivation—the discrepancy between what one anticipates and what one attains.
(Chapters 4 and 6)

Likewise, conventional wisdom dictates that Negro
Americans should be more content today than any previous point in America's history. After all, have Negro
gains not been faster in recent decades than any period
since Emancipation? Why, then, are many Negroes so
unusually restive, so openly angry, so impatient for further gains? Relative, not absolute, deprivation once again
provides a social-psychological explanation. The great
majority of Negroes in past years dared not cherish high
aspirations. While never satisfied with their lot, they,
like the Military Police, expected very little of life, and
they had to be content with what crumbs they did
receive. But Negro Americans in recent years hunger for
much more than crumbs. Like the Air Corpsmen, they
have tasted significant progress and can fully appreciate
what further progress could mean. Indeed, Negro aspirations have risen far more swiftly than Negro advances.
Thus, while better off in absolute terms than ever before,
Negroes today are relatively more deprived than they
were before the last twenty-five years of racial progress.

This important social-psychological principle underlies the Negro American protest of the 1960's. To trace
its operation, this chapter summarizes the actual gains
of recent years, lists the simultaneous psychological
losses of these same years, offers a psychological interpretation of the protest movement itself, and, finally,
ventures four predictions concerning the future of Negro protest.[1]

ACTUAL GAINS

The past quarter-century has witnessed the most rapid
actual gains in Negro American history. Consider this

[1] An earlier draft of this chapter appeared as "Actual Gains
and Psychological Losses: The Negro American Protest," *Journal
of Negro Education*, 1963 *Yearbook*, 32(4), 493-506.

sampling of recent advances culled from a variety of statistical sources:

The Negro's transition from rural Southerner to urbanite, North and South, continues apace. (526) Today's Negro Americans are more urban than white Americans; 72 per cent of all non-whites in 1960 resided in urban areas, three times the non-white urban percentage in 1900. The Negro has migrated particularly to the very largest of American cities. Thus, in 1960 over half of all non-whites in the nation lived in metropolitan centers with at least a half-million people. Mark the Negro's growth in America's five largest cities. Between 1940 and 1960, the non-white percentages in New York and Philadelphia more than doubled and in Chicago, Los Angeles, and Detroit nearly tripled.

Behind these data lie literally millions of individual stories of migration, of picking up stakes in rural areas and moving into strange and bustling cities. The period from 1950 to 1960 alone witnessed the mass movement of more than a half-million Negro Southerners to the Northeast, another half-million to the Midwest, and a third of a million more to the West. Consequently, Negro migration has not only involved a moving from farm to city, but also a moving out of the South into other parts of the country. Clearly, race relations are no longer the problem and domain of a single region; with almost as many Negroes residing outside the South as in it, racial matters are definitely a national concern.

These enormous demographic alterations contribute to Negro progress in several ways. To begin with, this massive migration has lifted the bulk of the Negro population out of those areas most resistant to racial change and into the cities where racial change is least resisted. Within the South, the old rural Black Belt—named for its rich black soil—has traditionally had counties where Negroes outnumbered whites. A symbol and center of racial discrimination, this area is now breaking up. Today only one Southern county in eight has more Negroes than whites, while Negro populations in Southern cities have been growing at rates only slightly less than those of Northern cities. Between 1950 and 1960, the absolute number of Negroes residing in Miami almost tripled; in Dallas and Oklahoma City, more than doubled; and in Houston and Little Rock, almost doubled. (223)

Moreover, this massive movement leads directly to a more sophisticated people capable of effective protest, a people more cognizant of what discrimination over the years has denied them. It also produces large concentrations of Negroes, facilitating communication and organization that simply could not be achieved in scattered rural districts. Finally, migration enables Negroes to benefit from the substantially higher urban standards of living. This factor greatly influences Negro progress in a wide range of domains: health, employment, business, income, housing, politics, and education.

As observed at the close of Chapter 4, life expectancy at birth for Negroes from 1900 to 1960 has increased twice as rapidly as that of whites. Much of this advance reflects the better medical care available in large metropolitan areas, and most of the advance has occurred in recent years. In relation to the nation as a whole, age-adjusted, non-white total mortality rates improved from 1950 to 1960 virtually as much as they had in the previous half century. (197)

Likewise, gains have been registered in upgraded employment. The first few years of the Kennedy Administration witnessed a substantial growth in middle- and high-level federal employment of Negroes. (236) Although the positions involved are still relatively few, the number of Negroes in responsible government service jobs (GS 5 through 18) shot up 20 per cent from July, 1961, through June, 1962, while the number of whites in comparable jobs increased only 6 per cent. Responsible postal employment (PFS 5 through 18) revealed a similar trend. Lower level federal positions (GS and PFS 1 through 4) showed more modest Negro gains. While federal employment comprises only a small fraction of the nation's jobs, this swift improvement in occupational upgrading demonstrates what well-directed, crash programs can accomplish.

Employment opportunities have gradually expanded in recent years for Negro youth in the professional and clerical categories as well as the more traditional service fields (13); and non-white males have made gains somewhat faster than white males during the 1950's in both the professional and operative job classifications. (112; see Figure 10, Chapter 7) Only a small portion of this professional and clerical progress, however, can be attributed to the development of Negro-controlled business itself, though some aspects of Negro business have prospered. The assets of Negro savings and loan associations, for instance, have multiplied over 32 times since 1947 (563), a rate roughly three times that of all savings and loan associations combined.[2] Similarly, commercial banks owned and operated by Negroes increased their assets from 5 million dollars in 1940 to about 53 million by 1960, a growth rate over five times faster than that of all commercial banks. (563) And the 51 Negro-controlled life insurance companies have doubled their assets since 1951 to a present total of at least 320 million dollars. (563)

These trends in turn generate income gains. From 1950 to 1960, the median annual income for individual non-whites fourteen years of age and older climbed 54 per cent and for non-white families 73 per cent. (192, 223) The Negro middle class swelled; the percentage of non-white families earning $6000 or more in 1961, 20 per cent, was over five times larger than in 1945. (223) The resulting purchasing power of Negroes has evolved into a potent factor even in the South. Thus, in 1961 it was estimated that the Negro participation in the total retail sales of ten standard metropolitan areas of the South amounted to 19 per cent, representing sales of almost two billion dollars. (223) "This is not only

[2] According to the *New York Times* (August 26, 1963, p. 37), savings and loan associations in general have expanded eleven times since 1945.

suggestive of the impact of aggregate and concentrated purchasing power in the Negro market," remarks economist Vivian Henderson, "but it is also indicative of the kind of economic potential to which southern race relations must adjust." (223, p. 11)

Increments in income are soon translated into better housing. The 1950's marked a doubling of the percentage of non-whites residing in census-defined "standard" housing. (560) And many Negroes became able for the first time to afford their housing without taking in boarders and extended family members; consequently, significantly fewer Negro households in 1960 included lodgers and three-generation families than in 1950. (142)

Important changes have occurred in political, as well as purchasing, power. Over a million more Negroes voted in 1962 than in 1950, and the power of this increased access to the ballot revealed itself in a wide range of elections. The first Negro elected to the Georgia legislature for generations won office in 1962, as did Negroes elected to statewide posts in Connecticut and Massachusetts. And it was no coincidence that the 1960 presidential campaign was the first in history where both major political parties vied intensively with one another as to which could write the stronger civil rights plank in its platform. Demographic shifts have established powerful concentrations of Negroes in most of the key electoral states: New York, Pennsylvania, Ohio, Michigan, Illinois, and California. In addition, Negro voters more than made the difference for Mr. Kennedy in 1960 in three crucial Southern states—North Carolina, South Carolina, and Texas.

Educational gains have also been evident. The percentage increments from 1940 to 1960 of Negro youth of all ages attending school are dramatic; and indices of educational quality, such as expenditures per pupil, number of pupils per teacher, and the academic preparation of teachers, have all risen in Southern schools for Negroes. (385) Educational attainments for the Negro adult population have climbed markedly in recent decades.[3] From 1940 to 1960, the percentage of Negroes who had attended college more than doubled (128); from 1950 to 1960, the percentage of Negroes who had completed high school rose from 14 to 22 per cent, a faster rate than that of whites; and from 1950 to 1960, the median school years completed by all adult Negroes increased over a grade, 6.9 to 8.2 years. (360) Particularly indicative is the advance made by the twenty-five-to-twenty-nine-year-old age group. Negroes in this key age category in 1940 had received a median of only 7 years of training, while similar Negroes in 1960 recorded a median of 11 years. (385)

These recent advances have had a profound psychological effect upon Negro Americans. Despair and hopelessness have declined, new and proud aspirations have taken hold, and a determined optimism about the future has developed. These trends became noteworthy by the early 1950's. A representative 1954 national public opinion poll asked: "On the whole, do you think life will be better for you or worse, in the next few years than it is now?" [4] Figure 12 provides the results. Of those with an opinion, 64 per cent of the Negro respondents felt life would soon be better. This figure compared with only 53 per cent of a white control sample equivalent to the Negro sample in region of residence, sex, age, education, and occupation. Observe also that this heightened Negro optimism, relative to comparable whites, is especially marked among the most deprived segments of the Negro population. Thus, the greatest relative optimism was evidenced by Negroes who were laborers, or had only a grammar school education, or resided in the South.

[3] Educational data cited throughout this chapter use the census definition for adults as all persons twenty-five years of age and older.

[4] These results were derived from a re-analysis by the author of data from Samuel Stouffer's large polling study, *Communism, Conformity and Civil Liberties*. These data were kindly furnished by the Roper Public Opinion Research Center, Williamstown, Massachusetts.

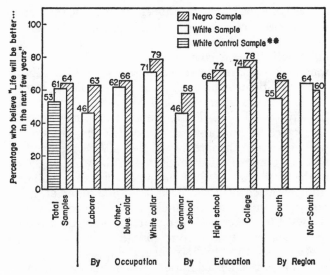

FIGURE 12—OPTIMISM FOR THE FUTURE

(Reanalysis of data from: S. A. Stouffer, *Communism, Conformity and Civil Liberties*. New York: Doubleday, 1955. Data furnished by Roper Public Opinion Research Center, Williamstown, Mass.)
** Equal to Negro Sample in age, sex, education, region and occupation.

The public school desegregation ruling of the Supreme Court, of course, made 1954 a vintage year for rising Negro aspirations. But recent poll data suggest that, if anything, this high level of optimism has risen further. A 1959 national survey found that Negro Americans felt they had personally lost ground during the previous five years; but their hopes for the next five years revealed a relative increment roughly twice that of white Americans. (251a) The 1963 *Newsweek* opinion survey of Negro Americans also uncovered revealing results: 73 per cent felt that the racial attitudes of whites would improve during the next five years; 63 per cent thought whites would accept racial change without violence; 85 per cent desired to own a private home; and 30 per cent believed it was qualified for elevation to professional or other white-collar employment. (382)

This same poll finds that much of this renewed hope for the future centers upon education. Although one in five families interviewed had a child who had dropped out of school before completing high school, 97 per cent wanted its children to finish high school. (382) Ever since Abolitionist schoolmarms implanted faith in learning in Negroes after the Civil War, they have traditionally valued education as a means of achieving full acceptance in American society; and several additional studies point to the intensity of this faith at the present time. One investigation conducted in the middle 1950's in the Northeast noted that a sample of Negro mothers strongly valued achievement in terms of a future orientation that usually accompanies high educational aspirations. (440) Indeed, 83 per cent of these mothers intended for their sons to go to college.

Studies of the children themselves further confirm this emphasis upon education as a means for upward social mobility. One research project of the early 1950's tested and interviewed Negro and white children of matched intelligence from a desegregated elementary school. (54) The Negro youngsters expressed higher levels of aspiration and more ambitious hopes for the future than the white youngsters. And a recent investigation of Negro high school students throughout the South reveals that they, too, harbor a great desire for further education. (467)

Some observers interpret such heightened educational aspirations as "unrealistic" and indicative that Negroes learn early to separate their hopes from the stark reality that generally confronts them. But another study done in the late 1950's of high school seniors in Kentucky discovered that most of the Negro children who had reached this level had surprisingly well-conceived plans for the future. (312) Negro seniors in this sample were not only more optimistic than the white seniors, but they shrewdly appraised their position in American society, their better chances for white-collar jobs in the North, and their need to end discriminatory barriers.

PSYCHOLOGICAL LOSSES

Slowly, imperceptibly, the frame of reference for many Negro Americans has shifted during the past few decades. While formerly most Negroes judged how well off they were by their own previous conditions, the rising expectations of the present are increasingly framed in terms of the wider society. Negro protest today is moving away from an exclusive emphasis upon desegregation and equal opportunity toward a broader demand for a "fair share" and advantages directly comparable to those of whites. This shift merits special attention, for the actual gains just reviewed were all relative to previous Negro conditions. But such advances are not enough to meet the hopes of a people beginning to contrast their still-lowly position with the rich abundance surrounding them. The hard truth is that the Negro's recent progress does not begin to close the gap between the two races. Consider once again each of the realms in which changes have occurred.

Despite the large-scale migration since 1915, substantial segments of the Negro population remain in the most hostile and deprived areas of the nation. Mere mention of county names—such as Greene and Monroe in Alabama, Lee and Terrell in Georgia, Carroll and Tate in Mississippi, McCormick and Williamsburg in South Carolina, Fayette and Haywood in Tennessee, and Prince Edward in Virginia—serves to remind us that several millions of Negroes still reside in rural areas of the South which are resisting racial change by almost every means possible. The high promise of change is barely beginning in these Black Belt counties.

There is also another aspect to the recent improvements in Negro American health. As pointed out in Chapter 4, life expectancy at birth still lags behind that of white Americans, though the discrepancy has shrunk to six to eight years. (359) And relative to white rates, non-white mortality rates for diabetes mellitus and cirrhosis of the liver actually increased between 1950 and

1960; this increase, however, may well reflect better reporting and diagnosis rather than actual retrogression. (197) The remaining racial disparities in health are principally due to conditions which can be drastically reduced with both improved medical care and a higher standard of living: tuberculosis, syphilis, childhood diseases, perinatal and maternal complications, etc. (Chapter 4)

Employment presents a similar picture. In spite of rapid upgrading in the past few years, Negroes employed by the federal government are still concentrated in the lower, blue-collar brackets and sparse in the upper, white-collar brackets (236); in most unionized industries, basic racial employment patterns remain unaltered (328); Negro youth suffer from almost twice the unemployment rate of white youth (Chapter 6); and Negro adults in general are still vastly underemployed, downgraded, and underpaid relative to comparably-educated segments of the white community. (112) The slow rise of Negro occupational trends during the 1950's is forcefully shown by projecting these trends into the future. (192) At the creeping 1950 to 1960 rate of change (Figure 10 in Chapter 7), non-whites in the United States would not attain equal proportional representation among clerical workers until 1992, among skilled workers until 2005, among professionals until 2017, among sales workers until 2114, and among business managers and proprietors until 2730! Obviously, such a pace is ridiculously slow for a people whose expectations for the immediate future are among the most optimistic in the nation; hence, the significant slogan of the 1963 March on Washington—"Jobs and Freedom Now."

The projected eight centuries necessary to close the racial gap among business managers and proprietors illustrate once more the exclusion of Negroes from executive roles in the general society and the minuscule size of Negro business. Even in the savings and loan field, a strong Negro business area, the assets of Negro-controlled institutions constitute only approximately three-tenths of one per cent of total assets;[5] and in the insurance field, the strongest Negro business area, the assets of all Negro-controlled companies constitute only a fraction of any one of the very largest companies. Although minor allowance must be made for a few publishing and insurance companies and financial institutions, the dour generalization of Franklin Frazier continues to hold true: ". . . 'Negro business,' which has no significance in the American economy, . . . [is] a social myth . . ." (171, p. 193)

Changes in Negro income relative to white income provide the most disappointing trend of the 1950's. The ratio of non-white to white median-family-income in 1959 (51.7 per cent) was virtually the same as in 1949 (51.1 per cent). (192) Korean War prosperity elevated the ratio to its highest point (56.8 per cent) in 1952, but since then white income gains have been markedly larger than those of non-whites. The racial discrepancy is especially great in the South, where in 1960 the median non-white family received $2687 less than the median white family; in no region, however, did the dollar difference narrow to less than $1500.[6] (223) This means that, although the absolute level of Negro family income rose throughout the 1950's, white family income rose proportionately faster.

This sharp racial differential in family income persists in spite of a larger average number of Negro family members working and larger families to support. Differential tax payments balance this inequity slightly; but Negroes typically obtain less for their consumer dollar.

[5] The total assets of Negro savings and loan associations are approximately 300 million dollars (563), while total assets of all associations passed the 100-billion-dollar mark during 1963 (*New York Times*, August 26, 1963, p. 37).

[6] One of the results of this relative lack of income improvement, as Chapter 1 suggested, is that Negro family disorganization actually worsened during the 1950's. From 1950 to 1960, the percentage of non-white, husband-wife families slipped from 78 to 74, while the percentage of non-white families headed by a female increased from 18 to 21. (142)

This is especially true in housing. While some housing gains occurred in the 1950's, the quality of Negro housing remains vastly inferior relative to that of whites. (560) For example, in Chicago in 1960, Negroes paid as much for housing as whites, despite their lower incomes. Median rents for both groups were $88, yet Negroes received much poorer accommodations. This situation exists because of essentially two separate housing markets; and the residential segregation that creates these dual markets "has increased steadily over past decades until it has reached universally high levels in cities throughout the United States, despite significant advances in the socio-economic status of Negroes." (507)

Even the accelerated political advances of Negro Americans leave much undone. Negroes still vote far less often than whites. Particularly in those Southern areas where racial change is most desperately needed, Negroes are least often found on the electoral rolls.[7] Indeed, there is a massive denial of the franchise in most of Alabama and Mississippi and large parts of Louisiana, Georgia, and South Carolina. (201) The proposed voting title of the 1964 Civil Rights Act provides limited help, but does not offer a definitive solution.

Finally, Negro education has yet to approach that generally available to whites. It remains in general "less available, less accessible, and especially less adequate." (385) In 1960, Negro college attendance was proportionately only about half that of whites (128); the percentage of adult Negroes who had completed college was considerably less than half that of whites; and the percentage who had completed high school was precisely half that of whites. (360) These gaps are especially serious, for as we have seen, Negro hopes for the future are so centered upon education that training of poor

[7] A recent ecological investigation of all of the Southern counties with at least one per cent Negroes demonstrates that Negro voting is proportionately greatest in those counties with high white and Negro incomes, fairly large percentages of Negro white-collar workers, and relatively few Negroes. (329)

quality at this stage could well undercut the determined thrust toward group uplift.

Thus, in each interrelated realm—health, employment, business, income, housing, voting, and education —the absolute gains of the 1950's pale when contrasted with current white standards. Numerous spokesmen for the status quo have boasted of the present status of the Negro in glowing international comparisons. Negroes in the United States today, goes one boast, have a consumer buying power comparable to that of similarly-populated Canada. And a larger percentage of Negroes, goes another, attends college than residents of the British Isles. But such glittering statements must not blind us to the fact of greatest psychological importance. Negro American standards have their psychological meaning relative to the standards of other Americans, not of Canadians or the British. The Negro American judges his living standards, his opportunities, indeed, even judges himself, in the only cultural terms he knows —those of the United States and its "people of plenty." Dr. Martin Luther King, Jr. made the point bluntly in his Washington March address: "The Negro lives on a lonely island of poverty in the midst of a vast ocean of material prosperity . . . and finds himself an exile in his own land."

The resulting relative deprivation is the fundamental basis of mass Negro American dissatisfaction today. But it is not the only factor. Special frustrations are created by the appearance of proud new African nations upon the world scene. Emerging Africa has a dual psychological effect upon Negro Americans. On the one hand, it generates racial pride and lifts self-esteem—especially among the darkest members of the group. (Chapter 1) On the other hand, it lends a desperate urgency to protest at home. Heretofore, Negro Americans have been the most sophisticated and respected black group in the Western world—regardless of their lowly position by American standards. But now many Africans can claim complete freedom, while Negro Americans still seek theirs. In this sense, then, independent African nations add to the Negro's keen sense of relative deprivation.

A similar phenomenon occurs regionally within the United States. Negro Northerners have typically prided themselves on being the products of the big-city North, on being superior to their Southern "country cousins." Yet Negro Southerners today lead the struggle for racial justice; many of them have willingly faced fire hoses, dogs, jail, and police brutality in order to demand and assert their rights; and one of them, Dr. King, has become the symbol of the protest movement throughout the country. A few Negro leaders in the South even hint wryly that the day may come when Negro Northerners will have to migrate southward to obtain true equality. And when Negroes in the North contrast their slow progress against de facto segregation in housing, schools, and employment with the dramatic desegregation of public facilities in many parts of the South, they must wonder if such wry hints do not possess some basis in truth.

Thus, the present-day Negro's feeling of being left behind springs from three sources. It derives partly from relating his situation to emerging Africa. For the Negro Northerner, it also stems from comparing his gains with those of his on-rushing Southern relatives. But its primary source is from contrasting his still meager lot with the abundance of other Americans.

ALL, HERE, NOW!

Intense relative deprivation in an age of rising expectations is the stuff out of which revolutions are made. But this revolution of 1963, with its ringing demand for "all, here, now," is a revolution only in a sense special to the Negro's unique role in American society.[8] An

[8] In the technical language of social science, the Negro American protest is a reform movement and not a revolution. This is true because the protest aims to change norms—the accepted rules of societal operation—and not to overturn basic values. The term "revolution" is used here, then, only in the popular sense of a major social movement demanding fundamental reforms.

understanding of this special form of revolution is requisite to any meaningful projection of the Negro American's status into the future.

This non-violent revolution does resemble more typical revolutions in some ways. The present movement has shifted in emphasis from legalism to direct action, from narrow objectives to a full-scale attack, from pockets of protest to a genuine mass movement cutting across divisions within the Negro community. (346) And like other mass movements, it has achieved a heightened militancy and urgency, a new sense that "even yesterday was too late." It also exhibits some of the irrationality common to all revolutions.

Nevertheless, this is a revolution with a basic difference. It aims to modify, not to overturn, the society it confronts; it seeks to amend, not to ravage. Negro Americans are so firmly rooted in and shaped by their land that their revolution is attempting merely to guarantee full participation in the society as it otherwise exists. In short, they do not wish to deprecate or destroy that which they wish to join. It is, then, a peculiarly conservative revolution, a fact that in many ways gives it a special force.

Such a conservative revolution acts out the culture's most cherished values; it dramatizes the "American dilemma" between high ideals and lowly practices. It does not offer new values, but demands that old values be realized. To suppress such a revolution would be to surrender the very foundations of the United States. There is in the long run, then, but one viable alternative —to move with history and achieve a racially integrated society in which skin color loses all relevance. This alternative is already recognized in the support given the protest by the federal government—a strange ally for true revolutionaries. Even if federal authorities have sometimes been too late with too little help, as in Albany, Georgia, and other Black Belt sites, the fact remains that the current Negro protest takes place within a generally permissive national atmosphere.

Moreover, this special type of revolution is supported to a considerable degree by white American opinion. There is a hard core of whites marching in demonstrations, going to jail, even facing death with Negroes. Though a small minority, these whites serve the vital function of keeping the confrontation from becoming a purely black versus white conflict. To be sure, there is also a hard core of white dead-enders, those who resist even token desegregation by burning crosses, exploding bombs, and assassinating Negro leaders. But the majority of white Americans range somewhere in between, and, while their attitudes often do not measure up to Negro expectations, they nevertheless contribute to the permissive atmosphere in a number of key ways.

To begin with, there is solid approval outside of the South of the Supreme Court's 1954 school desegregation ruling. Gallup polls show that 62 per cent of the nation, Negro and white, approves of the decision, with the proportion among non-Southerners reaching almost three out of four. (7, 147) School desegregation itself wins general approval outside of the South, as long as Negro children are not in the majority. In the South, although racial change is still widely opposed by white Southerners, such change is increasingly seen as inevitable. Gallup polls have repeatedly asked Southerners of both races if they thought "the day will ever come when white and Negro people will be going to the same schools, eating in the same restaurants, and generally sharing the same public accommodations." (11, 147) In 1957, only 45 per cent of the South answered "yes"; by 1958, 53 per cent did so; by 1961, 76 per cent; and by 1963, 83 per cent. In addition, among the 83 per cent who saw desegregation as inevitable in 1963, half believed it would come about completely within five years and another fourth believed it would occur within ten years. Thus, the majority of white Southerners clearly expects racial progress even while opposing it, and this widespread feeling of inevitability contributes importantly to the present milieu in which the Negro protest is operating.

The ground was prepared for these white opinions before the current revolution. During and since World War II, the stereotype of the Negro has undergone drastic modification. Witness the erosion of the racist contention that Negroes are innately stupid. (Chapter 5) The National Opinion Research Center asked Americans in a series of representative polls: "In general, do you think Negroes are as intelligent as white people— that is, can they learn just as well if they are given the same education and training?" In 1942, only 42 per cent of white Americans believed the two groups to be equally intelligent; by 1944, the figure was 44 per cent; by 1946, 53 per cent; by 1956, 78 per cent. (147, 247) This fundamental alteration of the image of the Negro acts to sharpen further white guilt over the "American dilemma."

There remain, however, serious limitations to white understanding of the Negro American. The majority of white Americans as yet neither identifies with Negro Americans nor senses the urgency of the present revolution. Most whites believe that Negroes are being treated fairly in the United States and that gradualism should be the rule in effecting desegregation. (7, 147, 383) Since these beliefs assuage guilty consciences, it is not surprising that Negro demonstrations which boldly challenge them are resented. In 1961, for example, national samples questioned by Gallup pollsters indicated that 64 per cent disapproved of the freedom rides and 57 per cent believed the rides would "hurt the Negro's chance of being integrated in the South." (147) Similarly, 65 per cent of white Northerners and 73 per cent of white Southerners interviewed in 1963 thought that "mass demonstrations by Negroes are likely to hurt the Negro's cause for racial equality." (10) Without denying the basic justice of the protest, many whites handle their guilt by complaining that Negroes are "pushing too hard

too fast." (7, 383) Yet some of these same people
realize upon reflection that Negroes do in fact make
maximum progress only when they confront the nation
directly with their demands.

Within this social-psychological context—severe relative deprivation among Negroes, an urgent, but basically
conservative, protest revolution, a supportive federal government, and a guilty, if gradualistic, dominant climate
of white opinion—four predictions for the future can be
ventured.

*First, Negro protests will continue to grow both in
intensity and depth.* As demonstrations persist, advances
will occur ever more rapidly. These advances serve to reward the protest and stimulate its continuance. "The
leaders sitting down together would, of course, be the
best way," frankly confided one Negro lady, "but we
found it didn't work and sit-ins did." (382, p. 34) Advances also serve to highlight further racial changes that
are needed. These effects are part of a widely-studied
psychological phenomenon known technically as "goal
gradient" and popularly as "running for home." As subjects in an experiment approach their final goal, they
typically gain a "second wind" and speed up their performance. Or in relative deprivation terms, protest success enlarges aspirations faster than actual gains can
meet; the result is deeper frustration and more insistent
demands. "The closer we come to the achievement of
our ideals," shrewdly observed a Civil Rights Commis-
sioner, "the more obvious and galling is the disparity."

Apart from its success, the current revolution will become increasingly intense because of the psychological
effects of the demonstrations themselves, mentioned in
the previous chapter. No protester, Negro or white,
comes out of a racial demonstration the same person he
was when he entered. Personal participation publicly
commits the protester; it gives him a new sense of actively influencing events rather than passively accepting
them; and it can provide him with greater confidence
and an enhanced self-image. All of these changes aid

him in undertaking additional protest. In short, demonstrations are both a symptom and a cause of psychological health. "My feets is tired," remarked an elderly Negro lady in the midst of the Montgomery bus boycott,
"but my soul is rested."

Furthermore, demonstrations instruct both participants and by-standers that segregation is a two-way
street, a process of role reciprocation. It takes two to
tango, and it requires the complicity of both whites and
Negroes to maintain patterns of segregation and discrimination. (Chapter 1) If Negroes disengage themselves from these patterns, racial barriers cannot long be
maintained. This insight, achieved in the midst of demonstrations, also makes further protest inevitable. "We
the Negro people are now not afraid," announced a
grocery store owner in a small Alabama town, "we have
woke up." (382, p. 17)

*Second, the protests will increasingly attract a larger
proportion of lower-income Negroes and shift from status
to economic goals.* The direct action phase of the revolution began in earnest when Southern college students
initiated in 1960 a wave of mass sit-in demonstrations
aimed at the desegregation of lunch-counters. The fact
that college students sparked this phase and that public
facilities were the initial targets is important; but direct
action weapons are now spreading and will continue to
spread to diverse segments of the Negro population with
primarily economic targets.

The fact that Negro college students ignited the direct action fuse involves a special irony. These youngsters
benefited from the best schools the South ever provided
Negroes. Though still not the equal of white education,
this improved training produced a relatively more sophisticated, self-confident generation. It also kindled,
through the mechanism once again of relative deprivation, a greater frustration over racial barriers that finally
exploded into militant social action. Like oil and water,
education and oppression do not mix.

The student presented the perfect symbol as the initiator of public demonstrations. Well-dressed and well-behaved, the Negro student epitomized the group's aspirations for social mobility and integration. His non-violent movement flew in the face of the segregationist stereotype of the Negro as violent yet subservient, degraded yet happy with his lot. The student was also less encumbered with fears from past mistreatment and less vulnerable to economic retaliation. In short, he was uniquely situated to transform public protest and going to jail into not only socially respectable acts but badges of high honor.

To become a full-fledged revolution, however, the movement has to incorporate all elements of the Negro community. The Montgomery bus boycott in 1955-1956 provided a preview of the power of a unified effort across class lines. But it required Bull Connor's police dogs and fire hoses in Birmingham in 1963 to capture the imagination of all segments of Negro America. Data from a national poll of Negroes in the summer of 1963 tell the story. (382) Fifty per cent felt the pace of racial change was far too slow; 80 per cent felt certain that demonstrations were effective; 4 per cent had already personally been jailed in the cause or had family members who had been; 40 per cent had already personally, or had family members who had taken part in a sit-in, marched in a mass protest, or engaged in picketing; and 48 per cent reported a willingness to participate in mass protests even if it meant going to jail. Clearly, the revolution is an authentic mass movement that unites many different Negro elements, and shows every promise of recruiting more adherents in the future.

As the proportion of lower-income participators climbs, the nature of the struggle's primary goals necessarily shifts from status to economic concerns. (Chapter 2) Poor Negroes are not importantly affected by the desegregation of the opera, expensive restaurants, or golf courses; they are chiefly interested in getting good jobs and sharing in the material abundance surrounding them. "Freedom" for them signifies inseparably both dollars and dignity. Yet relative occupational and income gains, it will be recalled, were the most disappointing indices of the 1950's. Consequently, 1963's wave of building-site demonstrations against racial discrimination in the building trades is sure to be merely the forerunner of attacks upon a variety of employment fields and economic problems.

Third, a more extensive use of local and national boycotts of consumer products will be made. The consumer boycott is a weapon yet to be fully exploited. But a number of localities, like Philadelphia and Nashville, have learned what well-organized Negro boycotting can accomplish. And national advertisers have made agreements with protest organizations to include Negroes in their television programs and advertisements in order to avert national campaigns against their products. A 1963 poll of Negroes reports that because of employment discrimination 29 per cent of its sample stopped buying in certain stores and 19 per cent stopped buying certain companies' products. (382) But this barely touches the potential. Sixty-three per cent of the sample stated that it would stop buying at a store if asked, including over two-thirds of the highest-income Negroes.

This mass willingness to participate in boycotts stems from two factors. The first is economic; boycotts are unusually well-suited for achieving the employment breakthroughs so desperately desired by low-income Negroes.[9] The second factor is psychological. As described in Chapter 2, there are three major types of responses hu-

[9] Not all boycotts, of course, gain effective leverage on economic problems. Thus, boycotts against whole industries (e.g., new automobiles) or the entire economy (e.g., no Christmas buying) may serve other protest aims, but are not ideally styled for battering down employment barriers. More directed are selective boycotts, campaigns to restrict sales of one particular company's stores or products. Such selective campaigns have the dual advantage of: (1) greater likelihood of success, for followers must make fewer alterations in their daily living; and (2) both firms whose sales decline and those whose sales correspondingly rise achieve healthy respect for the Negro's ability to influence profit margins.

man beings can make to oppression: they can move toward the oppressor and seek acceptance as an equal; they can move against the oppressor and aggressively express their frustration; and they can move away from the oppressor and seek to minimize painful contacts. Boycotts have the distinct psychological advantage of appealing to all three of these basic responses. Such campaigns move toward the oppressor by seeking to achieve desegregation; they move against the oppressor by encouraging group unity and aggressively upsetting the white-controlled economy; and they move away from the oppressor by requesting the participators merely to avoid the scene of conflict. For these reasons, it seems highly probable that boycotts will increase in number and scope.

Four, as the revolution proceeds through the coming years, some basic structural changes in American society will have to occur before viable race-relations solutions are possible. This prediction is based on the discussion in Chapter 7. The problems facing Negro American protest are considerably more complicated than merely battering down the walls of segregation. The skill with which the movement addresses itself to these structural issues, particularly the economic ones, is a critical determinant of its success in the near future. Indeed, success is dependent upon all of the factors mentioned in these predictions. Should the protest movement cool, should the involvement of lower-income Negroes and the shift in emphasis to economic goals not take place, should nationwide boycotts not be effectively mounted, should all types of necessary and decisive structural changes needed now by the American society be blocked, then obviously significant progress will not occur.

This is precisely what makes the 1960's and 1970's such crucial, yet promising, years for American race relations. The gravest danger is not interracial violence, as the mass media endlessly assert, but that this golden opportunity will not be fully utilized. The nation is ripe for sweeping racial change and is in fact changing. Except for the Black Belt South, the formal desegregation of public facilities will soon be a mopping-up operation. The critical question, then, is: Can the revolution deal with *de facto* segregation and the vast educational and economic issues still impeding Negro progress as effectively as it has dealt with legal segregation?

FREEDOM!

In Mississippi there is a tall, black-skinned young woman, Annelle Ponder, who contributes to the revolution as a voter registration worker. (564, p. 193) For her efforts, she was once beaten by police and thrown in jail in the little town of Winona. When friends visited her, they found her sitting in her cell, her face swollen and bruised, barely able to speak. She looked up at them, and managed to whisper one word: "Freedom!"

As in many revolutions, *freedom* has assumed a definition special to the situation. Freedom for protesting Negro Americans means a complete casting off of the inferior role of "Negro"; it means the cessation of all of the disabilities traditionally placed upon black skin by American society. It means the stilling of self-hatred. Freedom also means an end to claims of white superiority, to dire poverty, to the social conditions permitting inflated rates of disease and inadequate medical care, low intelligence test scores, and heightened crime rates. Freedom means, in short, the right to participate fully in American society with the dollars and dignity of other Americans.

REFERENCES

1. T. W. Adorno, Else Frenkel-Brunswik, D. J. Levinson, and R. N. Sanford, *The Authoritarian Personality.* New York: Harper, 1950.
2. E. R. Akers and V. Fox, "The Detroit Rioters and Looters Committed to Prison," *Journal of Criminal Law and Criminology,* 1944, 35, 105-110.
3. G. W. Allport, *The Nature of Prejudice.* Cambridge, Mass.: Addison-Wesley, 1954.
4. G. W. Allport, *Pattern and Growth in Personality.* New York: Holt, Rinehart and Winston, 1961.
5. G. W. Allport and B. M. Kramer, "Some Roots of Prejudice," *Journal of Psychology,* 1946, 22, 9-39.
6. Thelma G. Alper and E. G. Boring, "Intelligence Test Scores of Northern and Southern White and Negro Recruits in 1918," *Journal of Abnormal and Social Psychology,* 1944, 39, 471-474.
7. S. Alsop and O. Quayle, "What Northerners Really Think of Negroes," *Saturday Evening Post,* Sept. 7, 1963, 236, 17-21.
8. M. Alter, "Multiple Sclerosis in the Negro," *Archives of Neurology,* 1962, 7, 83-91.
9. American Institute of Public Opinion Press Release, July 21, 1959.
10. American Institute of Public Opinion Press Release, July 18, 1963.
11. American Institute of Public Opinion Press Release, July 19, 1963.
12. R. Ames, "Protest and Irony in Negro Folksong," *Science and Society,* 1950, 14, 193-213.
13. W. E. Amos and Jane Perry, "Negro Youth and Employment Opportunities," *Journal of Negro Education,* 1963 Yearbook, 32(4), 358-366.
14. Anne Anastasi, "Intelligence and Family Size," *Psychological Bulletin,* 1956, 53, 187-209.
15. Anne Anastasi, *Differential Psychology.* Third edition. New York: Macmillan, 1958.
16. Anne Anastasi and Rita D'Angelo, "A Comparison of Negro and White Pre-School Children in Language Development and Goodenough Draw-a-Man I.Q.," *Journal of Genetic Psychology,* 1952, 81, 147-165.

202

17. R. S. Anderson and Laurie M. Gunter, "Sex and Diabetes Mellitus: A Comparative Study of 26 Negro Males and 26 Negro Females Matched for Age," *American Journal of the Medical Sciences*, 1961, *242*, 481-486.

18. H. Aptheker, "Literacy, and the Negro and World War II," *Journal of Negro Education*, 1946, *15*, 595-602.

19. H. S. Ashmore, *The Negro and the Schools*. Chapel Hill: University of North Carolina Press, 1954.

20. D. P. Ausubel, "Ego Development among Segregated Negro Children," *Mental Hygiene*, 1958, *42*, 362-369.

21. S. Axelrad, "Negro and White Male Institutionalized Delinquents," *American Journal of Sociology*, 1952, *57*, 569-574.

22. Virginia M. Axline, "Play Therapy Procedures and Results," *American Journal of Orthopsychiatry*, 1955, *25*, 618-626.

23. G. R. Bach, "Father-Fantasies and Father-Typing in Father-Separated Children," *Child Development*, 1946, *17*, 63-79.

24. Margaret K. Bacon, I. L. Child, and H. Barry, III, "A Cross-Cultural Study of Correlates of Crime," *Journal of Abnormal and Social Psychology*, 1963, *66*, 291-300.

25. J. Baldwin, *Notes of a Native Son*. Boston: Beacon Press, 1955.

26. J. Baldwin, *Nobody Knows My Name*. New York: Dial, 1961.

27. A. Bandura and R. H. Walters, *Adolescent Aggression*. New York: Ronald, 1959.

28. W. S. M. Banks, "Rank Order of Sensitivity to Discrimination," *American Sociological Review*, 1950, *15*, 529-534.

29. N. Barnicot, "Coon's Theory of Evolution," *The Observer Weekend Review*, May 26, 1963, 24.

30. H. Baron, "Samuel Shepard and the Banneker Project," *Integrated Education*, April, 1963, *1*, 25-27.

31. L. N. Bass and H. B. Yaghmai, "Report of a Case of Hemophilia in a Negroid Infant," *Journal of the National Medical Association*, 1962, *54*, 561-562.

32. R. Bastide, *Sociologie et Psychanalyse*. Paris: Presses Univer. de France, 1950.

33. Leona Baumgartner, "Urban Reservoirs of Tuberculosis," *American Review of Tuberculosis*, 1959, *79*, 687-689.

34. J. A. Bayton, "The Racial Stereotypes of Negro College Students," *Journal of Abnormal and Social Psychology*, 1941, *36*, 97-102.

35. J. A. Bayton and Ethel F. Byoune, "Racio-National Stereotypes Held by Negroes," *Journal of Negro Education*, 1947, *16*, 49-56.

36. K. L. Bean, "Negro Responses to Verbal and Non-verbal Test Material," *Journal of Psychology*, 1942, *13*, 343-353.

37. R. H. Beattie, "Criminal Statistics in the United States,"

Journal of Criminal Law, Criminology, and Police Science, 1960, 51, 49-65.

38. D. Bell, *The End of Ideology.* Glencoe, Ill.: Free Press, 1959.

39. R. C. Bensing and O. Schroeder, Jr., *Homicide in an Urban Community.* Springfield, Ill.: Thomas, 1960.

40. R. F. B. Berdie, "Playing the Dozens," *Journal of Abnormal and Social Psychology,* 1947, 42, 120-121.

41. B. Berelson and Patricia J. Salter, "Majority and Minority Americans: An Analysis of Magazine Fiction," *Public Opinion Quarterly,* 1946, 10, 168-190.

42. E. M. Berger, "The Relation between Expressed Acceptance of Self and Expressed Acceptance of Others," *Journal of Abnormal and Social Psychology,* 1952, 47, 778-782.

43. E. M. Berger, "Relationships among Acceptance of Self, Acceptance of Others, and MMPI Scores," *Journal of Counseling Psychology,* 1955, 2, 279-284.

44. Viola W. Bernard, "Psychoanalysis and Members of Minority Groups," *Journal of the American Psychoanalytic Association,* 1953, 2, 256-267.

45. W. H. Bexton, W. Heron, and T. H. Scott, "Effects of Decreased Variation in the Sensory Environment," *Canadian Journal of Psychology,* 1954, 8, 70-76.

46. J. T. Blue, "The Relationship of Juvenile Delinquency, Race, and Economic Status," *Journal of Negro Education,* 1948, 17, 469-477.

47. B. S. Blumberg (ed.), *Genetic Polymorphisms and Geographic Variations in Disease.* New York: Grune and Stratton, 1961.

48. J. H. Boger, "An Experimental Study of the Effects of Perceptual Training on Group I.Q. Test Scores of Elementary Pupils in Rural Ungraded Schools," *Journal of Educational Research* 1952, 46, 43-52.

49. D. J. Bogue, *The Population of the United States.* Glencoe, Ill.: Free Press, 1959.

50. P. Bohannan (ed.), *African Homicide and Suicide.* Princeton, N. J.: Princeton University Press, 1960.

51. W. A. Bonger, *Race and Crime.* Translated by Margaret M. Hordyk. New York: Columbia University Press, 1943.

52. J. A. Book, "A Genetic and Neuropsychiatric Investigation of a North Swedish Population," *Acta Genetica et Statistica Medica,* 1953, 4, 1-100, 133-139, 345-414.

53. B. B. Bovell, "Psychological Considerations of Color Conflicts among Negroes," *Psychoanalytic Review,* 1943, 30, 447-459.

54. G. F. Boyd, "The Levels of Aspiration of White and Negro Children in a Non-Segregated Elementary School," *Journal of Social Psychology,* 1952, 36, 191-196.

55. W. C. Boyd, *Genetics and the Races of Man.* Boston: Little, Brown, 1956.

56. W. C. Boyd, "Genetics and the Human Race," *Science,* June 7, 1963, *140,* 1057-1064.

57. Gladyce Bradley, "A Review of Educational Problems Based on Military Selection and Classification Data in World War II," *Journal of Educational Research,* 1949, *43,* 161-174.

58. W. F. Brazziel, "Correlates of Southern Negro Personality," *Journal of Social Issues,* 1964, 20(2), in press.

59. H. C. Brearley, "The Negro and Homicide," *Social Forces,* 1930, 9, 247-253.

60. H. C. Brearley, *Homicide in the United States.* Chapel Hill: University of North Carolina Press, 1932.

61. H. C. Brearley, "The Pattern of Violence." In W. T. Couch (ed.), *Culture in the South.* Chapel Hill: University of North Carolina Press, 1934.

62. H. P. Brinton, "Negroes Who Run Afoul of the Law," *Social Forces,* 1932, *11,* 96-101.

63. A. J. Brodbeck and O. C. Irwin, "The Speech Behavior of Infants without Families," *Child Development,* 1946, *17,* 145-156.

64. I. N. Brophy, "The Luxury of Anti-Negro Prejudice," *Public Opinion Quarterly,* 1946, 9, 456-466.

65. F. Brown, "An Experimental and Critical Study of the Intelligence of Negro and White Kindergarten Children," *Journal of Genetic Psychology,* 1944, *65,* 161-175.

66. J. H. Burma, "Humor as a Technique in Race Conflict," *American Sociological Review,* 1946, *11,* 710-715.

67. J. H. Burma, "The Measurement of Negro 'Passing,'" *American Journal of Sociology,* 1946, *52,* 18-22.

68. R. V. Burton and J. W. M. Whiting, "The Absent Father and Cross-Sex Identity," *Merrill-Palmer Quarterly,* 1961, 7, 85-95.

69. M. G. Caldwell, "Personality Trends in the Youthful Male Offender," *Journal of Criminal Law, Criminology, and Police Science,* 1959, *49,* 405-416.

70. H. G. Canady, "The Effect of 'Rapport' on the I.Q.: A New Approach to the Problem of Racial Psychology," *Journal of Negro Education,* 1936, *5,* 209-219.

71. H. Cantril (ed.), *Gauging Public Opinion.* Princeton, N.J.: Princeton University Press, 1944.

72. L. Carmichael, "A Further Study of the Development of Behavior in Vertebrates Experimentally Removed from the Influence of Environmental Stimulation," *Psychological Review,* 1927, *34,* 34-47.

73. L. Carr and S. O. Roberts, " 'Social Action' as Related to Verbalized Attitudes, Self-Concept, and Background Fac-

tors," *American Psychologist*, 1963, *18*, 381 (abstract).
74. A. S. Carson and A. I. Rabin, "Verbal Comprehension and Communication in Negro and White Children," *Journal of Educational Psychology*, 1960, *51*, 47-51.
75. W. J. Cash, *The Mind of the South*. New York: Knopf, 1941.
76. H. R. Cayton, "The Psychology of the Negro under Discrimination." In A. Rose (ed.), *Race Prejudice and Discrimination*. New York: Knopf, 1951; 276-290.
77. S. N. F. Chant and S. S. Freedman, "A Quantitative Comparison of the Nationality Preferences of two Groups," *Journal of Social Psychology*, 1934, *5*, 116-120.
78. J. Chateau, "Le Milieu Professionnel du Père et l'Équilibre Caractériel des Enfants," *Enfance*, 1961, no. 1, 1-8.
79. R. Christie and Marie Jahoda (eds.), *Studies in the Scope and Method of "The Authoritarian Personality."* Glencoe, Ill.: Free Press, 1954.
80. W. M. Christopherson and J. E. Parker, "A Study of the Relative Frequency of Carcinoma of the Cervix in the Negro," *Cancer*, 1960, *13*, 711-713.
81. K. B. Clark, "Group Violence: A Preliminary Study of the Attitudinal Pattern of Its Acceptance and Rejection—a Study of the 1943 Harlem Riots," *Journal of Social Psychology*, 1944, *19*, 319-337.
82. K. B. Clark, "Candor about Negro-Jewish Relations," *Commentary*, 1946, *1*, 8-14.
83. K. B. Clark, "Desegregation: An Appraisal of the Evidence," *Journal of Social Issues*, 1953, *9*, 2-76.
84. K. B. Clark, "The Most Valuable Hidden Resource," *College Board Review*, 1956, No. 29, 23-26.
85. K. B. Clark, *Prejudice and Your Child*. Second edition. Boston: Beacon Press, 1963.
86. K. B. Clark and J. Barker, "The Zoot Effect in Personality: A Race Riot Participant," *Journal of Abnormal and Social Psychology*, 1945, *40*, 143-148.
87. K. B. Clark and Mamie P. Clark, "Racial Identification and Preference in Negro Children." In T. M. Newcomb and E. L. Hartley (eds.), *Readings in Social Psychology*. First edition. New York: Holt, 1947; 169-178.
87a. K. B. Clark and L. Plotkin, *The Negro Student at Integrated Colleges*. New York: National Scholarship Service and Fund for Negro Students, 1963.
88. R. E. Clark, "Psychoses, Income and Occupational Prestige," *American Journal of Sociology*, 1949, *54*, 433-440.
89. D. P. Clarke, "Stanford-Binet Scale L Response Patterns in Matched Racial Groups," *Journal of Negro Education*, 1941, *10*, 230-238.
90. J. A. Clausen, "Drug Addiction." In R. K. Merton and R. A.

Nisbet (eds.), *Contemporary Social Problems*. New York: Harcourt, Brace and World, 1961.

91. G. E. Coghill, *Anatomy and the Problem of Behavior*. New York: Macmillan, 1929.

92. A. K. Cohen, *Delinquent Boys: The Culture of the Gang*. Glencoe, Ill.: Free Press, 1955.

93. A. K. Cohen and J. F. Short, Jr., "Research in Delinquent Subcultures," *Journal of Social Issues*, 1958, *14*(3), 20-37.

94. A. K. Cohen and J. F. Short, Jr., "Juvenile Delinquency." In R. K. Merton and R. A. Nisbet (eds.), *Contemporary Social Problems*. New York: Harcourt, Brace and World, 1961.

95. J. S. Coleman, "Community Disorganization." In R. K. Merton and R. A. Nisbet (eds.), *Contemporary Social Problems*. New York: Harcourt, Brace and World, 1961.

96. Commission on Chronic Illness, *Chronic Illness in the United States*. Vol. IV. *Chronic Illness in a Large City: The Baltimore Study*. Cambridge, Mass.: Harvard University Press, 1957.

97. G. W. Comstock, "An Epidemiologic Study of Blood Pressure Levels in a Biracial Community in the Southern United States," *American Journal of Hygiene*, 1957, *65*(3), 271-315.

98. C. S. Coon, *The Origin of Races*. New York: Knopf, 1962.

99. R. M. Cooper and J. M. Zubek, "Effects of Enriched and Constricted Early Environments on the Learning Ability of Bright and Dull Rats," *Canadian Journal of Psychology*, 1958, *12*, 159-164.

100. T. C. Cothran, "White Stereotypes in Fiction by Negroes," *Phylon*, 1950, *11*, 252-256.

101. T. C. Cothran, "Negro Conceptions of White People," *American Journal of Sociology*, 1951, *56*, 458-467.

102. T. C. Cothran, "Negro Stereotyped Conceptions of the White Liberal," *Arkansas Academy of Science Proceedings*, 1951, *4*, 123-129.

103. F. R. Crawford, G. W. Rollins, and R. L. Sutherland, "Variations between Negroes and Whites in Concepts of Mental Illness and Its Treatment," *Annals of the New York Academy of Sciences*, 1960, *84*(17), 918-937.

104. D. R. Cressey, "Epidemiology and Individual Conduct: A Case from Criminology," *Pacific Sociological Review*, 1960, *3*, 47-58.

105. D. R. Cressey, "Crime." In R. K. Merton and R. A. Nisbet (eds.), *Contemporary Social Problems*. New York: Harcourt, Brace and World, 1961.

106. W. H. Crosby, "Diseases of the Reticulo-Endothelial System and Hematology," *Annual Review of Medicine*, 1957, *8*, 151-176.

107. F. M. Culbertson, "Modification of an Emotionally Held Attitude through Role Playing," *Journal of Abnormal and Social Psychology*, 1957, 54, 230-233.

108. Margaret W. Curti, "Intelligence Tests of White and Colored School Children in Grand Cayman," *Journal of Psychology*, 1960, 49, 13-27.

109. J. V. Dacie, *The Hemolytic Anemias: Congenital and Acquired. Part I: The Congenital Anemias.* Second revised edition. New York: Grune and Stratton, 1960.

110. W. Dameshek and F. Gunz, *Leukemia.* New York: Grune and Stratton, 1958.

111. R. G. D'Andrade, "Father Absence and Cross-Sex Identification." Unpublished doctoral dissertation, Harvard University, 1962.

112. W. G. Daniel, "The Relative Employment and Income of American Negroes," *Journal of Negro Education*, 1963 Yearbook, 32(4), 349-357.

113. R. K. Davenport, "Implications of Military Selection and Classification in Relation to Universal Military Training," *Journal of Negro Education*, 1946, 15, 585-594.

114. K. S. Davidson R. G. Gibby, E. B. McNeil, S. J. Segal, and H. Silverman, "A Preliminary Study of Negro and White Differences in Form I of the Wechsler-Bellevue Scale," *Journal of Consulting Psychology*, 1950, 14, 489-492.

115. A. Davis and J. Dollard, *Children of Bondage.* Washington, D. C.: American Council on Education, 1940.

116. A. Davis and R. J. Havighurst, "Social Class and Color Differences in Child-Rearing," *American Sociological Review*, 1946, 11, 698-710.

117. W. Dennis, "The Effect of Cradling Practices upon the Onset of Walking in Hopi Children," *Journal of Genetic Psychology*, 1940, 56, 77-86.

118. W. Dennis, "Causes of Retardation among Institutional Children: Iran," *Journal of Genetic Psychology*, 1960, 96, 47-59.

119. Celia S. Deschin, *Teen-Agers and Venereal Disease.* Atlanta: U. S. Department of Health, Education, and Welfare, 1961.

120. W. P. DeStephens, "Are Criminals Morons?" *Journal of Social Psychology*, 1953, 38, 187-199.

121. A. Deutsch, "The First U. S. Census of the Insane (1840) and Its Use as Pro-Slavery Propaganda," *Bulletin of Historical Medicine*, 1944, 15, 469-482.

122. M. Deutsch, "Minority Group and Class Status as Related to Social and Personality Factors in Scholastic Achievement," *Monograph of the Society for Applied Anthropology*, 1960, no. 2, 1-32.

123. M. Deutsch and B. Brown, "Social Influences in Negro-

White Intelligence Differences," *Journal of Social Issues,* 1964, 20(2), in press.

124. G. DeVos and H. Miner, "Algerian Culture and Personality in Change," *Sociometry,* 1958, 21, 255-268.

125. Mary H. Diggs, "Some Problems and Needs of Negro Children as Revealed by Comparative Delinquency and Crime Statistics," *Journal of Negro Education,* 1950, 19, 290-297.

126. D. A. Dobbins and B. M. Bass, "Effects of Unemployment on White and Negro Prison Admissions in Louisiana," *Journal of Criminal Law, Criminology, and Police Science,* 1958, 48, 522-525.

127. T. Dobzhansky, "A Debatable Account of the Origin of the Races," *Scientific American,* February, 1963, 208, 169-172.

128. H. H. Doddy, "The Progress of the Negro in Higher Education, 1950-1960," *Journal of Negro Education, 1963 Yearbook,* 32(4), 485-492.

129. J. Dollard, *Caste and Class in a Southern Town.* New Haven, Conn.: Yale University Press, 1937.

130. J. Dollard, "Dialectic of Insult," *American Imago,* 1939, 1, 3-25.

131. J. Dollard, L. Doob, N. E. Miller, O. H. Mowrer, and R. R. Sears, *Frustration and Aggression.* New Haven, Conn.: Yale University Press, 1939.

132. E. H. Dombey, "A Comparison of the Intelligence Test Scores of Southern and Northern Born Negroes Residing in Cleveland." Unpublished Master's thesis, Western Reserve University, 1933.

133. St. C. Drake and H. R. Cayton, *Black Metropolis.* Vol. 2, revised and enlarged edition. New York: Harper and Row, 1962.

134. C. M. Drillien, "Physical and Mental Handicap in Prematurely Born," *Journal of Obstetrics and Gynaecology* [British], 1959, 66, 721-728.

135. T. D. Dublin and B. S. Blumberg, "An Epidemiologic Approach to Inherited Disease Susceptibility," *Public Health Reports,* 1961, 76, 499-505.

136. R. J. Dubos, *Bacterial and Mycotic Infections of Man.* Philadelphia: Lippincott, 1952.

137. L. C. Dunn and T. Dobzhansky, *Heredity, Race and Society.* Revised edition. New York: New American Library, 1952.

138. O. W. Eagleson, "Comparative Studies of White and Negro Subjects in Learning to Discriminate Visual Magnitude," *Journal of Psychology,* 1937, 4, 167-197.

139. O. W. Eagleson and E. S. Bell, "The Values of Negro Women College Students," *Journal of Social Psychology,* 1945, 22, 149-154.

140. N. J. Eastman, *Williams Obstetrics.* Eleventh edition. New York: Appleton-Century-Crofts, 1956.

141. D. Echeverria, *Mirage in the West*. Princeton, N. J.: Princeton University Press, 1957.

142. G. F. Edwards, "Marriage and Family Life among Negroes," *Journal of Negro Education*, 1963 Yearbook, 32(4), 451-464.

143. S. Elkins, *Slavery*. Chicago: University of Chicago Press, 1959.

144. Mabel Elliott, "Crime and the Frontier Mores," *American Sociological Review*, 1944, 9, 185-192.

145. Mabel Elliott, "Perspective on the American Crime Problem," *Social Problems*, 1957-58, 5, 184-193.

146. R. W. Erickson, "On Special-Training-Unit Performance as an Index of Negro Ability," *Journal of Abnormal and Social Psychology*, 1946, 41, 481.

147. Hazel G. Erskine, "The Polls: Race Relations," *Public Opinion Quarterly*, 1962, 26, 137-148.

148. Arrah B. Evarts, "Dementia Praecox in the Colored Race," *Psychoanalytic Review*, 1913, 1, 388-403.

149. K. Eyferth, "Eine Untersuchung der Neger-Mischlingskinder in Westdeutschland," *Vita Humuna*, 1959, 2, 102-114.

150. R. E. L. Faris and H. W. Dunham, *Mental Disorders in Urban Areas*. Chicago: University of Chicago Press, 1939.

151. W. Faulkner, *The Mansion*. New York: Random House, 1959.

152. Federal Bureau of Investigation, *Uniform Crime Reports, 1960-61*. Washington, D. C.: U. S. Government Printing Office, 1961-62.

153. Federal Bureau of Prisons, *National Prisoner Statistics: Prisoners in State and Federal Institutions, 1950*. Leavenworth, Kansas, 1954.

154. Federal Bureau of Prisons, *National Prisoner Statistics: Prisoners Released from State and Federal Institutions, 1951*. Atlanta, Ga.: United States Penitentiary, 1955.

155. Federal Bureau of Prisons, *National Prisoner Statistics: Prisoners Released from State and Federal Institutions, 1952 and 1953*. Atlanta, Ga.: United States Penitentiary, 1957.

156. Federal Bureau of Prisons, *Federal Prisons, 1951-60*. No date listed.

157. Federal Bureau of Prisons, "Executions, 1961," *National Prisoner Statistics*, April, 1962, 28.

158. W. F. Fey, "Acceptance of Self and Others, and Its Relation to Therapy Readiness," *Journal of Clinical Psychology*, 1954, 10, 269-271.

159. W. F. Fey, "Acceptance of Self and Others: A Re-Evaluation," *Journal of Abnormal and Social Psychology*, 1955, 50, 274-276.

160. H. Finestone, "Cats, Kicks, and Color," *Social Problems*, 1957, 5, 3-13.

161. J. Fischer, "What the Negro Needs Most: A First-Class Citizens' Council," *Harper's*, July, 1962, 225, 12, 14-15, 18-19.

162. N. J. Fiumara, B. Appel, W. Hill, and H. Mescon, "Venereal Diseases Today," *New England Journal of Medicine*, 1959, 260, 863-868 and 917-924.

163. P. H. Forsham, A. E. Renold, and G. W. Thorn, "Diabetes Mellitus." In T. R. Harrison (ed.), *Principles of Internal Medicine*. New York: McGraw-Hill, 1958.

164. W. Fowler, "Cognitive Learning in Infancy and Early Childhood," *Psychological Bulletin*, 1962, 59, 116-152.

165. J. C. Franklin, "Discriminative Value and Patterns of the Wechsler-Bellevue Scales in the Examination of Delinquent Negro Boys," *Educational and Psychological Measurement*, 1945, 5, 71-85.

166. J. H. Franklin, *The Militant South: 1800-1861*. Cambridge, Mass.: Harvard University Press, 1956.

167. J. H. Franklin, *From Slavery to Freedom*. Second edition. New York: Knopf, 1961.

168. E. F. Frazier, "Problems and Needs of Negro Children and Youth Resulting from Family Disorganization," *Journal of Negro Education*, 1950, 19, 269-277.

169. E. F. Frazier, "The Negro Middle Class and Desegregation," *Social Problems*, 1957, 4, 291-301.

170. E. F. Frazier, *The Negro in the United States*. Revised edition. New York: Macmillan, 1957.

171. E. F. Frazier, *Black Bourgeoisie*. New York: Collier, 1962.

172. F. N. Freeman, K. J. Holzinger, and B. C. Mitchell, "The Influence of Environment on the Intelligence, School Achievement, and Conduct of Foster Children," *27th Yearbook, National Society of Social Science Education*, 1928, Part I, 103-217.

173. H. J. Friedsam, C. D. Whatley, and A. L. Rhodes, "Some Selected Aspects of Judicial Commitments of the Mentally Ill in Texas," *Texas Journal of Science*, 1954, 6, 27-30.

174. E. Fromm, "Selfishness and Self-Love," *Psychiatry*, 1939, 2, 507-523.

175. R. M. Frumkin, "Race and Major Mental Disorders: A Research Note," *Journal of Negro Education*, 1954, 23, 97-98.

176. J. L. Fuller and W. R. Thompson, *Behavior Genetics*. New York: Wiley, 1960.

177. M. L. Furcolow, "Tests of Immunity in Histoplasmosis," *New England Journal of Medicine*, 1963, 268, 357-361.

178. G. E. Gardner and Sadie Aaron, "The Childhood and Adolescent Adjustment of Negro Psychiatric Casualties," *American Journal of Orthopsychiatry*, 1946, 16, 481-495.

179. H. Garfinkel, "Research Note on Inter- and Intra-Racial Homicides," *Social Forces*, 1949, 27, 369-381.
180. H. E. Garrett, "Psychological Differences as Among Races," *Science*, 1945, *101*, 16-17.
181. H. E. Garrett, "A Note on the Intelligence Scores of Negroes and Whites in 1918," *Journal of Abnormal and Social Psychology*, 1945, 40, 344-346.
182. H. E. Garrett, "Klineberg's Chapter on Race and Psychology: A Review," *The Mankind Quarterly*, 1960, *1*, 15-22.
183. H. E. Garrett, "The Equalitarian Dogma," *Mankind Quarterly*, 1961, *1*, 253-257.
184. H. E. Garrett, "Rejoinder by Garrett," *Newsletter of the Society for the Psychological Study of Social Issues*, May, 1962, 1-2.
185. H. E. Garrett, "The SPSSI and Racial Differences," *American Psychologist*, 1962, *17*, 260-263.
186. W. C. George, *The Biology of the Race Problem*. New York: National Putnam Letters Committee, 1962.
187. A. R. Gilliland, "Environmental Influences on Infant Intelligence Test Scores," *Harvard Educational Review*, 1949, *19*, 142-146.
188. A. R. Gilliland, "Socioeconomic Status and Race as Factors in Infant Intelligence Test Scores," *Child Development*, 1951, *22*, 271-273.
189. E. Ginsberg, *The Negro Potential*. New York: Columbia University Press, 1956.
190. B. Glass, *Genes and the Man*. New York: Columbia University Press, 1943.
191. B. Glass, "On the Unlikelihood of Significant Admixture of Genes from the North American Indians in the Present Composition of the Negroes of the United States," *American Journal of Human Genetics*, 1955, *7*, 368-385.
192. N. D. Glenn, "Some Changes in the Relative Status of American Non-Whites, 1940 to 1960," *Phylon*, 1963, *24*, 109-122.
193. S. Glueck and Eleanor T. Glueck, *Unraveling Juvenile Delinquency*. New York: Commonwealth Fund, 1950.
194. Regina M. Goff, "Problems and Emotional Difficulties of Negro Children Due to Race," *Journal of Negro Education*, 1950, *19*, 152-158.
195. M. Gold, "Suicide, Homicide, and the Socialization of Aggression," *American Journal of Sociology*, 1958, *63*, 651-661.
196. W. Goldfarb, "Emotional and Intellectual Consequences of Psychologic Deprivation in Infancy: A Revaluation." In P. H. Hoch and J. Zubin (eds.), *Psychopathology of Childhood*. New York: Grune and Stratton, 1955.
197. M. S. Goldstein, "Longevity and Health Status of the Negro

American," *Journal of Negro Education, 1963 Yearbook,* 32(4), 337-348.

198. Mary E. Goodman, *Race Awareness in Young Children.* Cambridge, Mass.: Addison-Wesley, 1952.

199. H. Gordon, *Mental and Scholastic Tests Among Retarded Children.* London: Board of Education (Educational Pamphlet no. 44), 1923.

200. Pearl M. Gore and J. B. Rotter, "A Personality Correlate of Social Action," *Journal of Personality,* 1963, *31,* 58-64.

201. H. F. Gosnell and R. E. Martin, "The Negro as Voter and Office Holder," *Journal of Negro Education, 1963 Yearbook, 32*(4), 415-425.

202. I. I. Gottesman, "Genetic Aspects of Intelligent Behavior." In N. Ellis (ed.), *The Handbook of Mental Deficiency.* New York: McGraw-Hill, 1963; 253-296.

203. H. G. Gough, "A Nonintellectual Intelligence Test," *Journal of Consulting Psychology,* 1953, *17,* 242-246.

204. Mary Gower, "Physical Defects of White and Negro Families examined by the Farm Security Administration, 1940," *Journal of Negro Education,* 1949, *18,* 251-265.

205. J. S. Gray and A. J. Thompson, "Ethnic Prejudices of White and Negro College Students," *Journal of Abnormal and Social Psychology,* 1953, *48,* 311-313.

206. Susan W. Gray, "A Note on the Values of Southern College Women, White and Negro," *Journal of Social Psychology,* 1947, *25,* 239-241.

207. J. H. Griffin, *Black Like Me.* Boston, Mass.: Houghton, Mifflin, 1961.

208. M. M. Grossack, "Perceived Negro Group Belongingness and Social Rejection," *Journal of Psychology,* 1954, *38,* 127-130.

209. M. M. Grossack, "Group Belongingness among Negroes," *Journal of Social Psychology,* 1956, *43,* 167-180.

210. M. M. Grossack, "Group Belongingness and Authoritarianism in Southern Negroes—a Research Note," *Phylon,* 1957, *18,* 261-266.

211. M. M. Grossack, "Some Personality Characteristics of Southern Negro Students," *Journal of Social Psychology,* 1957, *46,* 125-131.

212. E. G. Guba, P. W. Jackson, and C. E. Bidwell, "Occupational Choice and the Teaching Career," *Educational Research Bulletin,* 1959, *38,* 1-12, 27-28.

213. Lillian Guralnick, *Mortality by Occupation and Industry Among Men 20 to 64 Years of Age: United States, 1950.* Washington, D. C.: U. S. Government Printing Office, 1962 (Vital Statistics Special Reports, 52(2)).

214. E. A. Haggard, "Social Status and Intelligence: An experimental Study of Certain Cultural Determinants of Meas-

ured Intelligence," *Genetic Psychology Monographs*, 1954, *49*, 141-186.

215. E. F. Hammer, "Frustration-Aggression Hypothesis Extended to Socio-Racial Areas: Comparison of Negro and White Children's H-T-P's," *Psychiatric Quarterly*, 1953, *27*, 597-607.

216. E. F. Hammer, "Comparison of the Performances of Negro Children and Adolescents on Two Tests of Intelligence, One an Emergency Scale," *Journal of Genetic Psychology*, 1954, *84*, 85-93.

217. C. F. Hansen, *Addendum: A Five-Year Report on Desegregation in the Washington, D. C. Schools.* New York: Anti-Defamation League of B'nai B'rith, 1960.

218. J. Harding and R. Hogrefe, "Attitudes of White Department Store Employees toward Negro Co-Workers," *Journal of Social Issues*, 1952, *8*, 18-28.

219. H. F. Harlow, "The Formation of Learning Sets," *Psychological Review*, 1949, *56*, 51-65.

220. P. A. Harper, L. K. Fischer, and R. V. Rider, "Neurological and Intellectual Status of Prematures at Three to Five Years of Age," *Journal of Pediatrics*, 1959, *55*, 679-690.

221. R. F. Harrell, E. R. Woodyard, and A. I. Gates, "Influence of Vitamin Supplementation of Diets of Pregnant and Lactating Women on Intelligence of Their Offspring," *Metabolism*, 1956, *5*, 555-562.

222. S. I. Hayakawa, "The Semantics of Being Negro," *ETC: A Review of General Semantics*, 1953, *10*, 163-175.

223. V. W. Henderson, *The Economic Status of Negroes: In the Nation and in the South.* Atlanta, Ga.: Southern Regional Council, 1963.

224. A. F. Henry and J. F. Short, Jr., *Suicide and Homicide.* Glencoe, Ill.: Free Press, 1954.

225. B. D. Herring, "Pernicious Anemia and the American Negro," *American Practitioner*, 1962, *13*, 544-548.

226. M. J. Herskovits, "On the Relation between Negro-White Mixture and Standing in Intelligence Tests," *Pediatrics Sem.*, 1926, *33*, 30-42.

227. M. J. Herskovits, *The Anthropometry of the American Negro.* New York: Columbia University Press, 1930.

228. Dorothy Heyman, "Manifestations of Psychoneurosis in Negroes," *Mental Hygiene*, 1945, *29*, 231-235.

229. C. Higgins and Cathryne Sivers, "A Comparison of Stanford-Binet and Colored Raven Progressive Matrices I.Q.'s for Children with Low Socioeconomic Status," *Journal of Consulting Psychology*, 1958, *22*, 465-468.

230. M. C. Hill and T. D. Ackiss, "Social Classes: A Frame of Reference for the Study of Negro Society," *Social Forces*, 1943, *22*, 92-98.

231. H. E. Hilleboe and B. W. Larimore (eds.), *Preventive Medicine*. Philadelphia: Saunders, 1962.
232. J. Himmelhoch, "Tolerance and Personality Needs: A Study of the Liberalization of Ethnic Attitudes among Minority Group College Students," *American Sociological Review*, 1950, *15*, 79-88.
233. E. A. Hoebel, *Man in the Primitive World*. Second edition. New York: McGraw-Hill, 1958.
234. J. E. Hokanson and G. Calden, "Negro-White Differences on the MMPI," *Journal of Clinical Psychology*, 1960, *16*, 32-33.
235. A. B. Hollingshead and F. C. Redlich, *Social Class and Mental Illness: A Community Study*. New York: Wiley, 1958.
236. J. Hope, II, and E. Shelton, "The Negro in the Federal Government," *Journal of Negro Education, 1963 Yearbook, 32*(4), 367-374.
237. Karen Horney, *The Neurotic Personality of Our Time*. New York: Norton, 1937.
238. Karen Horney, *Our Inner Conflicts*. New York: Norton, 1945.
239. C. I. Hovland, Enid H. Campbell, and T. Brock, "The Effects of 'Commitment' on Opinion Change Following Communication." In C. I. Hovland (ed.), *The Order of Presentation in Persuasion*. New Haven, Conn.: Yale University Press, 1957.
240. W. W. Howells, "Our Family Tree," *New York Times Book Review Section*, December 9, 1962, 3.
241. J. H. Hughes and G. C. Thompson, "A Comparison of the Value Systems of Southern Negro and Northern White Youth," *Journal of Educational Psychology*, 1954, *45*, 300-309.
242. F. S. Hulse, "Exogamie et hétérosis," *Arch. Suisses d'Anthropologie Générale*, 1958, 22, 103-125.
243. J. M. Hunt, *Intelligence and Experience*. New York: Ronald, 1951.
244. W. A. Hunt, "The Relative Incidence of Psychoneurosis among Negroes," *Journal of Consulting Psychology*, 1947, *11*, 133-136.
245. W. A. Hunt, "Negro-White Differences in Intelligence in World War II—a Note of Caution," *Journal of Abnormal and Social Psychology*, 1947, 42, 254-255.
246. J. G. Hurst, "Relationships between Performance on Preschool and Adult Intelligence Measures." Paper presented at the Annual Meeting of the American Psychological Association, held at Philadelphia, August, 1963.
247. H. H. Hyman and P. B. Sheatsley, "Attitudes toward Desegregation," *Scientific American*, 1956, *195*, 35-39.
248. R. R. Ireland, "An Exploratory Study of Minority Group

Membership," *Journal of Negro Education*, 1951, 20, 164-168.

249. A. P. Iskrant and E. Rogot, "Trends in Tuberculosis Mortality in Continental United States," *Public Health Reports*, 1953, 68, 911-919.

250. S. P. Ivins, "Psychoses in the Negro: A Preliminary Study," *Delaware State Medical Journal*, 1950, 22, 212-213.

251. E. G. Jaco, *The Social Epidemiology of Mental Disorders*. New York: Russell Sage Foundation, 1960.

251a. W. P. Janicki, "Cross-National Study of Satisfaction." Unpublished paper.

252. I. L. Janis and B. T. King, "The Influence of Role-Playing on Opinion-Change," *Journal of Abnormal and Social Psychology*, 1954, 49, 211-218.

253. M. Janowitz, *The Professional Soldier*. New York: Free Press, 1960.

254. M. D. Jenkins, "The Upper Limit of Ability among American Negroes," *Scientific Monthly*, 1948, 66, 399-401.

255. M. D. Jenkins, "Intellectually Superior Negro Youth: Their Problems and Needs," *Journal of Negro Education*, 1950, 19, 322-332.

256. M. D. Jenkins and Constance M. Randall, "Differential Characteristics of Superior and Unselected Negro College Students," *Journal of Social Psychology*, 1948, 27, 187-202.

257. W. W. Jenkins, "An Experimental Study of the Relationship of Legitimate and Illegitimate Birth Status to School and Personal Adjustment of Negro Children," *American Journal of Sociology*, 1958, 64, 169-173.

258. C. S. Johnson, *Growing up in the Black Belt*. Washington, D.C.: American Council on Education, 1941.

259. C. S. Johnson, "The Socio-Economic Background of Negro Health Status," *Journal of Negro Education*, 1949, 18, 429-435.

260. G. B. Johnson, "The Negro and Crime," *Annals of the American Academy of Political and Social Science*, 1941, 217, 93-104.

261. J. W. Johnson, *The Autobiography of an Ex-Coloured Man*. New York: Hill and Wang, 1960 (originally published by Knopf, 1912).

262. R. Johnson, "Negro Reactions to Minority Group Status." In M. L. Barron (ed.), *American Minorities*. New York: Knopf, 1957; 192-212.

263. F. N. Jones and M. G. Arrington, "The Explanations of Physical Phenomena Given by White and Negro Children," *Comparative Psychology Monographs*, 1945, 18(5), 1-43.

264. J. Kagan, L. W. Sontag, C. T. Baker, and Virginia Nelson,

"Personality and I. Q. Change," *Journal of Abnormal and Social Psychology*, 1958, 56, 261-266.

265. F. J. Kallman, "Twin Samples in Relation to Adjustive Problems of Man," *Transactions of the New York Academy of Science*, 1951, 13, 270-275.

266. A. Kardiner and L. Ovesey, *The Mark of Oppression*. New York: Norton, 1951.

267. J. R. Karns, "Tuberculosis in Medical Students at the University of Maryland," *American Review of Tuberculosis*, 1959, 79, 746-755.

268. B. P. Karon, *The Negro Personality*. New York: Springer, 1958.

269. B. D. Karpinos, "Visual Acuity of Selectees and Army Inductees," *Human Biology*, 1944, 16, 1-14.

270. B. D. Karpinos, "Racial Differences in Visual Acuity," *Public Health Reports*, 1960, 75, 1045-1050.

271. I. Katz and L. Benjamin, "Effects of White Authoritarianism in Biracial Work Groups," *Journal of Abnormal and Social Psychology*, 1960, 61, 448-456.

272. I. Katz, E. G. Epps, and L. J. Axelson, "The Effects of Anticipated Comparison with Whites and with Other Negroes upon the Digit-Symbol Performance of Negro College Students." Unpublished paper.

273. H. C. Kelman, "Attitude Change as a Function of Response Restriction," *Human Relations*, 1953, 6, 185-214.

274. M. Kempton, "Footnotes on an Anniversary," *Progressive*, December, 1962, 26, 53-56.

275. W. M. Kephart, *Racial Factors and Urban Law Enforcement*. Philadelphia: University of Pennsylvania Press, 1957.

276. A. C. Kerckhoff and T. C. McCormick, "Marginal Status and Marginal Personality," *Social Forces*, 1955, 34, 48-55.

277. B. T. King and I. L. Janis, "Comparison of the Effectiveness of Improvised Versus Non-Improvised Role Playing in Producing Opinion Changes," *Human Relations*, 1956, 9, 177-186.

278. S. A. Kirk, *Early Education of the Mentally Retarded*. Urbana, Ill.: University of Illinois Press, 1958.

279. Evelyn M. Kitagawa and P. M. Hauser, "Trends in Differential Fertility and Mortality in a Metropolis—Chicago." In E. W. Burgess and D. J. Bogue (eds.), *Research Contributions to Urban Sociology*. Chicago: University of Chicago Press, in press.

280. R. J. Kleiner and S. Parker, "Migration and Mental Illness: A New Look," *American Sociological Review*, 1959, 24, 687-690.

281. R. J. Kleiner and S. Parker, "Goal-Striving, Social Status, and Mental Disorder: A Research Review," *American Sociological Review*, 1963, 28, 189-203.

282. R. J. Kleiner, J. Tuckman, and Martha Lavell, "Mental Disorder and Status Based on Religious Affiliation," *Human Relations*, 1959, *12*, 273-276.

283. R. J. Kleiner, J. Tuckman, and Martha Lavell, "Mental Disorder and Status Based on Race," *Psychiatry*, 1960, *23*, 271-274.

284. O. Klineberg, "An Experimental Study of Speed and Other Factors in 'Racial' Differences," *Archives of Psychology*, 1928, *15*, no. 93.

285. O. Klineberg, *Negro Intelligence and Selective Migration*. New York: Columbia University Press, 1935.

286. Patricia Knapp and Sophia Cambria, "The Attitudes of Negro Unmarried Mothers toward Illegitimacy," *Smith College Studies in Social Work*, 1947, *17*, 185-203.

287. Hilda Knobloch and B. Pasamanick, "Further Observations on the Behavioral Development of Negro Children," *Journal of Genetic Psychology*, 1953, *83*, 137-157.

288. Hilda Knobloch and B. Pasamanick, "Environmental Factors Affecting Human Development before and after Birth," *Pediatrics*, 1960, *26*, 210-218.

289. Hilda Knobloch and B. Pasamanick, "Mental Subnormality," *New England Journal of Medicine*, 1962, *266*, 1092-1097.

290. Hilda Knobloch, R. Rider, P. Harper, and B. Pasamanick, "Effect of Prematurity on Health and Growth," *American Journal of Public Health*, 1959, *49*, 1164-1173.

291. Helen L. Koch, "The Social Distance between Certain Racial, Nationality, and Skin Pigmentation Groups in Selected Populations of American School Children," *Journal of Genetic Psychology*, 1946, *68*, 63-95.

292. P. R. Koehler, J. I. Fabrikant, and R. J. Dickson, "Observations on the Behavior of Testicular Tumors with Comments on Racial Incidence," *The Journal of Urology*, 1962, *87*, 577-579.

293. M. L. Kohn and J. A. Clausen, "Parental Authority Behavior and Schizophrenia," *American Journal of Orthopsychiatry*, 1956, *26*, 297-313.

294. D. Krech, R. S. Crutchfield, and E. L. Ballachey, *Individual in Society*. New York: McGraw-Hill, 1962.

295. Catherine Landreth and Barbara C. Johnson, "Young Children's Responses to a Picture and Inset Test Designed to Reveal Reactions to Persons of different Skin Color," *Child Development*, 1953, *24*, 63-80.

296. A. M. Lee and N. D. Humphrey, *Race Riot*. New York: Dryden, 1943.

297. E. S. Lee, "Negro Intelligence and Selective Migration: A Philadelphia Test of the Klineberg Hypothesis," *American Sociological Review*, 1951, *16*, 227-233.

298. E. S. Lee and Anne S. Lee, "The Differential Fertility of

the American Negro," *American Sociological Review*, 1952, 17, 437-447.

299. Harper Lee, *To Kill A Mockingbird*. New York: Popular Library, 1962.

300. A. B. Lerner, "Hormonal Control of Pigmentation," *Annual Review of Medicine*, 1960, 11, 187-194.

301. W. F. Lever, *Histopathology of the Skin*. Third edition. Philadelphia: Lippincott, 1961.

302. S. A. Levitan, *Youth Employment Act*. Kalamazoo, Mich.: Upjohn Institute for Employment Research, 1963.

303. E. A. Lew, "Cancer of the Respiratory Tract," *Journal of the International College of Surgeons*, 1955, 24, 12-27.

304. E. A. Lew, "Some Implications of Mortality Statistics Relating to Coronary Artery Disease," *Journal of Chronic Diseases*, 1957, 6, 192-209.

305. H. S. Liddell, "Conditioned Reflex Method and Experimental Neurosis." In J. M. Hunt (ed.), *Personality and the Behavior Disorders*. New York: Ronald, 1946; Vol. I, Chapter 12.

306. C. E. Lincoln, *The Black Muslims in America*. Boston: Beacon Press, 1961.

307. R. Linton, *Culture and Mental Disorders*. Springfield, Ill.: Thomas, 1956.

308. L. F. Litwack, *North of Slavery*. Chicago: University of Chicago Press, 1961.

309. R. Logan, *The Negro in American Life and Thought: The Nadir, 1877-1901*. New York: Dial, 1954.

310. N. J. London and J. K. Myers, "Young Offenders: Psychopathology and Social Factors," *Archives of General Psychiatry*, 1961, 4, 274-282.

311. H. H. Long, "The Intelligence of Colored Elementary Pupils in Washington, D.C.," *Journal of Negro Education*, 1934, 3, 205-222.

312. A. J. Lott and Bernice E. Lott, *Negro and White Youth: A Psychological Study in a Border-State Community*. New York: Holt, Rinehart and Winston, 1963.

313. N. M. Luger, "The Incidence of Lymphogranuloma Venereum as Determined by the Quantitative Complement-Fixation Test," *American Journal of Syphilis*, 1950, 34, 351-355.

314. D. B. Lynn and W. L. Sawrey, "The Effects of Father-Absence on Norwegian Boys and Girls," *Journal of Abnormal and Social Psychology*, 1959, 59, 258-262.

315. Eleanor E. Maccoby, J. P. Johnson, and R. M. Church, "Community Integration and the Social Control of Juvenile Delinquency," *Journal of Social Issues*, 1958, 14(3), 38-51.

316. S. Machover, "Cultural and Racial Variations in Patterns of

Intellect," *Teachers College Contributions to Education*, 1943, no. 875.

317. Barbara MacKenzie, "The Importance of Contact in Determining Attitudes toward Negroes," *Journal of Abnormal and Social Psychology*, 1948, 43, 417-441.

318. J. B. Maller, "Mental Ability and Its Relation to Physical Health and Social Economic Status," *Psychological Clinic*, 1933, 22, 101-107.

319. B. Malzberg, "Mental Disease among American Negroes: A Statistical Analysis." In O. Klineberg (ed.), *Characteristics of the American Negro*. New York: Harper, 1944; 373-395.

320. B. Malzberg, "Mental Disease among Negroes in New York State, 1939-1941," *Mental Hygiene*, 1953, 37, 450-476.

321. B. Malzberg, "Mental Disease among Native and Foreign-Born Negroes in New York State," *Journal of Negro Education*, 1956, 25, 175-181.

322. B. Malzberg, "Mental Disease among Negroes: An Analysis of First Admissions in New York State, 1949-1951," *Mental Hygiene*, 1959, 43, 422-459.

323. B. Malzberg and E. S. Lee, *Migration and Mental Disease*. New York: Social Science Research Council, 1956.

324. J. H. Mann, "The Influence of Racial Prejudice on Sociometric Choices and Perceptions," *Sociometry*, 1958, 21, 150-158.

325. J. W. Mann, "Group Relations and the Marginal Personality," *Human Relations*, 1958, 11, 77-92.

326. E. Marcovitz and H. J. Myers, "The Marijuana Addict in the Army," *War Medicine, Chicago*, 1944, 6, 382-391.

327. P. A. Marks and Ruth T. Gross, "Erythrocyte Glucose-6-Phosphate Dehydrogenase Deficiency: Evidence of Differences between Negroes and Caucasians with Respect to This Genetically Determined Trait," *Journal of Clinical Investigation*, 1959, 38, 2253-2262.

328. R. Marshall, "The Negro and Organized Labor," *Journal of Negro Education*, 1963 Yearbook, 32(4), 375-389.

329. D. R. Matthews and J. W. Prothro, "Political Factors and Negro Voter Registration in the South," *American Political Science Review*, 1963, 57, 355-367.

330. K. F. Maxcy (ed.), *Rosenau Preventive Medicine and Public Health*. Eighth edition. New York: Appleton-Century-Crofts, 1956.

331. J. M. May, *The Ecology of Human Disease*. New York: MD Publications, 1958.

332. M. Mayer, "The Good Slum Schools," *Harpers*, April, 1961, 222, 46-52.

333. J. L. McCary, "Reactions to Frustration by some Cultural and Racial Groups," *Personality*, 1951, 1, 84-102.

334. P. McCauley and E. D. Ball (eds.), *Southern Schools: Progress and Problems*. Nashville, Tenn.: Southern Education Reporting Service, 1959.

335. D. C. McClelland, *The Achieving Society*. Princeton, N.J.: Van Nostrand, 1961.

336. W. M. McCord and N. J. Demerath, III, "Negro Versus White Intelligence: A Continuing Controversy," *Harvard Educational Review*, 1958, 28, 120-135.

337. P. A. McDaniel and N. Babchuk, "Negro Conceptions of White People in a Northeastern City," *Phylon*, 1960, 21, 7-19.

338. Myrtle B. McGraw, "A Comparative Study of a Group of Southern White and Negro Infants," *Genetic Psychology Monograph*, 1931, 10, 1-105.

338a. Myrtle B. McGraw, "Need for Denial," *American Psychologist*, 1964, 19, 56.

339. F. McGurk, "Socio-Economic Status and Culturally-Weighted Test Scores of Negro Subjects," *Journal of Applied Psychology*, 1953, 37, 276-277.

340. F. McGurk, "On White and Negro Test Performance and Socio-Economic Factors," *Journal of Abnormal and Social Psychology*, 1953, 48, 448-450.

341. F. McGurk, "Psychological Tests: A Scientist's Report on Race Differences," *U. S. News and World Report*, September 21, 1956, 92-96.

342. F. McGurk, "Negro vs. White Intelligence—an Answer," *Harvard Educational Review*, 1959, 29, 54-62.

343. Helen V. McLean, "The Emotional Health of Negroes," *Journal of Negro Education*, 1949, 18, 283-290.

344. R. McQueen and B. Churn, "The Intelligence and Educational Achievement of a Matched Sample of White and Negro Students," *School and Society*, 1960, 88, 327-329.

345. M. Meenes, "A Comparison of Racial Stereotypes of 1935 and 1942," *Journal of Social Psychology*, 1943, 17, 327-336.

346. A. Meier, "Negro Protest Movements and Organizations," *Journal of Negro Education*, 1963 Yearbook, 32(4), 437-450.

347. Ann D. Merbaum, "Need for Achievement in Negro Children." Unpublished Master's dissertation, University of North Carolina, 1960.

348. R. K. Merton, "The Self-fulfilling Prophecy," *Antioch Review*, 1948, 8, 193-210.

349. R. K. Merton, *Social Theory and Social Structure*. Revised edition. Glencoe, Ill.: Free Press, 1957.

350. R. K. Merton and Alice S. Kitt, "Contributions to the Theory of Reference Group Behavior." In R. K. Merton and P. F. Lazarsfeld (eds.), *Continuities in Social Re-*

search: *Studies in the Scope and Method of "The American Soldier."* Glencoe, Ill.: Free Press, 1950.

351. Metropolitan Life Insurance Company, "Maternal Mortality in Recent Years," *Statistical Bulletin*, September, 1961, 42, 6-8.

352. Metropolitan Life Insurance Company, "Cystic Fibrosis: A Child Health Problem," *Statistical Bulletin*, March, 1962, 43, 3-5.

353. Metropolitan Life Insurance Company, "Reduction in Perinatal Mortality," *Statistical Bulletin*, May, 1962, 43, 6-8.

354. Metropolitan Life Insurance Company, "Recent Trends in Heart Disease," *Statistical Bulletin*, June, 1962, 43, 1-4.

355. Metropolitan Life Insurance Company, "Recent Trends in Diabetes Mortality," *Statistical Bulletin*, August, 1962, 43, 1-3.

356. Metropolitan Life Insurance Company, "Improved Mortality among Colored Policyholders," *Statistical Bulletin*, August, 1962, 43, 6-8.

357. Metropolitan Life Insurance Company, "The American Widow," *Statistical Bulletin*, November, 1962, 43, 1-4.

358. Metropolitan Life Insurance Company, "Cancer Mortality Trends among Urban Wage-Earners," *Statistical Bulletin*, December, 1962, 43, 1-3.

359. Metropolitan Life Insurance Company, "Progress in Longevity since 1850," *Statistical Bulletin*, July, 1963, 44, 1-3.

360. Metropolitan Life Insurance Company, "Nationwide Rise in Educational Level," *Statistical Bulletin*, August, 1963, 44, 3-5.

361. W. B. Miller, "Lower Class Culture as a Generating Milieu of Gang Delinquency," *Journal of Social Issues*, 1958, 14(3), 5-19.

362. G. Millstein, "A Negro Says It with Jokes," *New York Times Magazine*, April 30, 1961, 34, 37, 39-40.

363. Esther Milner, "Some Hypotheses Concerning the Influence of Segregation on Negro Personality Development," *Psychiatry*, 1953, 16, 291-297.

364. W. Mischel, "Preference for Delayed Reinforcement and Social Responsibility," *Journal of Social and Abnormal Psychology*, 1961, 62, 1-7.

365. W. Mischel, "Delay of Gratification, Need for Achievement, and Acquiescence in Another Culture," *Journal of Abnormal and Social Psychology*, 1961, 62, 543-552.

366. W. Mischel, "Father-Absence and Delay of Gratification: Cross-Cultural Comparisons," *Journal of Abnormal and Social Psychology*, 1961, 63, 116-124.

367. M. F. A. Montagu, *Man's Most Dangerous Myth: The Fallacy of Race.* Revised edition. New York: Columbia University Press, 1945.

368. M. F. A. Montagu, "Intelligence of Northern Negroes and Southern Whites in the First World War," *American Journal of Psychology*, 1945, 58, 161-188.
369. J. K. Morland, "Racial Recognition by Nursery School Children in Lynchburg, Virginia," *Social Forces*, 1958, 37, 132-137.
370. D. Morse, "Prehistoric Tuberculosis in America," *American Review of Respiratory Diseases*, 1961, 83, 489-504.
371. E. R. Moses, "Differentials in Crime Rates between Negroes and Whites, Based on Comparisons of Four Socio-Economically Equated Areas," *American Sociological Review*, 1947, 12, 411-420.
372. O. H. Mowrer and A. D. Ullman, "Time as a Determinant in Integrative Learning," *Psychological Review*, 1945, 52, 61-90.
373. W. I. Murray, "The I. Q. and Social Class in the Negro Caste," *Southwestern Journal of Anthropology*, 1949, 4, 187-201.
374. P. H. Mussen, "Differences between the TAT Responses of Negro and White Boys," *Journal of Consulting Psychology*, 1953, 17, 373-376.
375. P. H. Mussen and L. Distler, "Masculinity, Identification, and Father-Son Relationships," *Journal of Abnormal and Social Psychology*, 1959, 59, 350-356.
376. H. J. Myers and L. Yochelson, "Color Denial in the Negro: A Preliminary Report," *Psychiatry*, 1948, 11, 39-46.
377. J. K. Myers and B. H. Roberts, "Some Relationships between Religion, Ethnic Origin and Mental Illness." In M. Sklare (ed.), *The Jews: Social Patterns of an American Group*. Glencoe, Ill.: Free Press, 1958.
378. J. K. Myers and B. H. Roberts, *Family and Class Dynamics in Mental Illness*. New York: Wiley, 1959.
379. National Committee for Children and Youth, *Social Dynamite*. Washington, D.C.: National Committee for Children and Youth, 1961.
380. National Office of Vital Statistics, *Death Rates for Selected Causes by Age, Color, and Sex: United States and Each State, 1949-1951*. Washington, D.C.: U.S. Government Printing Office, 1959.
381. T. E. Newland and W. C. Lawrence, "Chicago Non-Verbal Examination Results on an East Tennessee Negro Population," *Journal of Clinical Psychology*, 1953, 9, 44-46.
382. *Newsweek* editors, "The Negro in America," *Newsweek*, July 29, 1963, 62, 15-34.
383. *Newsweek* editors, "How Whites Feel about Negroes: A Painful American Dilemma," *Newsweek*, October 21, 1963, 62, 44-57.
384. Eunice Newton, "Verbal Destitution: The Pivotal Barrier

to Learning," *Journal of Negro Education*, 1960, 24, 497-499.

385. Eunice Newton and E. H. West, "The Progress of the Negro in Elementary and Secondary Education," *Journal of Negro Education*, 1963 Yearbook, 32(4), 465-484.

385a. A. D. Noel, "Group Identification among Negroes: An Empirical Analysis," *Journal of Social Issues*, 1964, 20(2), in press.

386. H. Olansky, "The Harlem Riot: A Study in Mass Frustration," *Social Analysis*, 1943, 1, 1-29.

387. R. T. Osborn, "Racial Differences in Mental Growth and School Achievement: A Longitudinal Study," *Psychological Reports*, 1960, 7, 233-239.

388. D. S. Palermo, "Racial Comparisons and Additional Normative Data on the Children's Manifest Anxiety Scale," *Child Development*, 1959, 30, 53-57.

389. C. M. Palmer, H. E. Sprang, and C. L. Hans, "Electroshock Therapy in Schizophrenia: A Statistical Survey of 455 Cases," *Journal of Nervous and Mental Disease*, 1951, 114, 162-171.

390. S. Parker, R. J. Kleiner, and Rochelle M. Eskin, "Social Status and Psychopathology." Paper presented at the Annual Meeting of the Society of Physical Anthropology, held at Philadelphia, April, 1962.

391. B. Pasamanick, "A Comparative Study of the Behavioral Development of Negro Infants," *Journal of Genetic Psychology*, 1946, 69, 3-44.

392. B. Pasamanick, "Some Misconceptions Concerning Differences in the Racial Prevalence of Mental Disease," *American Journal of Orthopsychiatry*, 1963, 33(1), 72-86.

393. B. Pasamanick and P. H. Knapp (eds.), *Social Aspects of Psychiatry*, Washington, D.C.: American Psychiatric Association, 1958.

394. B. Pasamanick and Hilda Knobloch, "Early Language Behavior in Negro Children and the Testing of Intelligence," *Journal of Abnormal and Social Psychology*, 1955, 50, 401-402.

395. B. Pasamanick and Hilda Knobloch, "The Contribution of Some Organic Factors to School Retardation in Negro Children," *Journal of Negro Education*, 1958, 27, 4-9.

396. I. P. Pavlov, *Lectures on Conditioned Reflexes*. New York: International, 1928.

397. H. M. Payne, "Leading Causes of Death among Negroes: Tuberculosis," *Journal of Negro Education*, 1949, 18, 225-234.

398. J. E. Perkins, "The Stage is Set—a Program for More Effective Control of Tuberculosis in the United States," *Tuberculosis Abstracts*, October, 1954, 27, no. 10.

399. J. Peterson and L. H. Lanier, "Studies in the Comparative Abilities of Whites and Negroes," *Mental Measurement Monograph*, 1929, no. 5.

400. T. F. Pettigrew, "Negro American Personality: Why Isn't More Known?" *Journal of Social Issues*, 1964, 20(2), in press.

401. T. F. Pettigrew, "Skin Color and Negro American Personality." Unpublished paper.

402. T. F. Pettigrew, "Father-Absence and Negro Adult Personality: A Research Note." Unpublished paper.

403. T. F. Pettigrew, "Authoritarianism among Negro Americans." Unpublished paper.

404. T. F. Pettigrew, "The Negro Respondent: New Data on Old Problems." Unpublished paper.

405. T. F. Pettigrew and R. L. Nuttall, "Negro American Perception of the Irradiation Illusion," *Perceptual and Motor Skills*, 1963, 17, 98.

406. T. F. Pettigrew and Rosalind B. Spier, "The Ecological Structure of Negro Homicide," *American Journal of Sociology*, 1962, 67, 621-629.

407. T. F. Pettigrew and G. S. Tracy, "Correlates of Prison Adjustment." Unpublished paper.

408. E. L. Phillips, "Attitudes toward Self and Others: A Brief Questionnaire Report," *Journal of Consulting Psychology*, 1951, 15, 79-81.

409. J. H. Phillips and G. E. Burch, "Cardiovascular Diseases in the White and Negro Races," *American Journal of the Medical Sciences*, 1959, 238, 97-124.

410. J. Piaget, *The Psychology of Intelligence*. Translated by M. Piercy and D. E. Berlyne. London: Routledge and Kegan Paul, 1947.

411. D. M. Pillsbury, W. B. Shelley, and A. M. Kligman, *Dermatology*. Philadelphia: Saunders, 1956.

412. O. Pollack, "A Statistical Investigation of the Criminality of Old Age," *Journal of Clinical Psychopathology*, 1944, 5, 745-767.

413. W. S. Pollitzer, "The Negroes of Charleston (S.C.); A Study of Hemoglobin Types, Serology, and Morphology," *American Journal of Physical Anthropology*, 1958, 16, 241-263.

414. W. S. Pollitzer, "Review of Coon's 'The Origin of Races,'" *American Journal of Human Genetics*, 1963, 15, 216-218.

415. A. L. Porterfield and R. H. Talbert, "A Decade of Differentials and Trends in Serious Crimes in 86 American Cities by Southern and Non-Southern Pairs," *Social Forces*, 1952, 31, 60-68.

416. W. D. Postell, "Mental Health among the Slave Population

of Southern Plantations," *American Journal of Psychiatry*, 1953, *110*, 52-54.

417. Hortense Powdermaker, "The Channeling of Negro Aggression by the Cultural Process," *American Journal of Sociology*, 1943, *48*, 750-758.

418. D. O. Price and Ruth Searles, "Some Effects of Interviewer-Respondent Interaction on Responses in a Survey Situation." Paper presented at the Annual Meeting of the American Statistical Association, held in New York, December 30, 1961.

419. Public Health Service, V D *Fact Sheet, 1961*, Atlanta, Ga.: Public Health Service, 1962.

420. R. W. Pugh, "A Comparative Study of the Adjustment of Negro Students in Mixed and Separate High Schools," *Journal of Negro Education*, 1943, *12*, 607-616.

421. C. Putnam, *Race and Reason: A Yankee View*. Washington, D.C.: Public Affairs Press, 1961.

422. M. Rapoport, "Inborn Errors of Metabolism." In W.E. Nelson (ed.), *Textbook of Pediatrics*. Seventh edition. Philadelphia: Saunders, 1959.

423. A. J. Reiss, Jr. and A. L. Rhodes, "The Distribution of Juvenile Delinquency in the Social Class Structure," *American Sociological Review*, 1961, *26*, 720-732.

424. D. C. Reitzes, *Negroes and Medicine*. Cambridge, Mass.: Harvard University Press, 1958.

425. R. V. Rider, M. Taback, and Hilda Knobloch, "Associations between Premature Birth and Socioeconomic Status," *American Journal of Public Health*, 1955, *45*, 1022-1028.

426. F. Riessman, *The Culturally Deprived Child*. New York: Harper and Row, 1962.

427. H. S. Ripley and S. Wolf, "Mental Illness among Negro Troops Overseas," *American Journal of Psychiatry*, 1947, *103*, 499-512.

428. H. W. Roberts, "Prior-Service Attitudes toward Whites of 219 Negro Veterans," *Journal of Negro Education*, 1953, *22*, 455-465.

429. H. W. Roberts, "The Impact of Military Service upon the Racial Attitudes of Negro Servicemen in World War II," *Social Problems*, 1953, *1*, 65-69.

430. S. O. Roberts, "Socioeconomic Status and Performance on the ACE of Negro Freshmen College Veterans and Non-Veterans, from the North and South," *American Psychologist*, 1948, *3*, 266.

431. S. O. Roberts and L. Carr, " 'Social Action' Participation As Related to Selected Variables for Negro American College Students," *American Psychologist*, 1961, *16*, 398 (abstract).

432. S. L. Robbins, *Textbook of Pathology with Clinical Application*. Second edition. Philadelphia: Saunders, 1962.

433. Mary L. Robinson and M. Meenes, "The Relationship between Test Intelligence of Third Grade Negro Children and the Occupations of Their Parents," *Journal of Negro Education*, 1947, *16*, 136-141.

434. J. B. Roebuck and M. L. Cadwallader, "The Negro Armed Robber as a Criminal Type: The Construction and Application of a Typology," *Pacific Sociological Review*, 1961, *4*, 21-26.

435. S. R. Roen, "Personality and Negro-White Intelligence," *Journal of Abnormal and Social Psychology*, 1960, *61*, 148-150.

436. C. R. Rogers, *Client-Centered Therapy*. Boston, Mass.: Houghton Mifflin, 1951.

437. J. H. Rohrer, "The Test Intelligence of Osage Indians," *Journal of Social Psychology*, 1942, *16*, 99-105.

438. J. H. Rohrer and M. S. Edmonson (eds.), *The Eighth Generation*. New York: Harper, 1960.

439. A. W. Rose, "How Negro Workers Feel about Their Jobs," *Personnel Journal*, 1951, *29*, 292-296.

440. B. C. Rosen, "Race, Ethnicity, and the Achievement Syndrome," *American Sociological Review*, 1959, *24*, 47-60.

441. U. Rotondo, C. B. Vigil, C. G. Pachecho, J. Mariategui, and Beatriz De Degaldo, "Personalidad básica: Dilemas y vida de Familia de un Grupo de Mestizos," *Revista de Psicología (Lima)*, 1960, *2*, 3-60.

442. G. Saenger and Emily Gilbert, "Customer Reactions to the Integration of Negro Sales Personnel," *International Journal of Opinion and Attitude Research*, 1950, *4*, 57-76.

443. Nancy St. John, "The Relation of Racial Segregation in Early Schooling to the Level of Aspiration and Academic Achievement of Negro Students in a Northern High School." Unpublished doctoral thesis, Harvard University, 1962.

444. L. Savitz, *Delinquency and Migration*. Philadelphia: Commission on Human Relations, 1960.

445. F. R. Scarpitti, Ellen Murray, S. Dinitz, and W. C. Reckless, "The 'Good' Boy in a High Delinquency Area: Four Years Later," *American Sociological Review*, 1960, *25*, 555-558.

446. R. A. Schermerhorn, "Psychiatric Disorders among Negroes: A Sociological Note," *American Journal of Psychiatry*, 1956, *112*, 878-882.

447. C. F. Schmid, "Urban Crime Areas: Parts I and II," *American Sociological Review*, 1960, *25*, 527-542, 655-678.

448. A. Sclare, "Cultural Determinants in the Neurotic Negro," *British Journal of Medical Psychology*, 1953, *26*, 278-288.

449. N. A. Scotch, "The Vanishing Villains of Television," *Phylon*, 1960, 21, 58-62.

450. W. A. Scott, "Attitude Change through Reward of Verbal Behavior," *Journal of Abnormal and Social Psychology*, 1957, 55, 72-75.

451. W. A. Scott, "Attitude Change by Response Reinforcement: Replication and Extension," *Sociometry*, 1959, 22, 328-335.

452. Ruth Searles and J. A. Williams, Jr., "Negro College Students' Participation in Sit-ins," *Social Forces*, 1962, 40, 215-220.

453. Pauline S. Sears, "Doll Play Aggression in Normal Young Children: Influence of Sex, Age, Sibling Status, Father's Absence," *Psychological Monographs*, 1951, 65(6), (Whole no. 323).

454. R. R. Sears, Eleanor E. Maccoby, and H. Levin, *Patterns of Child Rearing*. Evanston, Ill.: Row, Peterson, 1957.

455. R. R. Sears, M. H. Pintler, and Pauline S. Sears, "Effects of Father-Separation on Preschool Children's Doll Play Aggression," *Child Development*, 1946, 17, 219-243.

456. M. Seeman, "A Situational Approach to Intragroup Negro Attitudes," *Sociometry*, 1946, 9, 199-206.

457. T. Sellin, "Race Prejudice in the Administration of Justice," *American Journal of Sociology*, 1935, 41, 212-217.

458. T. Sellin, "Crime and Delinquency in the United States: An Over-all View," *Annals of the American Academy of Political and Social Science*, 1962, 339, 11-23.

459. I. J. Semler and I. Iscoe, "Comparative and Developmental Study of the Learning Abilities of Negro and White Children under Four Conditions," *Journal of Educational Psychology*, 1963, 54, 38-44.

460. A. R. Shands, Jr., *Handbook of Orthopaedic Surgery*. St. Louis, Mo.: Mosby, 1957.

461. L. W. Shannon, "The Spatial Distribution of Criminal Offenses by States," *Journal of Criminal Law, Criminology, and Police Science*, 1954, 45, 264-271.

462. L. W. Shaw, S. Glaser, and A. H. Wyman, *Reported Tuberculosis Data*. 1962 edition. Atlanta, Ga.: Public Health Service, 1962.

463. L. W. Shaw and A. H. Wyman, *Reported Tuberculosis Data*. 1960 edition. Washington, D. C.: Public Health Service, 1960.

464. Elizabeth T. Sheerer, "An Analysis of the Relationship between Acceptance of and Respect for Self and Acceptance of and Respect for Others in Ten Counseling Cases," *Journal of Consulting Psychology*, 1949, 13, 169-175.

465. H. I. Sheppard, "The Negro Merchant: A Study of Negro

Anti-Semitism," *American Journal of Sociology*, 1947, *53*, 96-99.
466. M. Sherif, O. J. Harvey, B. J. White, W. R. Hood, and Carolyn Sherif, *Intergroup Conflict and Cooperation: The Robbers Cave Experiment*. Norman, Okla.: Institute of Group Relations, 1961.
467. M. Sherif and Carolyn Sherif, *Reference Groups: Explorations in Conformity and Deviance of Adolescents*. New York: Harper and Row, 1964.
468. Audrey Shuey, *The Testing of Negro Intelligence*. Lynchburg, Va.: Bell, 1958.
469. Audrey Shuey, Nancy King, and Barbara Griffith, "Stereotyping of Negroes and Whites: An Analysis of Magazine Pictures," *Public Opinion Quarterly*, 1953, *17*, 281-287.
470. C. E. Silberman, "The City and the Negro," *Fortune*, March, 1962, *65*, 89-91, 139-154.
471. R. L. Simpson, "Negro-Jewish Prejudice: Authoritarianism and Some Social Variables as Correlates," *Social Problems*, 1959, *7*, 138-146.
472. S. L. Singer and B. Stefflre, "A Note on Racial Differences in Job Values and Desires," *Journal of Social Psychology*, 1956, *43*, 333-337.
473. Mollie S. Smart, "Confirming Klineberg's Suspicion," *American Psychologist*, 1963, *18*, 621.
474. W. G. Smillie, *Preventive Medicine and Public Health*. Second edition. New York: Macmillan, 1957.
475. D. T. Smith, W. W. Johnston, I. M. Cain, and M. Schumacher, "Changes in the Tuberculin Pattern in Students between 1930 and 1960," *American Review of Respiratory Diseases*, 1961, *83*, 213-234.
476. S. Smith, "Language and Non-Verbal Test Performance of Racial Groups before and after a 14-Year Interval," *Journal of Genetic Psychology*, 1942, *26*, 51-93.
477. Society for the Psychological Study of Social Issues, "Guidelines for Testing Minority Group Children." Pamphlet in press.
478. L. W. Sontag, C. T. Baker, and Virginia Nelson, "Personality as a Determinant of Performance," *American Journal of Orthopsychiatry*, 1955, *25*, 555-562.
479. Southern Regional Council, "Did You Find That There Was Much Difference in the Ability of Negro Children to Receive and Profit by Instruction?" *Report No. L-13*, December 15, 1959.
480. Southern Regional Council, "Desegregation and Academic Achievement," *Report No. L-17*, March 14, 1960.
481. *Southern School News*: (a) May, 1958, *4*(11); (b) January, 1959, *5*(7); (c) May, 1959, *5*(11); (d) July, 1959, *6*(1);

(e) August, 1959, 6(2); (f) December, 1959, 6(6); (g) January, 1960, 6(7); (h) April, 1960, 6(10); (i) May, 1960, 6(11); (j) June, 1960, 6(12); (k) July, 1960, 7(1); (l) August, 1960, 7(2); (m) November, 1960, 7(5); (n) February, 1961, 7(8); (o) June, 1961, 7(12); (p) September, 1961, 8(3); (q) February, 1962, 8(8); and (r) June, 1962, 8(12).

482. J. Spirer, "Negro Crime," *Comparative Psychological Monographs*, 1940, 16, no. 81, 1-81.

483. F. H. Stallings, "A Study of the Immediate Effects of Integration on Scholastic Achievement in the Louisville Public Schools," *Journal of Negro Education*, 1959, 28, 439-444.

484. F. H. Stallings, "Racial Differences and Academic Achievement," *Southern Regional Council's Report No. L-16*, February 26, 1960.

485. J. M. Stalnaker, "Identification of the Best Southern Negro High School Seniors," *Scientific Monthly*, 1948, 67, 237-239.

486. J. Stamler, D. M. Berkson, H. A. Lindberg, W. Miller, and Y. Hall, "Racial Patterns of Coronary Heart Disease," *Geriatrics*, 1961, 16, 382-396.

487. J. B. Stanbury, J. B. Wyngaarden, and D. S. Fredrickson (eds.), *The Metabolic Basis of Inherited Disease*. New York: McGraw-Hill, 1960.

488. W. Stanton, *The Leopard's Spots: Scientific Attitudes Toward Race in America, 1815-1859*. Chicago: University of Chicago Press, 1960.

489. G. A. Steckler, "Authoritarian Ideology in Negro College Students," *Journal of Abnormal and Social Psychology*, 1957, 54, 396-399.

490. C. Stern, "The Biology of the Negro," *Scientific American*, October, 1954, 191(4), 81-85.

491. C. Stern, *Principles of Human Genetics*. Second edition. San Francisco: Freeman, 1960.

492. H. G. Stetler, *Comparative Study of Negro and White Dropouts in Selected Connecticut High Schools*. Hartford: Connecticut Commission on Civil Rights, 1959.

493. H. W. Stevenson and E. C. Stewart, "A Developmental Study of Racial Awareness in Young Children," *Child Development*, 1958, 29, 399-409.

494. D. D. Stewart, "Posthospital Social Adjustment of Former Mental Patients from Two Arkansas Counties," *Southwestern Social Science Quarterly*, 1955, 35, 317-323.

495. Dorothy Stock, "An Investigation into the Interrelations between Self-Concept and Feelings Directed toward Other Persons and Groups," *Journal of Consulting Psychology*, 1949, 13, 176-180.

496. G. D. Stoddard, *The Meaning of Intelligence*. New York: Macmillan, 1943.
497. Lois M. Stolz, *Father Relations of Warborn Children*. Palo Alto, Cal.: Stanford University Press, 1954.
498. S. A. Stouffer, E. A. Suchman, L. C. DeVinney, Shirley A. Star, and R. M. Williams, *The American Soldier: Studies in Social Psychology in World War II*. Vol. I. *Adjustment During Army Life*. Princeton, N.J.: Princeton University Press, 1949.
499. Lorene A. Stringer, "Academic Progress as an Index of Mental Health," *Journal of Social Issues*, 1959, *15*, 16-29.
500. E. K. Strong, Jr., "Are Medical Specialist Interest Scales Applicable to Negroes?" *Journal of Applied Psychology*, 1955, *39*, 62-64.
501. H. S. Sullivan, "Memorandum on a Psychiatric Reconnaissance." In C. S. Johnson, *Growing Up in the Black Belt*. Washington, D.C.: American Council on Education, 1941; 247-263.
502. H. S. Sullivan, *Conceptions of Modern Psychiatry*. New York: Norton, 1953.
503. M. B. Sussman and H. C. Yeager, Jr., "Mate Selection among Negro and White College Students," *Sociology and Social Research*, 1950, *35*, 46-49.
504. E. H. Sutherland, *White Collar Crime*. New York: Dryden, 1949.
505. E. H. Sutherland and D. R. Cressey, *Principles of Criminology*. Sixth edition, Philadelphia: Lippincott, 1960.
506. R. L. Sutherland, *Color, Class, and Personality*. Washington, D.C.: American Council on Education, 1942.
507. K. E. Taeuber and Alma F. Taeuber, "Is the Negro an Immigrant Group?" *Integrated Education*, June, 1963, *1*, 25-28.
508. F. Tannenbaum, *Slave and Citizen: The Negro in the Americas*. New York: Knopf, 1947.
509. H. A. Tanser, *The Settlement of Negroes in Kent County, Ontario, and a Study of the Mental Capacity of Their Descendants*. Chatham, Ontario: Shephard, 1939.
510. V. Theman and P. A. Witty, "Case Studies and Genetic Records of Two Gifted Negroes," *Journal of Psychology*, 1943, *15*, 165-181.
511. W. R. Thompson and W. Heron, "The Effects of Restricting Early Experience on the Problem-Solving Capacity of dogs," *Canadian Journal of Psychology*, 1954, *8*, 17-31.
512. W. R. Thompson and R. Melzack, "Early Environment," *Scientific American*, 1956, *194*(1), 38-42.
513. E. L. Thorndike and Ella Woodyard, "Differences within and between Communities in the Intelligence of Children," *Journal of Educational Psychology*, 1942, *33*, 641-656.

232   REFERENCES

514. R. L. Thorndike, "Community Variables as Predictors of Intelligence and Academic Achievement," *Journal of Educational Psychology*, 1951, *42*, 321-338.
515. H. Tomlinson, "Differences between Preschool Negro Children and Their Older Siblings on the Stanford-Binet Scales," *Journal of Negro Education*, 1944, *13*, 474-479.
516. Helen G. Trager and Marian R. Yarrow, *They Live What They Learn*. New York: Harpers, 1952.
517. R. D. Trent, "The Color of the Investigator as a Variable in Experimental Research with Negro Subjects," *Journal of Social Psychology*, 1954, *40*, 281-287.
518. R. D. Trent, "The Relation between Expressed Self-Acceptance and Expressed Attitudes toward Negroes and Whites among Negro Children," *Journal of Genetic Psychology*, 1957, *91*, 25-31.
519. R. Trumbull, "A Study in Relationships between Factors of Personality and Intelligence," *Journal of Social Psychology*, 1953, *38*, 161-173.
520. R. D. Tuddenham, "Soldier Intelligence in World Wars I and II," *American Psychologist*, 1948, *3*, 54-56.
521. R. D. Tuddenham, "The Nature and Measurement of Intelligence." In L. Postman (ed.), *Psychology in the Making*. New York: Knopf, 1962.
522. S. H. Tulchin, *Intelligence and Crime*. Chicago: University of Chicago Press, 1939.
523. United States Bureau of the Census, *U. S. Census of Population. General Social and Economic Characteristics, United States Summary.* Final Report PC (1)—1C. Washington, D.C.: U.S. Government Printing Office, 1962.
524. United States Commission on Civil Rights, *Civil Rights U.S.A.: Public Schools, Southern States 1962.* Washington, D.C.: U.S. Government Printing Office, 1962.
525. *United States News and World Report:* (a) September 28, 1956, *41*, 98-107; (b) October 5, 1956, *41*, 68-69; (c) October 12, 1956, *41*, 82-88; and (d) January 4, 1957, *42*, 92-100.
526. P. Valien, "General Demographic Characteristics of the Negro Population in the United States," *Journal of Negro Education*, 1963 Yearbook, *32*(4), 329-336.
527. P. Valien and Alberta P. Fitzgerald, "Attitudes of the Negro Mother toward Birth Control," *American Journal of Sociology*, 1949, *55*, 279-283.
528. J. W. Vander Zanden, "The Non-Violent Resistance Movement against Segregation," *American Journal of Sociology*, 1963, *68*, 544-550.
529. J. Veroff, J. W. Atkinson, Sheila C. Feld, and G. Gurin, "The Use of Thematic Apperception To Assess Motiva-

tion in a Nationwide Interview Study," *Psychological Monographs*, 1960, 74(12), (Whole no. 499).

530. Rita Volkman and D. R. Cressey, "Differential Association and the Rehabilitation of Drug Addicts," *American Journal of Sociology*, 1963, 69, 129-142.

531. H. Von Hentig, "Criminality of the Negro," *Journal of Criminal Law and Criminology*, 1940, 30, 662-680.

532. J. N. Walton, "Multiple Sclerosis." In T. R. Harrison (ed.), *Principles of Internal Medicine*. New York: McGraw-Hill, 1958.

533. E. A. Weinstein and P. N. Geisel, "Family Decision Making over Desegregation," *Sociometry*, 1961, 25, 21-29.

534. Edith Weisskopf, "Intellectual Malfunctioning and Personality," *Journal of Abnormal and Social Psychology*, 1951, 46, 410-423.

535. Beth L. Wellman and Edna L. Pegram, "Benet I. Q. Changes of Orphanage Preschool Children: A Re-analysis," *Journal of Genetic Psychology*, 1944, 65, 239-263.

536. F. R. Westie and D. H. Howard, "Social Status Differentials and the Race Attitudes of Negroes," *American Sociological Review*, 1954, 19, 584-591.

537. L. R. Wheeler, "A Comparative Study of the Intelligence of East Tennessee Mountain Children," *Journal of Educational Psychology*, 1942, 33, 321-334.

538. J. E. White, W. J. Strudwick, N. Ricketts, and C. Sampson, "Cancer of the Skin in Negroes: A Review of 31 Cases," *Journal of the American Medical Association*, 1961, 178, 845-847.

539. R. K. White, "Black Boy: A Value Analysis," *Journal of Abnormal and Social Psychology*, 1947, 42, 440-461.

540. Edna M. Whittaker, J. C. Gilchrist, and Jean W. Fischer, "Perceptual Defense or Response Suppression?" *Journal of Abnormal and Social Psychology*, 1952, 47, 732-733.

541. W. F. Whyte, *Street Corner Society*. Second edition. Chicago: University of Chicago Press, 1956.

542. E. Y. Williams and C. P. Carmichael, "The Incidence of Mental Disease in the Negro," *Journal of Negro Education*, 1949, 18, 276-282.

543. D. M. Wilner, Rosabelle P. Walkley, and S. W. Cook, *Human Relations in Interracial Housing*. Minneapolis: University of Minnesota Press, 1955.

544. D. C. Wilson and Edna M. Lantz, "The Effect of Culture Change on the Negro Race in Virginia as Indicated by a Study of State Hospital Admissions," *American Journal of Psychiatry*, 1957, 114, 25-32.

545. J. Q. Wilson, *Negro Politics*. Glencoe, Ill.: Free Press, 1960.

546. M. M. Wintrobe, "Sarcoidosis." In T. R. Harrison (ed.),

Principles of Internal Medicine. New York: McGraw-Hill, 1958; 1148-1151.

547. M. M. Wintrobe, *Clinical Hematology.* Fifth edition. Philadelphia: Lea and Febiger, 1961.

548. L. Wirth and H. Goldhamer, "Passing." In O. Klineberg (ed.), *Characteristics of the American Negro.* New York: Harper, 1944; 301-319.

549. P. Witty, "New Evidence on the Learning Ability of the Negro," *Journal of Abnormal and Social Psychology,* 1945, 40, 401-404.

550. P. Witty, "Reply to Mr. Erickson," *Journal of Abnormal and Social Psychology,* 1946, 41, 482-485.

551. P. Witty and M. D. Jenkins, "Intra-Race Testing and Negro Intelligence," *Journal of Psychology,* 1936, 1, 179-192.

552. M. E. Wolfgang, *Patterns in Criminal Homicide.* Philadelphia: University of Pennsylvania Press, 1958.

553. A. L. Wood, "Minority Group Criminality and Cultural Integration," *Journal of Criminal Law and Criminology,* 1947, 37, 498-510.

554. W. A. Woods and R. Toal, "Subtest Disparity of Negro and White Groups Matched for I. Q.'s on the Revised Beta Test," *Journal of Consulting Psychology,* 1957, 21, 136-138.

555. T. J. Woofter, Jr., *Black Yeomanry: Life on St. Helena Island.* New York: Holt, 1930.

556. W. D. Workman, Jr., *The Case for the South.* New York: Devin-Adair, 1960.

557. E. Works, "The Prejudice-Interaction Hypothesis from the Point of View of the Negro Minority Group," *American Journal of Sociology,* 1961, 67, 47-52.

558. R. Wright, *Black Boy.* New York: New American Library, 1951 (originally published by Harper, 1937).

559. Writers' War Board, *How Writers Perpetuate Stereotypes.* New York: Writers' War Board, 1945.

560. Marian P. Yankauer and M. B. Sunderhauf, "Housing: Equal Opportunity To Choose Where One Shall Live," *Journal of Negro Education,* 1963 Yearbook, 32(4), 402-414.

561. Marian R. Yarrow (ed.), "Interpersonal Dynamics in a Desegregation Process," *Journal of Social Issues,* 1958, 14, 3-63.

562. Marian R. Yarrow and B. Lande, "Personality Correlates of Differential Reactions to Minority Group-Belonging," *Journal of Social Psychology,* 1953, 38, 253-272.

563. H. B. Young, "The Negro's Participation in American Business," *Journal of Negro Education,* 1963 Yearbook, 32(4), 390-401.

564. H. Zinn, "The Battle-Scarred Youngsters," *The Nation*, 1963, *197*, 193-197.
565. M. Zuckerman, M. Baer, and I. Monashkin, "Acceptance of Self, Parents, and People in Patients and Normals," *Journal of Clinical Psychology*, 1956, *12*, 327-332.

NAME INDEX

SUBJECT INDEX